*Forms of
the
Fantastic*

Forms of the Fantastic

*Selected Essays
from the
Third International Conference
on the
Fantastic in Literature
and Film*

Edited by JAN HOKENSON
and HOWARD PEARCE

Contributions to the Study of Science Fiction and Fantasy, Number 20

GREENWOOD PRESS
New York • Westport, Connecticut • London

Library of Congress Cataloging-in-Publication Data

International Conference on the Fantastic in Literature
  and Film (3rd : 1982 : Florida Atlantic University)
  Forms of the fantastic.

  (Contributions to the study of science fiction and
fantasy, ISSN 0193–6875 ; no. 20)
  Bibliography: p.
  Includes index.
  1. Fantasy in art—Congresses. 2. Arts—
Congresses. I. Hokenson, Jan. II. Pearce, Howard D.
III. Title. IV. Series.
NX650.F36I58 1982   700   85–17746
ISBN 0–313–25035–9 (lib. bdg. : alk. paper)

Library of Congress Catalog Card Number: 85–17746
ISBN: 0–313–25035–9
ISSN: 0193–6875

First published in 1986

Greenwood Press, Inc.
88 Post Road West
Westport, Connecticut 06881

Printed in the United States of America

The paper used in this book complies with the
Permanent Paper Standard issued by the National
Information Standards Organization (Z39.48–1984).

10 9 8 7 6 5 4 3 2 1

Copyright Acknowledgments

The editors and publishers are grateful for permission to reprint from the following sources.

M. G. Lewis, *The Monk* (New York: Grove Press, 1952). Reprinted with permission from Grove Press, Inc.

C. S. Lewis, *That Hideous Strength* (London: The Bodley Head; reprint New York: Macmillan Paperbacks, 1965). Reprinted by permission of The Bodley Head.

Kenneth Patchen, *The Journal of Albion Moonlight.* Copyright 1941 by Kenneth Patchen. Reprinted by permission of New Directions Publishing Corporation.

Edmund Spenser, *The Faerie Queen*, ed. J. C. Smith (Oxford: Oxford University Press, 1909). Reprinted by permission of Oxford University Press.

Neilson/Hill: *Complete Plays and Poems of William Shakespeare* Copyright © 1942, renewed 1969 by Caroline Steiner and Margaret N. Helburn. Used with the permission of the Houghton-Mifflin Company.

Peter Beagle, *Lila the Werewolf.* Reprinted by permission of Capra Press, Santa Barbara. This material originally appeared in *Lila the Werewolf* by Peter Beagle, copyright © 1974.

"Cock a doodle do . . . ." reprinted from *The Annotated Mother Goose* edited by William S. and Ceil Baring-Gould. Copyright © 1962 by William S. and Ceil Baring-Gould. Used by permission of Clarkson N. Potter, Inc.

To Margaret Gaines Swann, patron of the International
Conference on the Fantastic and founder of The Thomas Burnett Swann
Fund. Without her generous support, the occasion for these
studies could not have transpired.

Contents

THE FANTASTIC AND SEXUALITY

GENRE AND FANTASTIC GAME PLAY

Figures

Preface

This volume contains twenty-six essays originally presented at the Third International Conference on the Fantastic in the Arts, in March 1982. One of the most vibrant interdisciplinary meetings in the United States, the Conference draws together scholars, artists, authors, and theorists from several countries in the Americas and Europe, all seeking to recognize and explore the tradition of the fantastic in literature and the arts. Annually almost three hundred papers are presented in art, literature, philosophy, film, psychology, sociology, history, aesthetics, and theory. This third volume of papers selected for publication reflects both the heterogeneity of the forum, with its multiple viewpoints on the mode of the fantastic, and the continuing joint effort to define the fantastic in a generally satisfactory way.

As in previous volumes, the essays suggest the range of problems involved in such a definition. Each essay was selected, first, for its intrinsic merit as exposition of a particular form of the fantastic, and second, as a contribution to the common endeavor to distinguish the fantastic from other modes, most notably realism and rationalism, and as an explication of the premises and techniques of the fantastic. Thus, the essays included here cross traditional boundaries of language or medium or period, by way of elaborating concepts of the fantastic derived from all its protean forms.

The title *Forms of the Fantastic* denotes standard notions of shape and structure with, however, particular stress on a third definition: the ideal or intrinsic character, the essential nature, of the fantastic as distinguished from the matter in which it is embodied or expressed. Although we are not Platonists, we have found that these essays taken together constitute a widely ranging effort to disengage from their contexts some consistent features of the fantastic. Each writer fully respects local habitations and names, even as he or she pushes the exposition of the text further, toward the character of the fantastic itself. Therefore, although to our dismay the essays seemed naturally to group themselves under certain rubrics, those rubrics as listed in the table of contents are not divisions so much as complementary aspects of diverse forms: The reader will find that, if carefully considered, the essays in each group illuminate the subjects and perspectives of the next. Whether from Elizabethan drama, German Romantic music, French Expressionist painting, or American science fiction, most texts studied exhibit common features: echoes of myth and epic, linguistic archaism or invention, and emphasis on freedom and, particularly in more recent texts, on the marvelous, on sexuality, and on reflexive gaming with genre. Although perspectives range from New Critical to deconstructive, the essays constitute investigations, eschewing conclusions for the sake of keeping open the common continuing inquiry into the nature of the fantastic.

Almost all considerations of genre and period have been subordinated to that inquiry. Thus, Shakespeare and Michael Mann cohabit "Freedoms of the Fantastic," just as the Grimms and Robert Coover together open the question of sexuality. We have made one exception to such collapsing of chronology, however, by beginning the volume with essays addressing the issue of period itself, notably exploring Romanticism and Modernism. Following essays on "Theoretical Approaches to the Fantastic" build vertically from those sample period bases with diachronic viewpoints from anthropology, phenomenology, and theology. Thereafter, essays thematically address various instances of the fantastic. We do not mean to argue that certain literary periods or movements are not particularly congenial to the fantastic, though they may be. Rather we hope that by first considering the fantastic in such disparate forms as German Romantic music and American Cubist film, the reader will best engage the subject, its broad dimensions and its specific richness.

*Forms of
the
Fantastic*

PERIODS OF THE FANTASTIC

The fantastic occurs in all the arts in all periods, from Hellenistic to contemporary. The following essays explore the role of the fantastic in two major periods of transition, suggesting that Romantic and Modernist writers stressed the fantastic in their efforts to break down rigid notions of person and genre. From their different viewpoints, both essays describe mixed media and transformations of genres as functions of the fantastic. What does it mean to speak of "verbal music" in Romantic verse? Are "Cubist materialism" and "Expressionist idealism" constatively distinct? Can attention to the fantastic as mode help us to apprehend more deeply such familiar notions as the enchanted realm of German Romanticism or textual registers that make possible the production of meaning in Modernism?

Between Two Worlds: Robert Schumann and German Romanticism

Donald H. Crosby

The affinity between German literature and German music, or—to put it more concretely—between German poets and German musicians, has never been more pronounced than in those remarkable decades clustered around the beginning of the nineteenth century. If one sharpens the focus a bit, one perceives that the specific era of German Romanticism—which falls roughly between 1790 and 1840—was especially rich in intellectual crosscurrents, in the flux of ideas and ideals. This was the era, after all, in which philosophy felt akin to literature, literature to folklore, folklore to history, history to painting, painting to poetry. But above all it was music, that most elusive, paradoxical, and yet universal of the arts, that "most German" of the arts, as it has been called, that most clearly placed its stamp on the spirit of the age. From Wilhelm Heinrich Wackenroder (1773–1798) to Heinrich Heine (1797–1856), there was scarcely a Romantic poet who, either intuitively or consciously, did not deal with music thematically or attempt to expand the limitations of the printed word in quest of a form of verbal music.

Given the fact that the Romantic era was one of intellectual and creative cross-pollination, it is not surprising that the admiration of German poets for the composers of the day did not go unreciprocated. Ludwig van Beethoven, whose ripening creative talents coincided with the developmental years of early German Romanticism, paid tribute to Johann Wolfgang von Goethe both through his song settings and through his powerful incidental music to the poet's drama *Egmont*. Franz Schubert, fusing his own melodic genius with the incredible outpouring of German lyricism, all but created that perfect amalgam of German poetry and music, the *Lied*, or art song. Later in the century, Richard Wagner, a come-lately Romantic, would realize in his operas that fusion of the arts, the *Gesamtkunstwerk*, that had been an unattainable ideal for the Romantics of the previous generation.

Within the formal time frame of Romanticism, however—that is to say between Wackenroder and Heine—there was no musician more passionately dedicated to the literature of the day, none more sensitively attuned to it, than Robert Schumann, that problematical, pivotal composer who might well be called the father of German musical Romanticism. Without making his music merely imitative of literature—that is to say without specifically seeking a "program" for his compositions—Robert Schumann was perhaps the most literary of German composers before Richard Wagner. Postponing value judgments for the moment, one might fairly claim that Schumann's abstract music, especially his piano music, comes closer to paralleling the moods, associations, and evocative power of literature than any other music written during his time. The very titles of some of his best-known piano compositions carry "literary"—for example, pictorial and/or emotional—implications: "Papillons," "Carnaval," "Faschingsschwank aus Wien," "Fantasiestücke," "Nachtstücke," "Kinderszenen," "Waldszenen," "Kreisleriana." Much has been made of the fact that Schumann himself took pains to point out that he added these titles only after he had composed the respective works[1]—as if somehow this shielded Schumann from the stigma of having created "program music."[2] Here two points must be made: Irrespective of whether the titles occurred to Schumann before, during, or after the actual period of composition, it is striking that he felt that these works would be incomplete without pictorial–emotional indicators; and in at least two cases—"Papillons" and "Kreisleriana" come immediately to mind—Schumann's inspiration sprang directly from the reading of literary texts, a fact that minimizes the importance of exactly when the titles might have been applied.

Schumann's birth year of 1810—he was born on June 8 in the Saxon town of Zwickau—placed him, auspiciously enough, in the chronological center of a German Romantic movement then in full flower. Some of the pioneers of German Romanticism, such as Wackenroder and Novalis, had, to be sure, gone to an early grave, and the great poet Friedrich Hölderlin had already lapsed into madness; but the ranks of the Romantics were still swelled by such spirits as Friedrich and August Wilhelm Schlegel, Heinrich von Kleist, Ludwig Tieck, Achim von Arnim, Clemens Brentano, Ernst Theodor Amadeus Hoffmann, Friedrich de la Motte Fouqué, Adelbert von Chamisso, Joseph von Eichendorff, Justinus Kerner, Ludwig Uhland, and Friedrich Rückert. Waiting in the wings, as it were, were young Romantics-to-be such as Heinrich Heine, Nikolaus Lenau, and Eduard Mörike. Bracketing Schumann's birth year were such monuments of German Romanticism as the collection of folk songs edited by Arnim and Brentano (*Des Knaben Wunderhorn*, 1806–1808) and the epochal compilation of fairy tales (*Kinder-und Hausmärchen*, 1812) published by the brothers Jacob and Wilhelm Grimm. The birth year itself brought the publication of Kleist's *Das Käthchen von Heilbronn*, Brentano's *Godwi*, and Hoffmann's *Ritter Gluck*. Casting a giant shadow over the entire era was the towering figure of Goethe himself, who in the year 1810 still had a remarkable 22 years of productivity before him. Small wonder that Robert Schumann, coming of age in these years of Germany's great literary renaissance, developed a lifelong love of literature that was to enrich and color his musical compositions from beginning to end.

Schumann's love for the literature of his day derived not only from the normal impulses of literary taste and appreciation but also from a deeper urging, a certain kinship he felt both with the authors he revered and with the fictional creations of their pens as well. The duality Schumann found in *Faust*, in the characters of Jean Paul Richter, in Chamisso's *Peter Schlemihl*, and above all in the tales of E. T. A. Hoffmann, reflected deeply rooted contradictions in his own nature; this dichotomy in his personality led to the uneasy coexistence, within Schumann, of what he called the "light" and "dark" sides of his nature. Schumann's early mental derangement, his attempted suicide, and his death in early middle age recall the constant fear of madness that racked Hoffmann, the madness of Lenz and Lenau, the suicide of Heinrich von Kleist, and the tragic mental demise of Friedrich Hölderlin.

Turning to Schumann's major piano compositions, one finds a novel written by Jean Paul Richter (1763–1825) serving as the inspiration for the set of piano pieces Schumann published under the title "Papillons" ("Butterflies"), Opus 2. Literary historians do not rank Jean Paul, as he is usually called, among the truly great writers of the Romantic era; indeed, the tone and content of his novels tend to place him on the periphery of the "Romantic school" of writing. Yet it was Jean Paul, rather than, say, Goethe, who exerted the most profound influence on Schumann, and who became "the master of his thought, his literary model and the constant example of his life."[3] Just before composing "Papillons," Schumann had reread Jean Paul's rambling novel *Die Flegeljahre*, and in Chapter 63, entitled "Larventanz" ("Dance of the Masks"), had found himself transported into the realm of the fantastic. Using the Baroque palace of the nobleman, Zablocki, as a *mise–en–scène*, Jean Paul had conjured up a Polish festival rich in symbols and allegory: the giant boot, walking by itself; the talking wig with its oracular pronouncements; the shifting identities of the masked dancers, Walt, Vult, and Vina. The twelve dance scenes Schumann grouped under the title "Papillons" may be regarded as musical pendants to the fantastic figures and phenomena of Jean Paul's "Larventanz": Here, too, one encounters carnival gaiety and sudden loneliness, heady exuberance and sobering melancholy, fleeting figures and bells tolling in the night. How exhilarating it must have been for the young composer to discover that through the genius of his own art, for example, through contrasts of rhythm, tempo, and tonality, he could meet an admired master on common ground.

Not surprisingly, the fact that "Papillons" has such a clearly defined literary provenance has sparked critical controversy regarding the interpretation of the work. Some critics, using Schumann's annotated copy of *Die Flegeljahre* as a guide, have tried to establish exact parallels between the dance suite and Jean Paul's masked ball; other critics deny any close parallels and point out that Schumann wrote the marginalia after he had composed the suite.[4] Without taking sides, one might make the observation that literature and music are two very distinct arts, each of which operates within its own laws and limitations. In the final number of "Papillons," for example, Schumann introduces a melody borrowed from a German folksong dealing with parting, thereby conveying the idea that the masked ball is winding down and the guests are preparing to depart homeward; he then adds a new theme, a puckish, whimsical melodic fragment possibly intended to destroy the illusion of the fantastic and to bring the revelers back to the plane of reality. These two themes are then combined with the "butterfly" theme that opened the suite, whereupon Schumann ingeniously weaves these three melodic strands together to form a final, rather weary dance before six strokes of the village clock—conveyed by repeated single notes—announce that the ball is over. Listening to this finale, one can understand why so many German poets envied the art of the composer. Unlike the writer, the composer can have several themes occupying the same space at the same time, as indeed Schumann does at the close of "Papillons." This simultaneously, alas, is beyond the achievement of the writer or poet, who deals not with diaphanous tones but rather with concrete words and concepts. Schumann may well have intended his "Papillons" to serve as a musical tribute to a beloved literary model, but what he created, paradoxically, was autonomous music that can be enjoyed independently of any model whatsoever.

The themes of masks and split identities carried over into an activity Schumann undertook as a practical complement to his nascent career as a composer: music criticism. In search of a livelihood—a finger injury had ended his hopes of becoming a virtuoso pianist—Schumann founded the *Neue Zeitschrift für Musik*, a journal that helped set the course for Germany's era of musical Romanticism. Like E. T. A. Hoffmann, his spiritual kinsman and only contemporary equal as a music critic, Schumann knew that the Romantic listener was an ecstatic visionary and that it was therefore the mission of the critic to go beyond mere analysis and to attempt to express the ecstasy and the vision. Determined to integrate his own split identities into his music criticism, Schumann hit upon the brilliant if whimsical idea of creating three fictive critical personae, each one himself, or at least part of himself. He named these alter egos Eusebius, Florestan, and Raro. Reduced to their essentials, Eusebius was the personification of dreamy melancholy, Florestan of poetical fire and impetuousness, and Raro, the *Meister*, of reason. Schumann the composer, like Schumann the critic, was the sum of all three parts, and it is a rare piece of music from his pen that does not bear the mark of Eusebius, Florestan, and Raro.

The multiform musical character of Schumann's piano compositions, already evident in "Papillons," is even more sharply etched in the great set of variations he composed when he was twenty-five and to which he ultimately gave the title "Carnaval." An outgrowth of Schumann's fascination with masks and doubles, "Carnaval" transports the listener once again to the Romantic world of the masked ball, that arena of the fantastic so congenial to the Romantic imagination. Between the stately "Preamble" and the final, rousing "March of the *Davids-*

bündler Against the Philistines,'' a parade of musical masks and portraits passes in review, sometimes in pairs: Pierrot and Harlequin, Eusebius and Florestan, Frederic Chopin and Nicolo Paganini. Behind the mask of "Chiarina" is none other than Schumann's beloved, Clara Wieck; her rival, a certain Ernestina von Fricken, peers from behind yet another musical veil. There are clowns, dancing letters, even mysterious, growling sphinxes.

Obviously the Romantic conceit of the masked ball, half-real, half-fantastic, struck a responsive chord in Schumann's musical imagination. In his musical masquerades, as in the literary masquerades of Jean Paul, Eichendorff, and Hoffmann, the permissible alternation between rigid form and free fancy, between the rational and the fantastic, relaxed the confinement of compositional laws and allowed for the free exercise of *Spieltrieb*, or aesthetic play. With its shifting identities and Dionysian atmosphere, the carnival supplies the perfect framework for the flights of the Romantic spirit: Here, through tricks of disguise, the protean Romantic persona can transform and transcend itself. To the pianist concerned more with mastering the notes of Schumann's "Carnaval"—and they are difficult enough—than with ferreting out literary parallels, this piano suite may well appear to be nothing more than a series of virtuosic variations on the four notes A, E flat, C, and B natural, which indeed it is.[5] To the student of Romanticism, however, "Carnaval" is one of the most extraordinary musical realizations of the half-playful, half-demonic world of the masked fête, that realm of fantasy and fantastic so inextricably woven into the fabric of German Romantic literature. Both points of view, despite the apparent contradiction, are, in fact, equally valid, since "Carnaval," for all its literary associations and evocations, is not bound to any programmatic format. Poetry it is, but it is a poetry that soars beyond the realm of speech to that intangible sphere occupied by music alone.

Schumann's next major piano composition, the C major "Fantasy," Opus 17, marked an even greater departure from a specific literary program. Indeed, if there was a non-musical model for the "Fantasy," then it was the turbulent romance between Schumann and young Clara Wieck, who was later to gain fame as the foremost woman pianist of her day. The main obstacle to the romance was the hostile and overly protective attitude of Clara's father, the celebrated piano teacher, Friedrich Wieck, who guarded his daughter—and prize pupil— as tenaciously as the fictive musician, Counselor Krespel, guards his daughter, Antonia, in Hoffmann's famous tale *Rat Krespel*. It was out of the anguish of separation, therefore, and perhaps also out of Schumann's will to overcome, that the great "Fantasy" was born. But despite this turn to pure music, Schumann had by no means lost faith in the power of words. In his printed instructions to the executant, he went beyond the usual Italian-language performance sugges- tions and substituted German-language instructions of strong psychological im- plications: "Durchaus fantastisch und leidenschaftlich vorzutragen" ("To be executed in a fantastic [for example, highly imaginative] and passionate manner'').[6] Furthermore, as a verbal clue meant for Clara's eyes, he inscribed on the title page some lovely lines by Friedrich Schlegel that, in the best Romantic tradition, seamlessly weld together colors, tones, and dreams:

> Durch alle Töne tönet
> Im bunten Erdentraum
> Ein leiser Ton gezogen
> Für den, der heimlich lauschet.[7]

(Midst all tones in earth's motley colored dream, one gentle tone is sounded for the secret listener.)

In perhaps none of Schumann's compositions for the piano do literary and musical impulses merge more seamlessly than in the set of pieces integrated under the title of ''Kreisleriana,'' Opus 16, a work completed in the year 1838. Johannes Kreisler was a fictional musician, a character created by E. T. A. Hoffmann for two series of *Kreisleriana* written in 1814 and 1815 and reintroduced in Hoffmann's later novel *Kater Murr*. Modeled in part on Hoffman himself, Kreisler is an amalgam of those musicians and music enthusiasts who, either thirsty for music or intoxicated by it, roam through the pages of Hoffman's tales. At the same time, Kreisler is more than just the alter ego of Hoffmann: He is the very incarnation of Romantic music, prefiguring such flesh-and-blood Romantics as Paganini and Franz Liszt, each of whom enthralled audiences as much through their hypnotic personalities as with their virtuosity.

For all Schumann's indebtedness to Hoffmann, the composer's ''Kreisleriana'' is not a musical transcription of Hoffmann's tales. The music bears no subtitles, and there is no ''plot'' other than the music itself. What Schumann's music conveys, rather, is a distillation of Kreisler's manic oscillation between the ecstasy of creation and those dark moments of self-destructive melancholy. If Hoffmann's Kreisler may be said to be intoxicated with the divine madness of music, then one may claim that Schumann was intoxicated in turn with the madness of Kreisler. ''Kreisleriana'' is also confessional music, as is much of Schumann's music, and one suspects that the composer's self-doubt and his troubled romance with Clara Wieck were powerful emotive components of the composition. Withal, the finale of ''Kreisleriana'' contains music that, for want of a better description, is perhaps the most ''Hoffmannesque'' that Schumann ever composed. Consisting of spooky-sounding melodic fragments superimposed on what the ear perceives as strange, bouncy, off-beat rhythms, this finale suggests the kind of music Hoffmann, himself a finished musician and composer, might have created for his ''Kreisleriana'' had his musical talent matched his genius as a teller of fantastic tales.[8] Since it did not, one must be thankful that there was a Robert Schumann to capture the very essence of the Hoffmann narrative and give it lasting musical form. It would be melodramatic to make Kreisler into Schumann's evil genius, or to hold this mere phantom responsible for the composer's madness and early death; for all his demonic power, Kreisler was no "homicidal *Doppelgänger*."[9] Yet it cannot be denied that with the displacement of Jean Paul by Hoffmann, with the substitution of Kreisler for Walt, Vult, and Wina of the *Flegeljahre*, a somberness came into Schumann's music, a tone that, coincidentally or not, had been absent from "Papillons" and "Carnaval." Like the figure of the sandman who haunts poor Nathanael in Hoffmann's gruesome tale *Der Sandmann*, Kreisler was to keep his hold on Schumann's imagination until the very end.

The "Fantasiestücke," Opus 12, comprises another set of pieces—"Fantasy Pieces"—composed under the spell of Kreisler, or at least under the spell of Hoffmann. The "Fantasiestücke" supplies fascinating examples of Schumann's genius for translating certain states of consciousness, certain moods, into tonal language. In these pieces Schumann turned his gaze to that "night-side" of experience that held such fascination for Novalis, Tieck, Eichendorff, Heine, and Hoffmann—indeed for almost every German Romantic writer and poet. The very titles of the pieces suggest the mood and ambiences Schumann sought to convey in the "Fantasiestücke": There is "In der Nacht," with its overtones of mystery; "Warum?"—the eternal question, often left unanswered by the Romantics; "Grillen" ("Whims"); and "Aufschwung" ("Soaring"). If there is one piece in the "Fantasiestücke" that might be singled out as being quintessentially Romantic—in the sense that it conveys the magically evocative mood characteristic of so many Romantic lyrics—it would surely be the opening piece, "Des Abends" ("At Time of Evening"). This short introduction, with its shifting tonality, its supple rhythms, its luminosity and liquescence, its limpid colors and mirror images, suggests a tonal complement to the "verbal music" heard in the finest lyrics of Goethe, Eichendorff, and especially Brentano, whose poem "Abendständchen" ("Evening Serenade") might be viewed as a verbal pendant to "Des Abends":

> Hör, es klagt die Flöte wieder,
> Und die kühlen Brunnen rauschen,
> Golden wehn die Töne nieder—
> Stille, stille, laß uns lauschen!

> Holdes Bitten, mild Verlangen,
> Wie es süß zum Herzen spricht!
> Durch die Nacht, die mich umfangen,
> Blickt zu mir der Töne Licht.[10]

(Hark: once more the flute begins its lament, / And cool springs burble. / In a golden aura the tones waft downward— / Hush, let us listen. / Sweet supplication, gentle yearning, / How sweetly it speaks to the heart! / Through the night surrounding me / There shines the light of tones.)

Schumann's "Kinderszenen," Opus 15, might not, at first glance, seem to have very much to do with literary Romanticism at all; but when one surveys the writings of the German Romantics, one finds that nostalgic veneration of childhood is one of the many common strands weaving their way through the works of Novalis, Tieck, Brentano, and other writers associated with the "Romantic school." In preparing his "Kinderszenen" for publication, Schumann again added titles to the individual pieces, thereby demonstrating once more how important a role verbal enhancement played in the projection of his musical thoughts. Not surprisingly, some of the titles added recall themes familiar from Romantic literature: "Of Distant Lands and Peoples," the opening piece, strikes an Eichendorffian tone of *Wanderlust*; "Scary Story," the eleventh piece, likewise recalls the eerie tales of Tieck and Hoffmann. The best-known piece, however, is the seventh, entitled "Träumerei," which conjures up the realm of dreams the literary Romantic found so congenial. The concluding piece, "Der Dichter spricht," might be interpreted as a bit of Romantic irony, since the poet lays aside his masks and reserves the final commentary on the suite for himself. Like the earlier "Papillons," the "Kinderszenen" was misinterpreted by some critics who felt that Schumann had been too literal, or programmatic, in depicting scenes of childhood. Indeed, one mean-spirited critic named Ludwig Rellstab claimed that Schumann had simply taken a howling child, set it down on top of the piano, and recaptured the child's moods in tones. Schumann parried with the observation that his "Scenes of Childhood" were symbolic, not literal, and that they were, in fact, backward glances toward the ephemeral state of childhood.[11]

Of similar provenance are Schumann's "Waldszenen," Opus 82, those mood-rich "Scenes of the Forest" that were composed in 1849 and hence fall outside that extraordinary first creative decade within which most of Schumann's major piano compositions were written. Notwithstanding their later date of origin, these musical nature miniatures, like the earlier suites, present an amalgam of the musical and literary elements of Schumann's compositional technique. Schumann knew the German forest first-hand from his boyhood in Saxony, an acquaintance deepened by the solitary "wood walks" he enjoyed in later years; hence, that dark, green forest that forms the habitat of so many Romantic tales was anything but a literary artifact for him. Indeed, one may claim that, like the German Romantic writers, Schumann found the forest not only an unending source of inspiration but a link to the German mythic past. Perhaps for this reason his "Waldszenen" is so successful in capturing the *Waldstimmung*, or mood of the woods, which is conveyed so magically both in the German fairy tales and in the matchless lyrics of Goethe and Eichendorff.

The titles chosen by Schumann to illustrate his "Scenes of the Forest" are reflective of the shifting moods and vistas of the woods: "Hunter on the Watch," "Lonely Flowers," "Haunted Spot," "Friendly Landscape," "Wayside Inn," "The Prophet Bird," "Hunting Song," and "Farewell." Significantly, Schumann originally prefaced each piece with a short poem or poetic fragment, but retained only one poem for the published score, a morbid lyric by Friedrich Hebbel entitled "Böser Ort" ("Evil Place"), which he prefaced to the piece "Haunted Spot." Sadly enough, this choice probably stemmed from the gradual darkening of Schumann's spirit and his slow descent into a world of hallucinations. The poem reads in part as follows:

Die Blumen, so hoch sie wachsen,
Sind blaß hier, wie der Tod,
Nur eine in der Mitte
Steht da in dunklem Roth.

Sie hat es nicht von der Sonne,
Nie traf sie deren Glut,
Sie hat es von der Erde,
Und die trank Menschenblut![12]

(The flowers, however high they grow, / Are here as pale as death. / Only one, standing in the middle, / Is dark red. / Her redness comes not from the sun, / Whose heat she has never felt. / Her color comes rather from the earth, / The earth that has drunk human blood!)

Already in the year 1840 Schumann had begun to find the solo piano inadequate for his ever-expanding musical imagination and had turned his attention to that genre that was to prove so congenial to him, the art song, or *Lied*. In all, Schumann was to compose 260 *Lieder*, and although they are inevitably uneven in quality, the best of them exhibit the same inexhaustible vitality, freshness, and richness, the same vivid coloring and resources of harmony, that one admires in the compositions for solo piano. Although Schumann's *Lieder* may sometimes seem to lack the spontaneity and the infinite melodic variety found in the songs of his great predecessor Franz Schubert, they are no less rewarding in their harmonic boldness, their psychological aptness, their atmospheric opulence, and their *Innigkeit*, that inward-directed immediacy characteristic of great German poetry and music alike. More than half of Schumann's songs were based on poems written by poets who were his contemporaries in the Romantic era: Heine, Rückert, Eichendorff, Kerner, Chamisso, Lenau, and Mörike. Perhaps it is this very contemporaneity, this lack of distance, or "time lag," that makes the union between words and music in Schumann's best songs seem so perfect. Admirers of German *Lieder* may well recall the almost magical setting Schumann composed for Eichendorff's "Mondnacht," a contemplative lyric that finds the poet standing awestruck on a starry night, sensing a *unio mystica* as his soul seems to merge with the cosmos:

Es war, als hätt der Himmel
Die Erde still geküßt,
Daß sie im Blütenschimmer
Von ihm nun träumen mäßt.

Die Luft ging durch die Felder,
Die Ähren wogten sacht,
Es rauschten leis die Wälder,
So sternklar war die Nacht.

Und meine Seele spannte
Weit ihre Flügel aus,
Flog durch die stillen Lande
Als flöge sie nach Haus.[13]

(It was as though heaven / Had softly kissed the earth / So that she, in a shimmer of blossoms, / Was now dreaming of heaven. / The breeze passed softly through the fields, / The corn swayed gently, / The woods rustled softly, / The night was bright with stars. / And my soul spread / Its wings widely, / Flew through the silent landscape, / As though it were flying home.)

Schumann's setting of "Mondnacht" is exemplary in its musical re-creation of the poem's mood and amplitude. First, a muted, arpeggiated chord descending from the treble creates an ambience suggestive of the spaciousness and repose of Eichendorff's star-bright nocturnal landscape; then the meditative, other-worldly musings of the first strophe are enhanced by a slender, almost diaphanous accompaniment barely intruding on the vocal line. As the poet's soul "expands its wings" and begins its spiritual flight "homeward," this delicate beginning is broadened harmonically and allowed to swell in volume, as if the poet's soul were being borne "on wings of song." Once more the arpeggiated chord is sounded, this time in a lower range of the piano, before the music, like the poem itself, becomes one with the silence of the cosmos.

"Mondnacht" is the gem of the songs grouped under the title "Liederkreis II" ("Cycle of Songs, II") and based on poems by Eichendorff; the other *Lieder*, lovely as they are, do not display so rare a combination of inspiration and craftmanship. With the cycle "Dichterliebe" ("Poet's Love," Opus 48), however, inspired by poems by Heinrich Heine, Schumann's genius as a *Lied* composer rose to that exalted plane previously occupied by Franz Schubert alone. Nor should that be cause for surprise: No poet spoke more directly to Schumann than Heine, that master of the minor-key love lyric whose wit and wisdom, whose irony and irreverence were fated to stamp him not only as the consummate poet of Romanticism but also as its valedictorian. Heine, like Schumann, was torn between two worlds: He was a Jew by birth who saw himself forced to conform to a predominantly Christian culture, a cosmopolitan often stifled by conservative provincialism, a German patriot who spent years of exile in France, a Romantic living and writing at the very threshold of realism. Written in 1840, the year of Schumann's marriage, "Dichterliebe" consists of musical settings of sixteen Heine poems, all of which are bound together by the theme of love, sometimes blissful and intoxicating, more often marked by yearning and melancholy. Schumann, finally happily married to his beloved Clara, obviously had not forgotten the vicissitudes that had marred and nearly destroyed his own romance. The seminal Romantic themes of *Sehnen und Verlangen*—yearning and desire—were as familiar to Schumann as they were to Heine; doubtless it was this kinship of the spirit, this first-hand experience of the joys and sorrows of love, that invested the opening song of "Dichterliebe," "Im wunderschönen Monat Mai" ("In the Beautiful Month of May"), with such poignance. When the poet sings of "yearning and desire," Schumann is wise enough to read between the lines, as it were, and to interpret these feelings as the expression of an unrequited love; hence, he allows the final cadence of his setting to hover in the air unresolved and—like the poet's love—unrequited.

As a final example of a perfect word–tone synthesis, one might cite the twelfth song of "Dichterliebe," entitled "Am leuchtenden Sommermorgen" ("On a Glowing Summer Morning"), a *Lied* that could have been written only in the Romantic era, where the "real" and the "unreal" worlds are so often willfully transposed. In his poem Heine conjures up a magic garden, one complete with talking flowers and a "sad, pale man" who seems like an intruder in this realm of the fantastic. Schumann, attuned as always to the mysteries of nature, provides the appropriate tonal complement to Heine's whimsical lyric in the form of arpeggiated chords that seem to rise and fall like so many luminous soap bubbles. Not coincidentally, the music seems devoid of any substance, deriving its charm instead from mere suggestion and from its broad spectrum of tonal color. Hence, this *Lied*, perhaps more than any other, affords access to that enchanted garden of Romanticism, that impossible yet so believable sphere of talking flowers, of fairytale figures, of unsolved mysteries and unanswered questions that was the province of an entire generation of German poets.

It was in this realm of the enchanted, the realm of poetry and music merged in the *Lied*, that the two worlds of Robert Schumann found ultimate convergence; here at last the soul of the poet and the soul of the musician were no longer in conflict but in harmony. In a sense, Schumann remained a true Romantic to the end—that is to say a quester, never satisfied, never tiring, always in search of what Novalis called "the blue flower," which to the German literary Romantics was the symbol of the unattainable, and which to Schumann was possibly some great opera or bold symphony never composed. Although the "real" world would ultimately be unkind to Robert Schumann, bringing mental derangement and an untimely death, his "inner" world, the world of enchantment and creativity, the world he bequeathed to posterity, remains with us today: harmonious, infinite, Romantic.

NOTES

1. A good selection of Schumann's letters in English translation can be found in *The Letters of Robert Schumann*, trans. Hannah Bryant (New York: Benjamin Blom, 1971). All letters cited refer to this volume. See Schumann's letters to Frau Henrietta Voigt (Summer 1834), 98, and Simonin de Sire (15 March 1839), 128.

2. Over the years, the term "program music" has acquired a pejorative connotation,

even though it is applied to such masterpieces as Beethoven's *Pastoral* Symphony and the Berlioz *Symphonie fantastique*.

3. See André Boucourechliev, *Schumann* (New York: Grove Press, 1959), 23.

4. Schumann himself seemed to hedge on the matter. See the conclusion of his letter to Frau Voigt in *Letters*, 98.

5. These notes can be written, following German nomenclature, as ASCH, a fact that allowed Schumann to indulge his whimsical inclination toward puns and cryptic formulations: Asch is the name of the hometown of Ernestina von Fricken, a rival of Clara Wieck for Robert's affection.

6. Robert Schumann, *Complete Works for Piano Solo* (New York: Kalmus, 1900), vol. 3, p. 90. Translations are mine.

7. Ibid.

8. Hoffmann did, in fact, compose an opera based on the Romantic figure of Undine, a water sprite. His music, however, was far more conventional than his prose writings and has survived only as a curiosity.

9. The phrase is Marcel Brion's, to whom I am indebted for many insights into the complex relationship between Schumann and the German literary Romantics. See his *Schumann and the Romantic Age* (London: Collins, 1956), 195.

10. Clemens Brentano, *Ausgewählte Werke* (Leipzig: Max Hesse's Verlag, 1904), vol. 1, p. 15.

11. For Schumann's rebuttal of Rellstab's criticism, see his letter of 5 September 1839 to H. Dorn in *Letters*, 132–33.

12. Friedrich Hebbel, *Sämtliche Werke* (Leipzig: Max Hesse's Verlag, 1891), vol. 1, p. 81.

13. Joseph von Eichendorff, *Werke* (Leipzig: Bibliographisches Institut, 1891), vol. 1, p. 282.

Modernism and the Representation of Fantasy: Cubism and Expressionism in *The Cabinet of Dr. Caligari*

Mike Budd

In the late nineteenth and early twentieth centuries, the Modernist movement revolutionized virtually all the arts, as novelists, playwrights, poets, painters, and other artists sought to respond to—and help create—the rapidly changing modern industrial world. Consciously defying traditional aesthetic conventions, these artists developed the strategies of reflexivity, montage, and spatial–temporal discontinuity. Painters like Edvard Munch and Paul Cézanne, for example, repudiated a positivist realism that had assumed that painting represents external facts the eye in isolation transmits to the mind. Instead, these and other painters acknowledged a reality produced as well by fantasies, emotions, sensory experiences, and memory—a reality science was proving to be multiform, relativistic, and dependent on the relation between subject and object.

Yet even as Modernism challenged the dominant aesthetic conventions of narrative, realism, and naturalism in the novel, theater, painting, and other arts, these conventions were borrowed and molded into a new discourse, more dominant than any of its antecedents, which would establish hegemony over the new medium of film in less than three decades. Though Modernist artists as well as critics and theorists usually thought of film during this period in terms of its essential qualities, its unique potential, what was really at stake was not film's essence but its cultural function, its social usage. And here the businessmen and entrepreneurs were far ahead of the avant-garde, for they had been from the first the bosses of those who developed film's technological base, and they were developing filmic forms and institutions responsive to a capitalist economy increasingly oriented toward consumption rather than production. The mode of film discourse developed by Hollywood and the other commercial film industries by around 1915 to 1920, which we may call realist narrative, was developed not so much in response to the needs of its burgeoning audiences, let alone the activities of Modernist artists, but rather in response primarily to the industrial and corporate requirements of film producers—specifically, their desire to ensure steady and growing consumption of their films in order to stabilize mass production based on an efficient division of labor.

From 1896 until about 1902, the "primitive" cinema exploited its own novelty with short scenes of celebrities, exotic locations, and magical fantasies. Its discourse was relatively unformed and inarticulate: Without a strong temporal structure, the films could not hold an audience's attention for long, while the camera framed everything in long shots, as diffuse tableaux, so that images and their relationships lacked formal and semiotic organization. In a commercial context, primitive cinema was insufficiently consumable; as form follows function, the development of realist narrative over the next decade or so would be largely subject to the constraints of an economy of consumption, in which films, like other industrial products, could be "used up," to produce demand for more.

Thus, while other determinants were undoubtedly significant, consumability was surely central to the discourse that became dominant. Film style, the recurrent and significant use of film techniques, began to be motivated—justified—almost entirely by narrative. Films told, and still tell, stories in a way that promotes empathy with characters and narration, that makes technique "invisible," and that "centers" the viewer as subject of a flatteringly omniscient narrational presence. One looks "through" the picture plane of a realist narrative film as one looks through the window-like frame of a Renaissance painting, and no wonder: The movie camera is a sophisticated development from the *camera obscura*, or darkened chamber, developed by Renaissance painters to help make their imitations of the "objective" world more scientifically precise through perspective. Realist narrative is based in an ideology of the visible, in which spectators are invited to accept the unexamined assumption that seeing is believing. This ideology does not reside in the technological apparatus itself, as those Modernist artists who deformed film images optically were to demonstrate during the twenties, but rather in the production of an imaginary *diegesis*, an illusionistic spatiotemporal continuity for the sole use of the narration.

By around 1915–1920, the discursive mode described above had developed a worldwide hegemony that it maintains, with minor modifications, to this day, which is to say that as an institution it is reproduced both economically and subjectively, through the circulation and exchange not only of money but also of meaning, value, and human emotions as commodities. Reinforced by the ideology of the camera as recorder, realist narrative militates against a critical self-consciousness in viewers, promoting itself as the only way of seeing or knowing, smoothing the seemingly self-evident path to pleasurable entertainment without consequences.[1]

A measure of the development of realist narrative during this early period is its flexibility in articulating registers or modes within itself. Prime among these are fantasy and dream, in which the conventionally "invisible" narration seeks to become partially and temporarily visible, motivated usually by the subjectivity of a character. Thus, fantasy can be *contained* within "reality," omniscient narration holding its "subjective" counterpart within a stable frame of reference, the homogeneous authority of the narration established in its very invisibility. A fantasy unmarked as subjective might be puzzling or unsettling, even unconsumable; the marking can be done at the beginning and end of the fantasy, or throughout; it can be done with optical devices that distort the image or with deviations from a naturalistic *mise-en-scène*; but always it says implicitly, "Someone is telling/imagining this," since it reminds the audience of itself— and, of course, provides an alibi for the invisible narration that seems to be told by no one, or just appears, apparently without a source of enunciation.

The vicissitudes and contradictions involved in the articulation of these registers can be seen in a particularly intricate and fascinating text, *The Cabinet of Dr. Caligari* (1919). I am less interested in the meaning or content of fantasies than in the ways these registers are or are not distinguished, in the particular textual strategies that make possible the production of meaning by viewers but do not determine that meaning.

The Cabinet of Dr. Caligari provides a special opportunity for examining the assumptions of realist narrative texts, since it exists at the limit point of this discourse: It tells a story within a coherent, realist, diegetic space and time, but its settings, costumes, and acting all participate to an uneven degree in the Modernist revolt against the conventions of realism. Thus, the articulation of fantasy in *Caligari* produces and is produced by the unique tension between realist and Modernist modes within the film itself. And we may approach the problem more precisely, perhaps, by a further distinction between Modernisms— between German Expressionism, a style and movement to which *Caligari* is clearly indebted, and the more radical Cubism, to which the film apparently owes nothing, but which, on closer inspection, can provide three areas of comparison with which to tease out the assumptions of the film's representation of fantasy. Particular textual processes implicate larger modes and mixtures of modes, and by measuring these processes in relation to the dominant discourse and its heterogeneous Modernist alternatives, we may be able to illuminate, reciprocally, both structure(s) and event, systems and processes.

Recent scholarship on Cubism argues a new interpretation of this style. Concentrating on the "true" Cubism of Georges Braque and Pablo Picasso from about 1909 until the First World War, writers such as Douglas Cooper see these artists engaged not so much in testing conceptual theories or mathematical formulas about space and time, but primarily in searching for ways of representing the tangible reality, the *materiality* of objects in the world, but *without* the illusionism of the Renaissance tradition.[2] Thus, there is a tension in Cubism between the materiality of the three-dimensional objects represented on the canvas and the equally material two-dimensional flat surface of the canvas itself. The representation of volume through faceting, temporal simultaneity, abandonment of naturalistic one-source light, and movement toward flatness—these characteristics of Cubism are produced by that tension, which rejects abstraction as a devaluation of the visible world and illusionism as a devaluation of the concrete world of forms on the canvas. In this view, then, Cubism is predominantly a *materialist* style, whereas Expressionism would be *idealist*, a search for objective equivalents or expressions of inner states.

In their radical attack on the dominant modes of representation in Western painting, Braque and Picasso went through at least three stages, introducing three new kinds of elements or techniques. First, they denied Renaissance perspective by denying its basis, the illusion of recession into a three-dimensional space. Second, they introduced lettering and words onto the surfaces of their canvases, as opposed to the illusionistic space "behind" that canvas. Finally, they applied real objects—newspapers, chair caning, imitation wood-grain paper—to produce the first collages, the "pasted papers." Clearly, Picasso and Braque maintained the aforementioned tension even as they moved toward flatness; they almost always included painted or drawn figures in their collages, for example. The Cubism of this period, it may be argued, represents perhaps the most radical dimension of the Modernist movement in painting, since it struck at the very heart of the realist tradition—the imitation of perspective and three dimensionality. And *The Cabinet of Dr. Caligari* develops strategies comparable with those of the Cubists.

Whereas Cubism attacked recession and perspective directly, leading the eye instantly back to the surface of the canvas even as it sought out depth cues, *Caligari* distorts and exaggerates perspective, setting up crazy angles, slanting walls, impossible spaces. In this film, spectators are usually more aware of two-dimensional forms than they are when the naturalistic settings of most realist narratives predominate, but the continuity of diegetic space and time reinforces the opposite tendency, the illusion of looking through a window, or a series of windows, conveniently placed, always anticipating our questions, simultaneously answering and asking new questions with new spaces. The characters are walking around in a three-dimensional space, however deformed or theatrically stylized.

In perhaps the best-known shot in this famous film, Cesare, kidnapping Jane, carries her across the rooftops within such a deranged perspective that many viewers are startled at how few steps it takes him to navigate what appeared to be such a deep space. This surprise is based on the triumph of illusion rather than its denial, on the eye-fooling device of a deranged perspective without the usually full lighting to provide us with the depth cues for measuring that derangement as in most of the rest of the film. Cesare is usually read as a character at one with this insane environment, yet this event is a disjunction between his movements and that space. What is at stake here is the motivation for the film's deviations from the conventions of realist narrative: In a film about insanity, viewers are invited to read Modernist transgressions as indications of the mad fantasies of characters, whether Caligari and Cesare or Francis, the narrator. Thus, a viewer's surprise at this shot is in the disjunction between two illusions, that of "normal" perspectival three-dimensional space and that of an exaggerated but equally three-dimensional space—in contrast to the Cubist disjunction of three-dimensional and two-dimensional spaces. The film maintains an illusionistic diegetic space: Cesare's movements bring us back to the stability of a familiar spatial mode even as they reveal the Expressionist deformation. The film constantly hedges its bets, usually "placing" its deviations in relation to a norm so that it can "place" insanity in relation to the sanity of its own narrational enunciation.

Braque and Picasso began to subvert or ignore recession very early, bringing their forms up to the surface of the canvas. But *Caligari* wants both to produce a coherent story space and to designate that space (ambiguously) as mad; so perspective becomes a constant problem, a source of tension within the text's operation. This is nowhere clearer than in the piazza scene. Francis has followed Caligari to the asylum, and enters a new kind of space.

Whereas the rest of the film denies a middle ground, here there is an emphasis on it, a spaciousness. The open piazza leads to a classical tripartite arch, an architectural formation common in the Renaissance, and admired for its grace, precision, and logic. But compare the rendering of piazza and arch in a work as clearly Renaissance as Raphael's *The School of Athens* (1510–1511) to its replication in *Caligari*. Raphael's painting literally shows us how linear perspective recedes from the foreground in orthogonals which meet at the vanishing point in the background through the arrangement of tiles in the piazza. In *Caligari*, this perspective is reversed. It is Francis, the narrator, who stands at the vanishing point—yet that point is not in the background, but in the foreground. Distance irrationally advances.[3]

The contradictions of space in *Caligari* are focused in this shot, with the Expressionism of the reversed and irrational perspective meeting the classical rationality of the three arches. Our narrator commands the center of this irrational space, and he will later attack the benevolent psychiatrist who attempts to usurp this place, in the action that marks him as mad. This action allows most viewers retrospectively to designate Francis as the "source" of the reversed perspective, the motivation for a Modernism branded as hallucinatory fantasy.

The Cubists introduced a second radical innovation into their paintings: Letters and words further materialized the picture plane. Two aspects of *Caligari* bear comparison here. First, like other silent films, *Caligari* uses written intertitles for dialogue and narration. But these intertitles, unlike those in other films, are presented, at least in the film's original German version, in a graphic style that matches the Expressionist *mise-en-scène*. This device can have the effect of emphasizing the two-dimensional design of the images, of making the film's space flatter and less naturalistic. Yet insofar as Expressionist design is read as "mere" fantasy, this lettering becomes not material but ethereal, an illusion motivated by the illusion of character.

But *Caligari*, like Cubism, also introduces lettering into the image itself. This more unusual step occurs when Dr. Caligari is first in the grip of his Faustian obsession with power over Cesare. As he walks through the garden, the German words for "You must become Caligari" appear all around him as a projection of his own compulsions. Apparently, at least some of these were intended by the filmmakers to appear as if on the walls and other objects within the diegetic space; but they were filmed using a rather obvious transparency or double-exposure process, and so lose whatever illusion of perspective was intended and, at least in currently extant sixteen-millimeter prints, become entirely flat. It is a disconcerting scene, but again, the flatness is largely recuperated into the diegetic space, since Caligari looks at the letters, reacts to them, and makes them a part of "his" space; so that the film can once again disavow its address to us, the audience, can once again deny its own materiality with the alibi of fantasy.

Finally, the Cubists, in introducing real objects into their paintings, "called the bluff" of the illusionist tradition in the flatness of their collages. Yet in maintaining some drawn or painted figures in these "pasted papers," Braque and Picasso preserved that tension, that ironic self-consciousness so characteristic of Cubism in their juxtaposition of painted objects and real objects. *Caligari*, too, juxtaposes "real" and painted objects, but the tension is inadvertent rather than intentionally ironic. Many commentators have pointed out the contradiction of having human characters move against such an obviously painted background—the illusion is threatened, and characters look disconcertingly material. Yet the contradiction is not there with Caligari and Cesare, who are at one with this environment. It is most pronounced with those characters marked as sane throughout—the police, the townspeople, and especially the doctors, who seem to have no relation to their surroundings at all. The heterogeneity of acting styles in the film, ranging from the Expressionist stylization of Caligari and Cesare through the conventional silent film histrionics of Francis and Jane to the restrained and relatively naturalistic portrayal of the white-coated doctors, is no accident but a symptomatic contradiction produced by the contradictory projects of the film. On the one hand, there is the necessity for stylistic consistency between setting and character: This is provided by, but limited to, Caligari and Cesare. But, on the other, in a realist film in which setting seems to be motivated by insanity in a character, and in which that insanity will be suddenly and unexpectedly switched from a character to the narrator of the story itself, there is need for a stable reference point against which to measure the fantasies of madness or their absence. Unlike most realist narrative films, *Caligari* abandons the stability of naturalist settings, but must retain it in the representation of authoritative characters. The Cubists juxtaposed the real and the painted in an ironic comment on the illusionistic tradition they opposed; *Caligari* unintentionally makes its naturalistic characters seem more "real" in their relation to painted sets because the film is still based in the illusionistic tradition it can only partially and ambivalently oppose.

Artistic extremism . . . receives its legitimacy from the tradition it negates. Hegel taught that wherever something new becomes visible, immediate, striking, authentic, a long process of formation has preceded it and it has now merely thrown off its shell. Only that which has been nourished with the life-blood of the tradition can possibly have the power to confront it authentically; the rest becomes the helpless prey of forces which it has failed to overcome sufficiently within itself.[4]

In the Cubists' sustained rebellion, there was the freedom of fantasy. *Caligari*'s representation of fantasy conceals its opposite, the fantasy of innocent immediacy, the fantasy of fantasy without representation.

NOTES

1. The critique of narrative and realism summarized here derives from a still-controversial body of theory and analysis, much of it first published in the British journal *Screen* during the 1970s. Although the following do not represent a unified position, they constitute a range of interrelated texts: Roland Barthes, *S/Z*, trans. Richard Miller (New York: Hill and Wang, 1974); Rosalind Coward and John Ellis, *Language and Materialism* (London: Routledge and Kegan Paul, 1977); David Bordwell and Kristin Thompson, *Film Art: An Introduction* (Reading, MA.: Addison-Wesley, 1979); Noel Burch, *To the Distant Observer* (Berkeley: University of California Press, 1979); Stephen Heath, *Questions of Cinema* (London: Macmillan, 1981); Peter Wollen, *Readings and Writings* (New York: Schocken Books, 1983); David Bordwell, Kristin Thompson, and Janet Staiger, *The Classical Hollywood Cinema: Film Style and Mode of Production to 1960* (London: Routledge and Kegan Paul, 1984).

2. Douglas Cooper, *The Cubist Epoch* (New York: E. P. Dutton, 1970), 37–58 and passim.

3. Many of the ideas and some of the words in the present article were developed with Nancy Ketchiff during a summer seminar, "Toward a Theory of Modernism: An Interdisciplinary Approach," led by Professor Harvey Gross of the State University of New York at Stony Brook and sponsored by the National Endowment for the Humanities. I am greatly indebted to Dr. Ketchiff for her keen insights and articulate analysis of the function of visual forms in *Caligari*.

4. Theodor W. Adorno, "Arnold Schoenberg 1874–1951," in *Prisms*, trans. Samuel and Shierry Weber (London: Neville Spearman, 1967), 155.

THEORETICAL APPROACHES TO THE FANTASTIC

What is the fantastic? These essays, as replies to that question, reveal preconceptions about natural law, moral and immoral power, object and subject, truth and appearance. They examine the fantastic as an index to preconceptions that either underlie the text as givens or set into motion the threatening play of paradox.

The Ethical Status of Magic

William Schuyler

There is considerable disagreement among scholars as to whether magic is good or evil. This disagreement rests in large part on ambiguity and confusion, not to mention self-interest, envy, and general malevolence. Therefore, I shall take the time to define several common terms in the interests of clarity and precision before tackling my main subject.

Nature is the subject matter of physics, chemistry, biology, and (perhaps) psychology. Natural law comprises the principles that govern the behavior of nature. The supernatural includes all that is, but is not part of nature. Magic is whatever is done to make use of the supernatural.

Nothing here requires the supernatural to be unordered. It may very well have a nomological order every bit as constraining as natural law is on nature. The point is that such laws of the supernatural would not be laws of nature.

In order to deal with the ethical issues I raise below, it will be useful to have available a threefold distinction among different types of ethical theories. An *act-centered* theory is one in which rightness or wrongness attaches to the nature of an act performed (or omitted). No account of consequences or motives is taken. The Ten Commandments are a familiar example, but several species of ethical intuitionism also qualify. A *consequence-centered* theory is one in which only the values of the consequences of an act are taken into account. The nature of the act and the motives for it are ignored. The most familiar example will be utilitarianism. A *motive-centered* theory takes into account only motives, ignoring consequences and natures of acts. Kant's system is a good example.

All three types have their weaknesses, which they try more or less successfully to conceal. Each of them can be combined with either or both of the others.

Although magic has usually received sympathetic treatment in fantasy, there are points of view from which it simply cannot be tolerated. The Judeo–Christian tradition is a major case in point. The Bible says, "Thou shalt not suffer a witch to live'' (Exodus 22:18), and this injunction has been followed with much greater enthusiasm than the one against adultery. What sort of reasoning could be behind this?

I was at some pains earlier to define "nature." In Roman Catholic theology, it is held that man's behavior must be in accord with "natural law" in order to be morally correct. The domain of magic is the supernatural. Does it follow that anyone who traffics in magic is not behaving in accord with natural law?

Not yet. First it must be shown that the use of magic breaks natural law. The supernatural might be an extension of the natural, as is the case in Jack Vance's *Dying Earth*, where mathematics is the foundation of magic. But it might equally well be that the natural and the supernatural are fundamentally different. In Alexei and Cory Panshin's *Earth Magic*, Haldane attains magical powers by his dealings with the Goddess Libera; but his companion, the magician, Oliver, does not believe in the gods and has been confirmed in his skepticism by a look through a telescope that showed a putative god to be only a moon. Here science and magic coexist uneasily. In either case, magic might override natural law, though it need not.

Yet it would be wrong (in the context of the Christian doctrine of natural law) for human beings to invoke the supernatural in either case. For mankind to act rightly is to follow the natural law, but unlike other beings we have free will. We are able to choose to act in ways that do not accord with natural law.

In *That Hideous Strength*, C. S. Lewis explains that the effect of dealing with supernatural beings (for they are, he holds, the source of magic) is that any human being who does so is inevitably diminished in just those areas that make him or her human. This consequence happens even if the beings wish us well, which is not always the case. For Lewis, then, the moral aspect of natural law, which tells us not to stray outside its bounds, is consequence centered. In *Black Easter*, James Blish confirms Lewis's position on the source of magic, but he goes on to remark that the Church holds magic to be anathema. This sounds like an act-centered position, but it was taken because of the consequences of permitting magic and is thus consequence centered.[1]

Of course, that is not all there is to it. Many people would like to be able to use magic for virtuous purposes, so they say. Thus is born the dubious distinction between black magic and white magic, based on motive-centered or consequence-centered considerations, perhaps both. The distinction is dubious because in the theories we are discussing good motives and good consequences cannot outweigh the bad consequences and the risks, as Blish points out.[2] So much for the view of magic against which the majority of contemporary writers of fantasy react.

The most obvious place to attack this theory is on its doctrine of natural law and its ramifications. First, one could argue that since the notion of natural law properly construed does not encompass ethics, it cannot be used to justify a ban on magic. Second, one could argue that the notion of natural law properly construed does not allow a distinction between natural and supernatural. This line has two branches: in the first, the gradation between natural and supernatural is so smooth that one simply moves insensibly from one to the other; in the second, the laws of magic are indeed emergent with respect to natural law, but so are the laws of chemistry with respect to physics, and the cases are exactly analogous. In both branches the distinction between natural and supernatural is seen as merely traditional. Third, one could reject the whole notion of natural law. The underlying premise here is that there is no real order in the world.

It is easy to make a case for the first approach. Although both the law of gravity and moral law are part of natural law, we can break the latter but not the former. Why not make a distinction between laws we cannot help but obey and laws that we may choose not to obey? The reason for putting them on the same footing is that both kinds of law are held to emanate from God; but even within Christian theology, a strong case can be made for saying that what is good is independent of God's will. In that case, morality would be independent of God and could not be conflated with natural law, which would emanate from God. In Hilbert Schenck's *At the Eye of the Ocean*, Abel Roon is sure that his visions of the ocean and his innate understanding of Water Speech are magical. He sees no conflict between magic and religion, no doubt because his gift does not require commerce with supernatural beings. This is magic of another kind, one that is neither so taxing to the moral faculties nor so dangerous as the Christian version. Accordingly, there is no reason to reject it in this consequence-centered ethical system, whether or not that system emanates from God. In Abel's case, it apparently does not originate with God and would be distinct from natural law regardless of whether that issued from God.

The second approach in both its branches usually presupposes that natural law is morally neutral. That is not at all the same as accepting a distinction between natural law and moral law, which is what we would get if the first approach were successful. It could still be that some kinds of knowledge are good or bad in themselves. ("There are some things that man was not meant to know," as the old scientist is always saying to his brash young colleague in bad movies.)

An excellent example of non-neutrality on the first branch is to be found in Geoffrey Household's *Sending*. There, the Old Religion gets very sympathetic treatment. It is pictured as destroying anyone who would misuse it by turning back the forces unleashed by the miscreant upon himself. Moreover, a bold claim is staked: The Old Religion, not Christianity, is the place to look for a true understanding of nature and natural law.

There is a certain plausibility to this, since the Old Religion paid careful attention to the propitiation of nature gods down to the local level. However, it seems to go against the definition I proposed above of "nature" as the subject matter of physics, etc. It need not do so. Even in physics as we know it, there are distinctions among theoreticians, experimentalists, and engineers. The engineers do things that appall the less practically oriented, but their infernal machines work. What we have in *The Sending* is understanding at the engineers' level. Perhaps the implicit theory behind practice there is not the same as ours, but we have no guarantee that quantum mechanics is the ultimate truth.

As I said, however, taking magical knowledge as ethically neutral is a more common stance. Fritz Leiber's *Conjure Wife* is an excellent example. The sociologist hero simply puts magical rituals into symbolic logic, and lo! we have scientific principles no stranger than what passes for science in sociology today. No natural boundary between science and magic exists.

The other branch of the second case embodies a contrary point of view: There is a difference between magic and science, though not a difference in kind. Randall Garrett's stories about Lord Darcy and Master Sean fit here. In their world, the Church has been persuaded that the laws of magic are natural law. There is no barrier there to a rigorous scientific investigation of magic, and this occurs. In this world, Lord Darcy is a detective in the tradition of Sherlock Holmes, using dazzling displays of reason to solve apparently impossible crimes. But Master Sean is more than a Watson: He is a forensic sorcerer invaluable to Darcy, who does not have the talent to gather the kinds of evidence that Master Sean can make available through his spells. As for what we would regard as science, it is mostly dismissed as superstition, although technology has developed well enough.

Garrett's works suggest that one can do magic without doing physics, as well as the contrary. Science as we know it and magic have parallel sets of laws, either or both of which can be investigated scientifically. The main difference between black and white magics is the purpose to which each is put. Here is a motive-centered analysis, which leaves magical knowledge ethically neutral. A use of a spell will be black or white magic depending on why it is used but not on its nature or its consequences. Of course, some very destructive spells will obviously have more potential black uses than white, and some curative spells more white uses than black, but the principle remains.

The third case might seem a philosopher's whimsy. How can it be claimed that there is no real order in the world when we see order all around us? Both theologians and philosophers of science have interesting things to say about this matter, but no more so than what Roger Zelazny says in his "Amber" series. The story starts out as an elaborate alternate-worlds fantasy; but gradually we learn that some shadow worlds are more ordered than others, and that there is a progression from order to disorder in the shadow worlds that has its poles in Amber and the Courts of Chaos. Eventually we learn that the order epitomized in Amber is not natural but imposed. The natural state of affairs is chaos. There is no *natural* law.

Magic in these circumstances is something quite different from what it is in the other cases. It is not an alternative or addition to science, because without natural law there is no science.

The ethical status of this magic is puzzling, since it is not clear whether good and evil are created or have an independent existence. Perhaps magical knowledge here is not inherently good or evil; but it is hard to be sure, since the main characters are apparently egoistic hedonists at best. If they sometimes have regrets, it is mostly for present inconvenience caused by their past acts. There seems to be no distinction between black and white magics. What we seem to have is a consequence-based method of judging the morality of magical deeds, but it is certainly not utilitarian.

There are, then, several sharply distinct ideas of what magic is, and these go hand in hand with different ideas of natural law. Magic in its various guises may be judged in terms of different ethical theories. However, no view of magic, except highly integrated ones like the Christian view, is uniquely tied to a particular kind of ethical theory. Christian literature almost always distinguishes black magic from white on the basis of motive, but there is no reason in principle why the two could not be distinguished by the nature of the act performed or by its consequences.

I do not presume to have solved a problem but to have revealed its true complexity. The multitude of approaches to magic in literature may be further multiplied by recognition of ignored possibilities. I am better pleased with this than I would have been with a definitive solution that settled the ethical status of magic once and for all. There is something to be said for not saying the last word.

NOTES

1. James Blish, *Black Easter* (1968; reprint, New York: Avon, 1979), 28–29, 40.
2. Ibid., 40.

The Disenchantment of Magic

Jules Zanger and Robert G. Wolf

Recent twentieth-century fantasy literature has undergone a shift in attitude toward magic and the role magic plays in the lives of the characters in its stories. Briefly stated, the shift is from one in which magic is part of the background of the story and is an intrinsically immoral, threatening force to one in which magic and its attainment are the central key to the resolution of the plot and in which magic is an intrinsically neutral force just as easily used for good as for evil.

In the older, predominantly British view, magic and its practitioners may set the problem around which the plot revolves, but the hero is not himself or herself a magician, and the resolution of the problem involves non-magical (usually moral) effort on the part of the hero. The hero is everyman (or everychild), while the practitioners of magic (wizards, witches, demons, necromancers, etc.) are at best of ambiguous value. Usually they are the enemy, whose magic must be overcome; occasionally they assist the hero, but then their goodness is coupled with a relative inferiority in their magical ability as compared with the abilities of the foe. The magician is either evil and powerful or good but, for a variety of reasons, ineffective.

In the newer view, which appears to be predominantly American, magic not only sets the problem but is the principle of resolution. The hero is a version of the sorcerer's apprentice, who overcomes by becoming a better practitioner than his opponent. The hero is a specialist in magic who triumphs by mastering the technology of magic, not by essentially non-magical or moral effort. Magic is not an undifferentiated background to the story, but a device whose inner workings must be articulated as the main avenue for the triumph of good. Both these views coexist today. The older view is dominant in recent British fantasy, while the new view is prominent in recent American fantasy. American fantasy writers

as a group produce stories showing both views; British fantasy writers almost
never write stories evidencing the newer view.

Both the older and the newer views spring from the social situations of the
authors and their audiences and particularly from the social impact of modern
science and its attendant technology upon the writing community.

The connection between evil and magic is a traditional one, so widely accepted
that, until recently, "evil magician" could be regarded as a single compound
noun. The origins of this connection probably go back to the Garden itself, where
the subtle serpent eternally disrupted the coincident Divine and natural designs
of things by his willful deception of Adam and Eve. In our earliest fantasy
literature, magic tends to be regarded as both willful and deceiving. It is willful
in that it opposes human will to the order of the creation, violating the laws of
nature made by God to perform what are, in effect, pseudo-miracles. It is
deceiving in that its intention is to trick the Christian into betraying his faith. It
is also deceiving in that its effects are ultimately illusory rather than real: That
is, they deal with appearance rather than the essential reality of the creation.
Thus, ugly crones may be made to appear young and beautiful, filthy hovels
may be transformed into palaces—for as long as the spell serves. Archimago,
the evil magician of Edmund Spenser's *Faerie Queene*, or John Milton's Comus
were precisely such masters of illusion, creating false images of virtue to dupe
the innocent. But all these illusions could be dispelled by the touch of holy water
or, alternatively, of cold iron, or by a child's honest gaze, or by the sign of the
cross, or even by the rising of the sun.

The magician makes his real or illusory alterations of the natural order through
the exertion of power, through binding spells and conjurations, through the
control of demons, through the manipulation of forces. This emphasis on power,
control, manipulation, and force is in contrast with the function of the saint,
who may achieve ends also out of the natural order, but who employs prayer
and supplication. The saint says, "Thy will be done"; the magician orders,
"My will be done." In this regard, the false miracles, the acts of magicians and
witches, are usually acts of transformation and alteration; the good miracles
performed by saints and heroes are acts of restoration. Since magic employed
power to alter the natural order of the creation, it was always tinged with impiety,
and even good "white" magic was of precarious virtue.

This essentially Christian view of magic was to change at the beginning of
the nineteenth century. When Faust, rather than Archimago, became the dominant image of the magician, the idea of magic as impiety was to become
subordinated to the idea of magic as forbidden knowledge. The idea of a body
of knowledge that can bring death to its learner is a traditional one, having its
major source in Genesis, but it was to receive its definitive reembodiment in
Johann Wolfgang von Goethe's Faust, who risks damnation to acquire the secrets
of the universe. His ambitions are more subtle than those of Christopher Mar-

lowe's Dr. Faustus, who is tempted to lose his soul by wealth, power, and the beauty of Helen of Troy. Although in his dealings with Mephistopheles Goethe's Faust still represents an older view, in his desire for knowledge and experience he suggests the heroic Romanticism of a new age, an age of science and technology. In this shift, the magician emerges ambivalently as both demonic and Promethean. The distance from Dr. Faustus to Dr. Faust is great; the distance from Dr. Faust to Dr. Frankenstein is short, and from there, the Wizard of Menlo Park is only a step away. The extreme polarization of good and evil that marked the older pattern of magician was to be rivaled by a new pattern in which increasingly gray areas appeared. Nathaniel Hawthorne's alchemist–scientist, Aylmer, in ''The Birthmark'' and Mark Twain's Connecticut Yankee suggest the ambivalence of feelings toward the new magician of the century: the awe and gratification, and the increasing distrust. As the century wore on, the miracles of power and energy that were released in turn released the demons of urban slums, social unrest, and revolution. Romanticism, which had begun as a revolutionary movement, became, in its second generation, counterrevolutionary, opposing skepticism with faith and science with fantasy. In this new fantasy, magicians were still evil, but their evil was no longer cast simply in Christian terms. Instead, the magicians had become the technologists of magic, motivated not so much by the satanic desire to subvert the souls of their victims as by all-too-human greed and ambition and the desire for power. The changes they made were no longer mere illusion but terrible and real enough.

E. T. A. Hoffmann's evil magician, Coppelius, represents an early version of this pattern. He creates in Coppelia, a mechanical doll, an illusion of living beauty so perfect that her lover is driven to madness and death when he learns that she is compounded of gears and cogs. In this sense, Coppelius is a magician of illusion, but in a new and prophetic sense he is also a magician of technology whose magic is only a higher degree of the engineer's art.

J. R. R. Tolkein's Sauron, coming at the end of the dominance of this pattern, was to be its highest achievement, combining incredible power with an insatiable appetite for evil. His land of Mordor is transformed by his arts in what looks remarkably like Charles Dickens's Coketown in *Hard Times*.

In opposition to these masters of evil are heroes and, occasionally, good magicians. These good magicians, however, are rarely the center of the action, serving usually as aides and advisors or in some ancillary role. Their magic is never by itself adequate to defeat that of the evil magicians, so that, conventionally, evil magicians are opposed by human heroes who may be aided by good magicians. These good magicians are not only inadequate themselves to overthrow evil, they are often awkwardly absent at crucial moments or simply inept. Merlin is sleeping in Nimue's cave at the last great battle with Mordred; Gandalf is perched on a mountain peak waiting for an eagle through much of the action; Cadellin Silver Brow, in Alan Garner's *Weirdstone of Brisingamen*, must guard the sleepers during the final battle; Peter Beagle's Schmendrick in

The Last Unicorn is not a very good magician; and the Wizard of Oz is simply a fraud. Supported by these bending reeds, the hero or heroine must shoulder the burden of the good fight.

This emphasis on a human rather than a magical protagonist made fantasy an essentially moral *agon*, pitting individual human courage and decency against preternatural power. Fantasy echoed in its own terms the contemporary plight of individuals confronted by social and technological forces so vast as to dwarf them. But unlike naturalism's depiction of inevitable human defeat in works like Stephen Crane's *Maggie* or Theodore Dreiser's *American Tragedy*, fantasy offered a vision of individuals triumphant over the opaque power of evil.

An obvious feature of the newer view of magic in fantasy literature is the altered role of the magician. No longer is the good magician an ancillary to the non-magic hero; the hero is himself a practicing magician. The resolution of the plot often involves the hero's mastering the technology of magic and utilizing it to defeat the foe. The earliest instance of this trend of which I am aware is Fritz Leiber's *Conjure Wife*, published in 1942, in which the hero, Norman Saylor, in order to rescue his wife from the sorcery of the wives of his rival faculty members in the Sociology Department of Hempnell College, is forced to become a sorcerer himself. Saylor, by the end of the story, is matched against three witches and defeats them on their own ground.

In *Conjure Wife*, magic is open to practice by any, including the hero, who wish to learn the appropriate methods. Ursula Le Guin's *Wizard of Earthsea* trilogy also features a sorcerer, Ged, who overcomes his obstacles by study of the basic principles of magic. In both cases, the study does not involve any basic alteration of the fundamental character of the hero—a good man before learning magic, he retains his character, adding only an extrinsic body of information.

A related version is that in which magic is viewed as appropriable only by those with an inborn talent. The hero is presented as being a member of this privileged group; study mainly sharpens an innate ability, much as perhaps the trained musician must have built upon an already present musical ability. The *Riddle of Stars* trilogy by Patricia McKillip develops this theme: The hero, Morgan, to understand his heritage must master the principles of the Land Rule that governs the realms in which he travels. Only through such mastery—which is clearly open only to Morgan—can he hope to oppose the magic of two separate sets of evil magicians.

The *Deryni* and *Camber* trilogies of Katherine Kurtz also utilize the notion of magic being open only to a select group, in this case the Deryni. In *Deryni Rising*, the defeat of the evil sorcerers involves the efforts of two heroic magicians, one of whom, Kelson, finally defeats the sorceress through the growth of his own magic abilities. Finally, the *Dark Is Rising* sequence by Susan Cooper revolves around the growth of yet another magus, Will Stanton, belonging to a select group of magicians fated to combat the forces of the Dark. (This effect is rather as if the *Ring* trilogy focused on Gandalf and his colleagues to the exclusion of men and hobbits.)

Coupled with the elevation of the wizard to the status of main protagonist is a revised view of magic itself. Magic has become a counterpart of science, having a law-like structure, achieving objectively verifiable results, and open to all who learn its ways. *Conjure Wife* again sets out the basic point. Saylor, utilizing his scientific training as an anthropologist, gathers together a multitude of variant spells, translates them into the arcane language of modern symbolic logic, and, by logical analysis, distills them down into a set of basic formulas that uncover the intrinsic structure of magical laws. (Jack in Roger Zelazny's *Jack of Shadows* uses the post–1942 device of a computer to do exactly the same thing.) Empowered by the use of spells invoked in their pristine form, Saylor (and Shadow Jack) is easily able to overmatch his adversaries. (Saylor's approach is parallel to that of the atomic scientists who at the same time—1942—were also analyzing phenomena, drawing out from them the underlying principles and using the knowledge gained to build spells capable of easily overmatching their enemies.)

Ged, in *The Wizard of Earthsea*, also moves from crude nature conjuring to a Faustian understanding of the basic structure of the world, in this case a knowledge of the true names that attach to all objects in reality, a knowledge that allows Ged to manipulate those objects. Perhaps the most elaborate development of this idea is Kenneth Hardy's *Master of Five Magics* in which the hero, in order to obtain the fair princess whom he imagines he desires, must learn the inner workings of five different branches of magic. In each instance, the hero's new-gained knowledge allows him to fulfill a task, although the consequence of his success compels him only to further apprenticeship in a new branch of magic.

Magic in each of these stories is a force, not a tool to create illusion, as in one branch of the older tradition; it is a force that can be utilized by any good or evil person with knowledge and skill enough to wield it. The hero is characterized by his greater studiousness and greater innate talent, which puts him into the privileged position of being better at his craft than his opponents. While it is a force, though, it is not a force opposed to the right order of things, as in the older tradition, but is itself one of the forces of nature. The scientific metaphor of the "force of gravity," the "electromagnetic force," or the "atomic force" has been applied to the magical realm. There is no harmony of nature disrupted by an alien force; nature itself is a product of competing forces that interact and can be taken advantage of. Magic has become science, and the work of the magician is applied science, a technology complementary to the technology of the real world. The magician has become an engineer, and as technology is viewed as basically neutral, magic is also capable of both good and evil, depending upon the prior stance of the technician. The forces of magic can be used as easily by both hero and villain. The only claim to victory that good has is through a superior use of the techniques of sorcery.

This disenchantment and trivialization of magic and assimilation to technology are particularly evident in a series of tales in which technology and science are juxtaposed within the same story. In some cases, they blend together smoothly; in others, magic defeats technology. In still others, technology, in a dim echo of the *Connecticut Yankee*, overpowers the magic. But in all, magic and technology are competing forms of *gnosis* that interact on the same plane.

In stories such as Poul Anderson's *Operation Chaos*, magic is seen as the basis of an alternative technology. Werewolves get jobs in Hollywood movies; witches work in discovering oil resources; refrigerators are powered by Maxwell's Demon. (This brand of fantasy goes back to *Conjure Wife*'s contemporary in John W. Campbell's *Unknown* and Robert Heinlein's *Magic Incorporated*.) To discover how a salamander operates, the hero turns to an atomic physicist who quotes Werner Heisenberg's Uncertainty Principle, a principle much more arcane than any of James G. Frazier's principles of magic. To harrow hell, the hero and heroine must master non-Euclidean geometry and the manifolds of shifting space times.

In Zelazny's *Changeling*, the magician, Pol, is faced with his changeling counterpart, Mark, who has mastered a high technology. In the ensuing battle, which is depicted as replaying an older conflict of magic and technology, science is again defeated and cast out of the alternative earth. In the battle, dragons face fighter planes, and the forces of magic prevail, albeit with great difficulty.

In other stories, the conflict ends differently. The archetypical instance is Ralph Bakshi's film *Wizards*, in which, at the final duel between the Disney-like good wizard and the Gandalfish evil wizard, good prevails when the good wizard pulls out a .45 automatic and blows away the evil wizard who is in the middle of an elaborate, uncompleted spell. Less succinctly presented, such a resolution occurs near the beginning of Brian Daley's *Doomfarers of Coromande*, when the hero, Gil MacDonald, and the crew of his tank are transported from Vietnam to Coromande in order to defeat a fire-breathing dragon. (In Anderson's *Three Hearts and Three Lions*, which for the most part fits into the older paradigm of magic, the engineer–scientist hero, Holger Carlson, defeats another fire-breathing dragon by analyzing the thermodynamic properties of the combustion system of the dragon and dousing it with water, causing a boiler explosion within the creature.) In Christopher Stashoff's *Warlock in Spite of Himself* and *King Kobald*, the hero, Rod Gallowglass, and his faithful, though defective, robot–horse companion, Fess, defeat the forces of magic by means of a superior technology that they disguise as magic. In Fred Saberhagen's *Empire of the East*, the mythical talisman, Elephant, which must be discovered in order to destroy the evil magician, Eckuman, turns out to be an atomic-powered tank; the evil magician is finally destroyed by the power inherent in a fire extinguisher.

Obviously, the changes described here cannot be explained by any single cause. Changes in the nature of writers and audiences, the impact of current events, the influence of literary models and critical pressure—all can be seen as at least significantly responsible.

At the risk, then, of appearing reductivist, I would like to examine a few of the forces that helped transform a dominant literary stereotype. One particular influence appears to have been that much of the fantasy writing incorporating the later view of magic and the magician was written by writers within the American science fiction tradition. *Conjure Wife*, which I have pinpointed as the earliest example of the newer view, was published in John W. Campbell's *Unknown*, the companion journal to his *Astounding*. Within the pulp science fiction field, *Astounding* marked a shift paralleling and preceding that in fantasy. Much older American science fiction, especially that associated with Hugo Gernsbach's *Amazing*, emphasized man against monster, with spectacular space battles involving miraculous technological advances enabling the human heroes to overmatch their alien adversaries. Campbell, beginning in 1937, introduced a smaller-scale brand of pulp fiction, stressing problems that had to be solved by the heroes and dwelling upon the progressive stages of the solution and the nuts and bolts of the engineering techniques that provided the solution.

The writers of the new American fantasy were essentially approaching magic as a Campbell-trained writer approached science fiction. Specifically, the two models of the magician in the new fantasy are adaptations of models of the scientist–hero used in the engineering science fiction in *Astounding*. One model in the newer fantasy was the individual who analyzes the fundamental principles of magic and learns the techniques that are open to all who study them seriously. The other model in this new fantasy was that of the individual, a member of a select group of people, who refines an innate talent to do magic.

One model in science fiction is that of the hero as practitioner of the scientific method (a method, in principle, open to all). Stories such as George O. Smith's *Venus Equilateral* series of Isaac Asimov's *Foundation* series posed specific puzzles for the protagonists. The action of the story is the development of the engineering hardware (or sociological theory) needed to solve the problem. Thus, in Murray Leinster's "First Contact," the problem is to return to earth safely without being traced by the aliens. The action of the story is the formulation and rejection of various hypotheses that purport to solve the problem. (The archetype here seems to be Campbell's "Who Goes There?") More typical, perhaps, are stories—such as the *Venus Equilateral* stories—where a newly built machine is needed to solve a problem, such as contact with a spaceship at an unknown point in its orbit. These stories stress the mastery of scientific theory and its use in overcoming obstacles, much as the budding magician must learn the magical theory and use it.

The other science fiction model of the period relevant here comprises the stories that characterize the hero as mutant or evolutionary advance. In these stories, such as A. E. Van Vogt's *Slan*, the hero has a new ability—usually some psychic power—and the action of the story involves his realization of his nature and his struggle to master his own wild talent, which confers superiority over the common human herd, now seen as an evolutionary dead-end. The innovation within the Campbell tradition is that the mutant now functions as *hero*, not monster. The young magician who has to master his own innate, unsharable talent for magic is the obvious parallel.

Both models have a long science fiction development, beginning in the period around the Second World War, and speak to the self-image of the science fiction reader, who is positively oriented toward science and shares in a belief in its value. A significant part of the science fiction audience (and a substantial part of the later American fantasy audience) is one involved in technology and one that gains its livelihood and social utility from a mastery of such technology and its underlying theories. In recent fantasy, such theories are taken as paradigms for all of reality, including its magical side.

Perhaps as significantly as any, the influence of World War II can be seen as germinating popular icons that also helped to shape the image of the new magician. If you can accept, for the sake of argument, the identification I have offered of the magician in fantasy with the scientist and the technologist, this influence becomes clearer. The prestige of the scientist–technologist had, of course, been on the rise since the seventeenth century, but this increase was to make a quantum leap during World War II.

Certainly no other war was so profoundly dominated by the scientific magicians: Radar, the V2s, and finally the atomic bomb were only the most highly visible evidences of a war that was fought as crucially in the laboratories and factories as on the battlefields. The dropping of the bomb on Hiroshima finally transformed, in a single blinding flash, a war of men into a war of magicians. The circle of conjurers in the cavern under Stagg Field was to receive, perhaps unfairly, the credit for winning the war: The achievements of generals and heroes and footsloggers all were diminished in the fallout of the bomb. From the scientific community that created it, two particular public figures emerged: Albert Einstein and Robert Oppenheimer. Each, through the shaping of the media, came to embody one aspect of the magician figure. Albert Einstein, with his great poodle cut, shuffling in his bedroom slippers and playing the fiddle, became for the popular public the embodiment of the old magician, powerful and wise certainly, but a little absent minded, a little comic, a theoretician, a useful aide but no hero. T. H. White's comic Merlyn surely owes something to Albert Einstein.

Oppenheimer, however, virile, lean, aloof, intellectual—the maker of the bomb—was something else again. He was no mere theoretician, and there was nothing comic about him. Here was the new magician, and one who, disconcertingly, had ideas beyond making himself useful. Albert Einstein could be patronized by a shallow press, the public, and the political establishment. Oppenheimer never could be, and his fate at their hands reminds us of Coriolanus's. But if he posed a threat to one segment of the public, for another much smaller group he was, and is, regarded as an ideal of scientific achievement, of personal integrity, and of political responsibility.

A third scientist of quite another kind achieved sufficient public recognition to be admitted into our pantheon and offered still a third version of the new magician: Wernher von Braun, who, in the ridiculous ease with which he transferred his allegiance from Hitler's Germany to the United States, demonstrated with cheerful finality the absolute amorality of magic and its reduction to an expedient technology.

Finally, in the most general way, we can say that the shift in the conception of the magician owes a great deal to the shift in the character of the writing community, especially in America. The masters of nineteenth- and early twentieth-century fantasy—George MacDonald, Andrew Lang, Charles Williams, Tolkien—who offered the earlier version of the magician, came from a humanistic, literary culture that saw itself threatened by the prestige and power of the new scientific–technological–industrial complex. Consequently, they tended to identify magic with the usurpation of traditional power, with social dissolution, and, on the aesthetic level, with the transformation of a green and pleasant rural world into a blighted, blackened factory slum. The writers of the newer version come usually from universities in which the humanities wing has made its peace with, not to say capitulated to, the scientific–technological wing. C. P. Snow's two cultures may still divide the curriculum, but it is the scientific and technological one that often pays for both. The writing community today comes from and writes for a class in which the literary culture is itself to some degree nurtured and maintained by the scientific culture, rather than threatened by it.

This new symbiotic relationship helps generate the hero–magician. To some extent, then, the new version of the magician is more responsive and more appropriate to the world that engenders it than is the old. On the other hand, our new faith in magic may be an expression of our loss of faith in the ability of ordinary men and women to confront the evil we face.

The Exploding Matrix: The Episode of the Bleeding Nun in M. G. Lewis's *Monk*

Nancy Caplan Mellerski

Irène Bessière, in her 1973 essay entitled *Le Récit fantastique: la poétique de l'incertain*, describes the mechanism of the fantastic as the coexistence of two distinct discourses, both of which are inadequate to account for a supernatural event in the text.[1] These two discourses—the empirical (physical law, dream, delirium, illusion) and the meta-empirical (mythology, occultism, theology)— stem from disparate roots (real–unreal), are inevitably juxtaposed, cannot be reconciled, and thus mutually exclude one another.[2] The dialectic of the empirical and the meta-empirical is a constant one, proceeding by repetition and multiplication, each succeeding occurrence of the fantastic event provoking further possibilities that, because they are equivalent, lead ultimately to no resolution.[3] In this respect, the fantastic is the obverse of the classic detective narrative, where repetition of events leads inexorably and reductively to discovery and solution, and causality is reaffirmed. In the fantastic text, however, while cause and effect *appear* to have a particular linear relationship, the metaphoric is a force as powerful as the metonymic, and relationships are therefore maintained equally by causality and formal unity.[4]

It is precisely this dialectical relationship between the metonymic and the metaphoric that characterizes M. G. Lewis's *Monk*. The episode of the Bleeding Nun, which occupies most of Chapter 4, is noteworthy in two respects. In the first place, it demonstrates fictionally the kind of repetition and duplication that Bessière cites as essential in the fantastic. Simultaneously, it serves as a matrix for narrative echoes, reflections, and identifications that affect the remainder of the novel. In other words, just as the natural world of the novel is forever altered by the intrusion and the reappearances of the supernatural, in the guise of the Bleeding Nun,[5] so the structure of the text is endlessly perturbed by fragments of Beatrice's story that echo throughout the course of later events.

The appearance of Beatrice is facilitated by a tripartite structure that, through

repetition, achieves a movement from superstition through trickery to the supernatural.[6] In the course of this transformation, the event (the apparition of the
nun) passes through three separate discourses: cultural, real, and unreal. The
nun is first a part of family folklore; second, she is impersonated by Agnes; and
finally, she makes her fantastic appearance. In each of her presences she remains
physically the same, yet the viewpoints of those who perceive her are radically
altered. The event thus passes from "pretextual" tradition to a reality that can
be only textual, and in so doing precludes a single explanation. Beatrice may
be *both* a product of family mythology *and* a result of Raymond's delirium.
Neither of these solutions is totally acceptable, however, and their inadequacies
necessarily establish the nun as a supernatural being. Through foreshadowing,
therefore, the episode of the Bleeding Nun becomes retroactively valid; through
repetition, it acquires *a priori* reality.[7]

The Bleeding Nun first appears in a folkloric context. Raymond comes upon
Agnes occupied in drawing, and is struck by her very realistic portrait of Beatrice.
Agnes explains the family legend in a tone of "burlesqued gravity,"[8] and makes
it evident that, as distinct from her relatives and previous generations, she does
not believe in superstition: "I have too much reason to lament superstition's
influence to be its victim myself. However, I must not avow my incredulity to
the baroness; she entertains not a doubt of the truth of this history" (p. 154).
Agnes's disavowal of the legend, coupled with an oblique reference to her own
unhappy destiny caused by yet another superstition (her mother had promised
Agnes to the nuns of St. Clare if she should survive the pregnancy), serve to
condemn an older generation whose irrationality will be responsible for its progeny's unhappiness. Interestingly, Agnes's remarks on superstition are directed
toward both the sacred and the profane. She does not distinguish between her
mother's trust in prayer and the Bleeding Nun's legend, and she thus equates
divine intervention and spectral apparition on a larger scale as elements of
folklore.

Ironically, however, it is Agnes's rationality that will ultimately cause her to
be the victim of her own elaborate hoax. Because Agnes cannot soften her aunt's
heart to allow her to escape the convent to which her parents have consigned
her, she will impersonate the Bleeding Nun at the moment when Beatrice is
scheduled to make her quintennial appearance. By devising the plan of using
Beatrice's legend as a cover for her own escape from Lindenberg castle, Agnes
employs superstition as a method of defeating those most tied to it. The stage
is thus set for the second of three discourses, that of trickery.

Peter Brooks rightly underlines the passage in which Raymond awaits Agnes's
appearance disguised as the Bleeding Nun as the moment of "disjunction" in
the text, the properly Gothic moment where nature conspires to "receive and
produce the supernatural."[9] The description of the partly ruined and melancholy
castle, its gates opened "in honor of the visionary inhabitant" (p. 165), fore-
shadows the fact that whatever control the rational younger generation has ex-
ercised is about to slip away. But Raymond cannot know what the text already

knows. When the nun does appear, she does so in a manner that recalls precisely the original discourse in which she was introduced; her rosary, veil, and bloodied dress assure Raymond that the trick has worked. The rational, it would seem, have cheated the superstitious of their due. Raymond carries the nun into the coach that will bear the couple away from the weight of family superstition and domination.

The victory is, of course, only a temporary one. The nocturnal ride to freedom quickly becomes a nightmarish journey through the forest in an atmosphere charged with the satanic (p. 167). Yet even after the carriage crashes, and Raymond's wounds attest to the reality of his experience, he never imagines that his companion is not Agnes. It is not until the nun reappears in the full strength of the supernatural that Raymond finally accepts the possibility that the specter can exist. As if to drive home the inevitable, Beatrice begins the pattern of verbal echo when she repeats the pledge that Raymond had originally addressed to her when he believed her to be Agnes in disguise: "Raymond, Raymond, thou art mine; Raymond, Raymond, I am thine" (p. 170).

Raymond fights mightily against the pressure of the irrational; he conceals the source of his melancholy and debilitating illness, even as the supernatural visits of the nun chain his "limbs in second infancy" (p. 172). The repeated visits of Beatrice, however, ultimately drive him to make use of the same folklore he and Agnes had previously dismissed, or used only to perpetuate the hoax. To save himself, he gives himself over entirely to the exorcising Wandering Jew, who persuades Beatrice to reveal why she is tormenting Raymond. Here the circle closes: Just as Agnes is a victim of a family curse, destined for the convent, so Raymond is chosen because of a family tie to Beatrice. The nun is a Cisternas, related four generations back to Raymond. Raymond's task, to lay the bones of Beatrice in his family vault, coincides textually with the news that it is too late to save Agnes: She has—literally this time—taken the veil, and been buried herself in the convent.

At its most reductive, the episode of the Bleeding Nun may be illustrated in the following paradigm: Beatrice wants in (into the family burial vault); Agnes wants out (out of the social burial vault, that is, the convent to which her family has destined her). Both women circulate around the pivot, Raymond, who becomes both a real and a legendary lover, unwittingly a savior for Beatrice and a condemner of Agnes. Both Beatrice and Agnes pursue essentially a mirror-image objective: Beatrice wishes only to escape her role as a spectral nun at Lindenberg, and to repose on a real funeral bier in the Cisternas family castle; Agnes wishes only to escape the metaphoric funeral bier in the convent to which the Lindenberg faction has consigned her, in order to marry into the Cisternas family castle.

The concept of the mirror image is already present in the text when Agnes shows Raymond the portrait of Beatrice, and later announces her plan to make use of the legend—that is, to *become* the Bleeding Nun for the time it takes to make her escape. Yet Agnes's plan will fail not only within the confines of

Chapter 4. Once she has assumed the guise of the nun, the text will not allow her to shed it. Agnes's destiny will resemble Beatrice's, as much as Beatrice's destiny, it is revealed, resembled that of Agnes. The Wandering Jew relates the Bleeding Nun's story once he has succeeded in breaking the spell of the supernatural:

Beatrice Cisternas took the veil at an early age, not by her own choice, but at the express command of her parents. She was then too young to regret the pleasures of which her profession deprived her: but no sooner did her warm and voluptuous character begin to be developed, than she abandoned herself freely to the impulse of her passions, and seized the first opportunity to procure their gratification. This opportunity was at length presented, after many obstacles which only added new force to her desires. She contrived to elope from the convent, and fled to Germany with the baron Lindenberg. (p. 182)

Curiously, Beatrice's history presents a voyage that is analogous to that of Agnes. Dishonored, the nun fled the convent in order to take up residence at Lindenberg and devote herself to the sensual. Agnes, dishonored, will devote her energy to the opposite trajectory: she seeks to flee the convent in order to take up residence at the Cisternas castle, pursuing the maternal, and hence the moral.

Clearly, the resemblance between Agnes and Beatrice ought to stop, then, at the moment when the spectral nun's debauchery and depravity are further revealed by the exorcist. In fact, however, the full implications of the Agnes–Beatrice identification are not explored until Chapters 10 and 11, when Agnes is discovered buried alive in the vault of the convent and later recounts the tale of her imprisonment. Agnes, it is evident, has traded the convent for the tomb, just as Beatrice had done.

Like the nun before her, Agnes is described on her bier as pale and haggard; she carries a rosary, and is chained to her bed of straw. When she speaks, she does so in the same "hollow" tones as Beatrice (pp. 355–57). Agnes *entombed* is as much a loathsome vision for Don Lorenzo as was Beatrice *untombed* for Raymond. The two men experience precisely the same reactions on beholding the real ghost and the false one:

I gazed upon the spectre with horror too great to be described. My blood was frozen in my veins. I would have called for aid, but the sound expired ere it could pass my lips. My nerves were bound up on impotence, and I remained in the same attitude inanimate as a statue. (p. 170)

He felt a piercing chillness spread itself through his veins. . . . Lorenzo stopped: he was petrified with horror. He gazed upon the miserable object with disgust and pity. He trembled at the spectacle: he grew sick at heart: his strength failed him, and his limbs were unable to support his weight. (p. 335)[10]

Agnes's deliverance from the tomb and her restoration to life thus duplicate inversely the history of the Bleeding Nun.

As noted earlier, the resemblance between Agnes and Beatrice cannot be pushed too far. Agnes's moral life in no way reproduces that of the nun. There is, however, one character who echoes Beatrice's lack of faith to the cloth: This is, of course, Ambrosio. Peter Brooks notes that Ambrosio's "drama is in fact the story of his relationship to the imperatives of desire. His tale is one of Eros denied,"[11] as is, on a less tragic, or only picaresque scale, that of Agnes and Raymond. Ambrosio is a worthy successor to Beatrice in depravity. Her story, which also includes erotic passion, debauchery, atheism, profanity, incest, and murder, culminates in an event that prophesies Ambrosio's murder of Antonia:

The fatal night arrived. The baron slept in the arms of his perfidious mistress, when the castle bell struck "one." Immediately, Beatrice drew a dagger from underneath her pillow, and plunged it into her paramour's heart. (p. 183)

The echoes of Beatrice's story are not confined to the scene of Antonia's murder in the vaults of the convent. Earlier, in Chapter 9, Ambrosio and Antonia are the victims—or so they believe—of a spectral visit by Antonia's murdered mother. Here, the ghost of Elvira also passes through three distinct discourses (supernatural, folkloric, and comic), which have their analogues in the appearances of the Bleeding Nun in Chapter 4.

Antonia is the first to see the ghost of her dead mother, and the vision occurs within the framework of the conventional Gothic moment: a stormy night, howling wind, flickering candles, low moans and sighs (pp. 310–11). The ghost of Elvira speaks in the same sepulchral tones as the nun. When the landlady, Jacintha, repeats the story of the vision, she embellishes it according to her superstitious nature, just as the baroness has earlier described Beatrice. Jacintha says:

The face was Donna Elvira's . . . but out of its mouth came clouds of fire; its arms were loaded with heavy chains, which it rattled piteously; and every hair on its head was a serpent as big as my arm. (p. 316)

The final appearance of Elvira's ghost is, in fact, a non-appearance: Ambrosio spies a figure in white as he awaits the effects of the drug he has given to Antonia. The intruder turns out to be the servant, Flora, and Elvira's supposed spectral intervention is quickly laid to rest (p. 328). The text here has accomplished a degraded analogue to that of the episode of the Bleeding Nun. Repetition here, in Chapter 9, has ensured the illusion of the supernatural; previously, it ensured the illusion of rationality. Ambrosio's plot to flee with Antonia is facilitated, whereas Raymond and Agnes were thwarted.

What is the reader to make of this particular instance of reprise? Our understanding of its function may be enhanced by brief mention of other examples of textual mirrors in the novel. We have already seen that the chapter relating the episode of the Bleeding Nun contains its own mirror in the figures of Agnes and

Beatrice. A secondary echo occurs in the way Beatrice pledges herself to Raymond: The baroness, Agnes's aunt, has already done the same (p. 148). Both women mistake Raymond for their lover (both even faint in his arms), an error that textually justifies Agnes's banishment and Raymond's haunting—that is, future developments simultaneously picaresque and fantastic.

We should, of course, expect precisely this sort of development, because the text has prepared us for it. There is, after all, another instance of an error that will pave the way for the interplay of the real and the supernatural. This is a crucial one, occurring in Chapter 2: Ambrosio mistakes the demonic Matilda for a man. Matilda will sap Ambrosio's strength, as Beatrice does Raymond's; their vampiric qualities balance each other in both plots. Matilda and Ambrosio begin their illicit passion in the garden, just as Beatrice and Raymond meet for the first time in the garden at Lindenberg. Toward the end of the novel, Matilda conjures up the image of Lucifer for Ambrosio (p. 274), exactly as the Wandering Jew conjured up that of Beatrice for Raymond (pp. 179–80). Similarly, in the latter part of the novel, Matilda attempts to make Antonia sleep for Ambrosio; at the same time, Theodore attempts to wake Agnes for Raymond. Finally, the destinies of both Agnes and Antonia converge, in double necrophilia, in the vaults of the convent of St. Clare, where Ambrosio sends Antonia, dishonored in erotic love, to her death; and where Lorenzo exhumes Agnes, her honor regained in maternal love, for resurrection. Thus, the Raymond–Agnes nexus is an echo of the Matilda–Ambrosio denouement.

Peter Brooks notes that the climaxes of the two central plots of *The Monk* are played out in the "multilayered" catacombs of the convent, and indicates that the sepulcher represents the "interdicted regions of the soul," the area where all characters are "driven unconsciously . . . to confront their destinies."[12] He reasons that such a labyrinthine locale is apt for a novel whose principal thrust is "the transformation of the Sacred into taboo."[13] However, as shown here, such convergence is not dependent upon setting (the real) alone. On a formal level, metaphoric discourse in the text has predestined the two plots to converge on the convent. Agnes's curse, early in Chapter 2, supplies the impetus for this conclusion. She says to Ambrosio, who has refused her mercy:

But the day of trial will arrive. Oh! when you yield to impetuous passions; when you feel that man is weak, and born to err; when, shuddering, you look back upon your crimes, and solicit, with terror, the mercy of your God, oh! think upon your cruelty! think upon Agnes, and despair of pardon. (p. 72)

This speech, which occurs above ground in the cathedral, will be realized below ground, in the labyrinthine vaults of the convent, suggesting that the metaphoric second level of reading is the more "real."

Agnes's malediction needs only the example of the Bleeding Nun to propel it toward realization. Beatrice creates a model for the destiny that awaits those who yield to desire. Simultaneously, she seeds the text with elements that make it impossible for the double denouements to occur elsewhere than in the convent—from which Beatrice herself had originally eloped. Such reflection, in turn, means that Ambrosio's destiny, as predicted by Agnes, is yet another example of the *mise-en-abyme*, similar to Agnes's drawn portrait of Beatrice.

My suggestion of formal unity through metaphoric association has, of course, been amply studied in other contexts by Jean Ricardou in *Problèmes du nouveau roman*. Ricardou argues that the *mise-en-abyme* is both a matrix of a text, and, at the same time, an element that can explode, leaving fragments and inflections everywhere in succeeding pages.[14] Clearly, the Bleeding Nun fulfills both functions, on both the picaresque and the fantastic levels. As a matrix, Beatrice supplies examples for both Ambrosio and Agnes; fragmented, the episode is generalized throughout the novel on both the real and the supernatural levels. The nun is therefore an intruder both literally and figuratively—or, both metonymically and metaphorically. Though her bones are laid to rest at the end of Chapter 4, Beatrice's presence, it may be said, continues to haunt the entire narrative.

NOTES

1. Irène Bessière, *Le Récit fantastique: la poétique de l'incertain* (Paris: Larousse, 1973), 62.

2. Ibid., 32.

3. Ibid., 34.

4. Ibid., 209.

5. Peter Brooks, "Virtue and Terror: *The Monk*," *ELH* 40 (1973): 254.

6. Bessière, *Le Récit fantastique*, 109.

7. See ibid., 185, 203: "Par la logique du reflet, la consécution devient, dans la narration, permutation, substitution."

8. Matthew Gregory Lewis, *The Monk* (New York: Grove Press, 1952), 152. Further references appear in the text.

9. Brooks, "Virtue and Terror," 255.

10. The speech is by Raymond; the description is of Lorenzo.

11. Brooks, "Virtue and Terror," 257.

12. Ibid., 258.

13. Ibid., 259.

14. Jean Ricardou, *Problèmes du nouveau roman* (Paris: Seuil, 1967), 185.

The Shining as *Lichtung*: Kubrick's Film, Heidegger's Clearing

Howard Pearce

In relating Stanley Kubrick's film *The Shining* to Martin Heidegger's thought, I point to an essential paradoxical or ironic vein in Heidegger's theory of truth; in its application to aesthetics, especially contemporary theory; and in the mode of art I have chosen as an example. My assumptions about truth, aesthetics, and the particular work seek finality, clarity, certainty, seriousness, while at the same time, in a phenomenological perspective, allowing tentativeness and uncertainty about values. It is still difficult for us late in the twentieth century to give up or even to modify the preconceptions built into Western thought, the "logocentrism" of the Socratic tradition.[1] Our assumptions about art are still torn between demanding immediate, "useful" seriousness and requiring easy satisfactions. *The Shining* might fulfill either requirement, but seems rather recalcitrant, pleasing many on neither count. The reviewers' complaints in general concern their feeling that Kubrick seems to be self-indulgent, pleasing himself rather than considering us. Pauline Kael begins her review with the rather sardonic observation that if the movie "is about anything that you can be sure of, it's tracking."[2] That is, Kubrick the artist is merely playing around with cinematic techniques, exploiting the medium and the audience.

These assumptions can, I think, be illuminated by turning to Heidegger. Heidegger tries to relocate truth and place it in temporal structures as opposed to the traditional dichotomizing of truth and appearance. For Heidegger, as he argues in "The Origin of the Work of Art," truth can only "appear," and in appearing it involves the revelation, unconcealment, or uncovering (*alethia*) of Being (*Sein*), which resides only in temporality and beings (*Seiendes*).[3] This unconcealment does not reveal permanence, as logos, as something other than appearances, but does reveal consistency of structural relationships within and extending beyond the immediate. It does not struggle beyond the testing ground of experience toward absent forms of permanence.

Given this ostensible depreciation of truth, the way we approach it becomes critical. Ideal, permanent forms must be brought into question, along with our imposition of those forms on appearances. That imposing or forcing is our habitual practice, and our motions toward truth in appearances must become a "letting be" or appear (*lassen*). The position we must assume, then, is a sort of give and take rather than a demand on the objectivity before us. "We let something ready-to-hand *be* so and so *as* it is already and *in order that* it be such" (p. 84).

If in the aesthetic experience we try to "let appear," we are inclined neither to accept the artist along with the text as pure presence nor to discount the artist as utterly absent. Letting appear is not bound to any absoluteness, even absolute presence. It involves rather a readiness, an anticipation, wherein structures and relationships of previous experience are in play beforehand. And those structures are allowed to appear along with the concrete presentation. Beings "ready-to-hand" are presented *as* something, as not simply discovered but recognized, as involved in relationships that inform our relationship with them. The artist appears, then, in a more complex set of relationships, and as a less discrete being, than when we think of him as mind governing text. Kubrick is there in and for *The Shining* involving the idea of the artist as he is related to this work, his other work, his ideal relationships, his "business," audiences, other artists, etc. These relationships are still mimetic, but more multiply reflective than traditional mimetic theories allow. The *idea* of the artist emerges as reflected in the text and in the manifold structures of reality and imagination that can be understood in terms of that presence.

My considering possible "forestructures" of aesthetic theory has generated an implicit question about their underlying values. Heidegger's lesson seems to lead again and again to that paradox: Of what value is truth itself when it has been brought down to dependence on appearances? What good is art, after all, that is in turn dependent on the uncertain consequences of that theory of truth? Reduced to slight significance, even triviality, the work of art is placed in jeopardy, becoming mere pastime, a quick easy lesson, or play. Consistent with Heidegger's theory, however, is the strong tendency toward letting be, contemporary art's apparent willingness to take that risk. If art is "nothing much," like William Carlos Williams's "Red Wheelbarrow," it resists an understanding that asks of it too much in the way of value systems already understood and finally structured. Ask directly what it *means*, and it answers, "Nothing much." But such art is indeed paradoxical. It allows interpretation, itself taking the position of letting be. It allows us to treat it as we please, using it for a moment's pastime, getting some little message, appreciating whatever is lapidary about it, or even, if we will, reaching for deep symbolic or philosophical meanings.

The paradox itself, as an intentionally present structure, requires the absent, past, imaginative structures upon which we play if we are to play at all. The naive audience deals with those structures, in his or her assumptions about art and artists, their limitations and powers, their relations and values. But art is not simply something to be set apart from reality, either as escape from it or reflection of it; it is rather among the structures of reality, revealing the world and at the same time concealing it in art's own appearances. Here again, Heidegger tries to overcome those oppositions that in their presumed finality seem to close down that interplay to idealist dualities. *Da-sein*, being-in-the-world, is radically grounded and can come to understandings only in temporality. He is not subjectivity antecedent to his own experiences in the world, and he cannot rise above the modifications and adjustments he makes at any given moment, adjustments based on present experience added to that of other moments. Thus, all previous structures of understanding and imagination are always vulnerable to transformation in the presence of this particular experience—if we let them be.

That structuring always involves what in the painting can be called "background," the fading into darkness or falling away into absence that is, in reality, both temporal and spatial. That structure of appearance within the condition of loss, or "falling away," produces "anxiety." We do not live merely in an alien surrounding that is chaos and darkness. The utter possibility of apprehending that condition *as*, so to speak, the "void" can happen only within the context of the human and familiar as well as the unknown, the present as well as the absent. We never entirely escape the metaphysical by thinking ourselves into the presence of familiar, secure structures, either purely physical or purely ideal. Neither mechanist science nor logic saves us from our temporal state. If the condition of life as appearances opens us to the possibilities of meaningfulness and coherence, it leaves us as well open to the anxieties, even the horrors, that come out of the darkness, the unknown.

At this point, I trust the reader has anticipated me in harking back to the horror film. The aesthetic structures we bring to bear on *The Shining* may occur in the way of self-defense. If we object that this film "fails" because it does not make us feel the terror as powerfully and as directly as the horror film should (meaning "as some other films *do*"?), we are both asking for that felt structure of "falling away" and at the same time imposing on it our intellectually secure placement in a world of seemingly enduring forms. Our securities are, of course, *felt* as assuredly as the metaphysical dread that we want to put away from us. That felt dread can invade and trouble our peace unless it can be isolated and dealt with from our safe position in reality. If, for the audience, the film objectifies the horror and dissolves it, it has become a glimpse of something "else" that can be quickly dispelled, a mere toying with a void that is not, after all, real.

With a little more consideration, however, we can begin to approach the structures as appearances, light from a screen in a dark theater, both as they reveal meaningful structures and as they open us up to, as they appear out of, the darkness. We can entertain the phenomenal structures and our own fore-structures, including those of art and reality. We can recognize them not only as phenomena but as involving underlying structures of repetition, reflection, mimesis. We can appreciate the radical structures of presence and absence, understanding and abyss (*Abgrund*), security and anxiety, Being and Nothing-ness.[4] And we can hope to realize the interdependence, interpenetration, and mutual implications of the polarities in these formulations.

The Shining occurs as elaborate sets of dualities that are mutually reflective, phenomenal images understandable immediately and in a limited way. The fact that we want to explain them, but feel that we cannot quite, as a finally coherent structure, a transcendent unity—that is, perfection of form in the discrete object matched by our capability to reflect the absolute form subjectively—does not detract from the "dilapidations" of form we apprehend in the event. Mirrors, for instance, recur as phenomena but most assuredly, now and then, add up.[5] Mirrors in the ghostly bar are bright, reflecting most clearly, as if untroubled by the shadows of time. But mirrors can be dislocating as well, producing in the audience a slight start, for instance, when the letters on Jack's shirt first appear backward, and we then discover we are seeing them in a mirror. More violently inverting reality is the image "murder" seen in flashes by Danny and later spelled by him on the door. Danny's complex orthographical inversions seem to show him trying to show Wendy mirroring per se, in that he begins with reflected image, which needs correction by the mirror. Murder is not just there at that moment in the past or here at this upcoming moment. It is itself negotiating toward those moments when it can break forth, when it can be uncovered.

Reflections among characters similarly entail the doubling of images and in addition generate a sense of uncertain motions in time. The two girls, murdered by their father, appear in two ways, as doll-like creatures beckoning Danny to play and as mangled, bloody corpses. Danny's imaginary playmate, Tony, is a double who at times can speak for Danny, and into whom Danny can retreat when as Jack's son his life is threatened. The woman in the bath is Wendy's antithetical image, Wendy being wife—devoted, understanding, faithful—and the woman being seductress—beautiful, dangerous. And the woman's threat-ening nature is revealed when the mirror shows her opposite nature: She appears in the reflection and again in the bath aged, even putrescent, the old hag who has taken the form of princess in order to entice.

Implicit in these instances of the human image is the uncertain sense of time out of which they appear. Shining involves the individual not only in transcendent subjectivity, extrasensory perception of others' subjectivity, but also temporal transcendence, the shining forth of past events. Events of the moment anticipate repetitions of the past, the plot developing from Jack's being warned about the previous caretaker's having slaughtered his family. And past events seem to suggest, like "murder" spelled backward, not a simple "then" as opposed to "now," but gradual inclination of times to reflect others. The final image of Jack places him in the collective image, the photograph, where he has taken his place in that earlier time.

The film is structured, then, on manifold repetitions that involve both discrete images and particular moments in exchanges of identities. Those exchanges set in motion transactions that require more than identification of opposites or duplicates. The idea of dualities is temporalized in that our active, interpretive engagement is temporal. We must act among the always-escaping appearances as we inevitably try to place them in a logocentric frame. We are "putting" the work of art "together," as for Wallace Stevens's "Someone Puts a Pineapple Together."

Locations in *The Shining* manifest places as setting for the activities of life and art, and they, too, are reflective. The hotel itself seems at once a setting removed from life and the ground of involvement in life. Interior scenes range from the kitchen, where services are performed, to the grand, well-appointed drawing rooms, ballroom, and bar. The interiors dramatize the stark functionality of the work areas in contrast to the lavish decorations of the "playrooms." The hotel has been constructed as a playground for the wealthy. It is, however, the place Jack has selected for retreat from the world, not to play but to fulfill his most serious ambition, to work on his writing. It becomes, finally, the ostensibly Edenic place wherein utmost horror appears. The work–play, life–art antithesis yields what appears as it will appear, the uncontrollable, destructive force that emerges from the darkness beyond work and play.

The hedge maze reflects the hotel as an artful construction, even more overtly so because its function is to engage guests in negotiating corridors successfully. Wendy identifies the kitchen as a maze, remarking that she would need a "trail of bread crumbs" to find her way. The literal maze sets artist–designer at odds with audience–gamesters. Ullman says it was "famous," played in by movie stars and royalty, but that "you would need an hour" to find your way out. Like the hotel, it exposes the irreducibility of reality to the play–seriousness dichotomy; for though Wendy and Danny experience it as a diversion and on a bright autumn day make their escape, Danny's final journey into it, at night and in the snow, is a flight of terror, and Jack, stalking him in the snow, does not escape. The maze again reflects the hotel in this "tracking," for while Jack literally tracks Danny in the maze, Wendy tracks him in the maze-like corridors of the hotel. Danny, like Daedalus, escapes only by his wits, covering his tracks and walking backward in his own footprints.

As reflexive image the maze repeats not only the hotel but also the larger, encompassing work of art, the film itself. Tracking is repeated in Kubrick's tracking. As Daedalus the artist appears in the maze and in the writer–artist Jack, Kubrick appears in the film. If the film has appeared on first viewing as a moment's pastime, superficial and undemanding entertainment, it becomes nevertheless a reflector of presences and also of things unseen. If it is, as Bill Warren observes, "an elegant, graceful and hypnotic production," it is attractive like the hotel, a scenic delight.[6] If it becomes a problem in interpretation, alluring and seemingly without satisfactory resolution, it shares with the maze the quality of entrapment. If, like the seductive lady, it "turns rotten" as it places frightful images before our eyes, perhaps that is because it forces us to confront not only its represented horror but also the deeper (or shallower?) horror that it cannot resolve, perfectly structure, or delimit within the bounds of our understanding. It opens us up to the anxieties felt in our confronting the void, to the possibility of death in the maze, the persistence of terrible deeds descending upon us from the past, the impossibility of insignificant art saving us from the vagaries of life.

Our hope, then, for release from the maze back into the life we control in living is not destroyed. We can even reject the film as we return to our well-lighted place, our intellectual security. Danny tries to repudiate the image of the slaughtered bodies of the girls by reminding himself that they are like "pictures" in a book, "not real." But we might continue to return to the "elegant, graceful and hypnotic" maze that leads in many turnings toward darkness. The hotel itself, we recall, is not simply an Arcadian retreat. It was built of blood and desecration. To provide pleasure for the rich, it humiliated the Indian dead, being built on their burial ground, and Indian blood was risked in the uprisings when the hotel was under construction. Perhaps the movie's recurrent "symbol," so apparently gratuitous, needs to be thought of in terms of the hotel's origins. Blood spilling from elevator shafts might be less a hyperbolic metaphor of the several murders that take place in the hotel than a revelation of its essential nature as a being founded in collective violation. We may even entertain the idea of the hotel itself as sentient being. Halloran says that it has "something that's like shining." And Lloyd, the bartender, refusing Jack's money, will only enigmatically explain Jack's benefactor as being "orders from the house."

Seen in this way, hotel and film are double images of immediate design, the pleasures of art, which let appear antithetical chaos, meaninglessness, and horror. The hotel lets the ghosts appear—masquers, drinkers, sensualists—because they, like the forces of destruction, seem both to possess it and to be possessed by it. The film reveals not only through the hotel but also through its own structures that lead toward uncertainty. Art has opposed itself to that dark otherness, the unknown, uncontrolled, unspoken, unrepresented, only to let its opposite appear as involved in the design itself. Since the hotel itself, as Halloran says, has "something that's like shining," it and the film have the power to produce images, to "show," to let appear, visual images that are either beautiful or terrifying, that reveal and conceal and consequently promote our trying to organize, to bring together, discrete and apparently contradictory appearances.

Seen phenomenologically, shining, like art, is the transcendence of bondage to the mechanics of time and place. Transcendence can involve us, in genuine ghost stories as in religious apprehensions of reality, with the dead and with deity. Spiritual forces are "there" and real. But if beliefs in those supernatural manifestations of Being are "suspended," in Edmund Husserl's terms "bracketed," still our impulse to transcendence is grounded in our human nature and in our physical condition in the natural world, "earth." We try as *Da-sein* to apprehend dimensions of reality that transcend empirical data. We try to "get outside" our own isolated subjectivity. We connect with other subjectivities; we apprehend structures of relationships that are not simply perceived; we engage in acts of the imagination that interpolate, extrapolate, extend, confirm meaningfulness and purposefulness, in art as in life. As reflectors of the artist, we contribute to his patterning of events and images by seeing meaningfully.

Shining, as given in the forestructures of *The Shining*, is the same sort of activity. Systems of purpose are manifest in the appearances of empirically inexplicable beings. There is always the possibility that from the vantage of empiricism neither the designs we see in the film nor the "unreal" beings in the representation are "real." Indeed, as poetic images, objects not merely of the senses but also of the imagination, they negotiate between the real and the unreal. The film may be nothing much but patterns of images, for the artist "abstract" art, for us a moment's pleasure in seeing it. But as soon as we begin to interpret those impressions as if coherent, meaningful, purposeful, we are engaging in acts of transcendence. To respond imaginatively to the work of art is to allow the uncovering, the clearing, the lighting of Being.

Art, then, is not discretely inferior or superior to truth. Audience and art are inextricably involved in a revelation of Being, willy-nilly, as structures are opened up, put into play. Reflexivity is more than reduplication, since the reflections and repetitions provoke us to transcendence, discovery of absences. The exact nature of Halloran's shining helps to explain coherence in the represented events themselves. He sees in a limited way, since shining is not total intelligibility and does not explain everything in context. What he sees is what he anticipates, the danger in room 237. He receives those images in Miami, and as a result returns with his mind on Danny's and Jack's vulnerability. He knows of many events in the hotel's history, but is especially concerned with what has transpired in that room. It is we who have had our attention focused on the slaughter in 1970. Since he is not anticipating Jack as ax-murderer, he walks into the hotel unarmed and is himself vulnerable to the unseen. These conclusions I draw about Aristotelian "probability" are based in acts of the imagination. Our imagination, like Danny's shining, is a receptiveness to those flashes that are there in the appearances but that in addition involve us in explaining their values, relationships, and meanings (even when we busy ourselves explaining away ghosts or artist's intentions, trying to secure ourselves in empirical states). We are receiving out of the darkness intimations that seem to want understanding, and that we want in turn to understand as coherences.

Shining in the representation is a matter of appearances, epiphanies, that are grounded in the uncertain relationships of presences. If, as discrete phenomena, they appear in cinematic art metonymically, they allow us to flow in the sequence of sense impressions. But images of shining reach toward transcendence. They involve subjective transcendence in that, as Danny and Halloran show, another's thoughts can be "read" without a text, a spoken language. In their shining, images seen may be of distant events occurring at the moment, for example, Halloran's "seeing" the activities in room 237, the woman as threat to Danny and Jack. They may transcend time as well as space, as images from the past or the future. And they may be imaginatively transcendent, the blood pouring from elevator doors, which as an event we take to mean "something," though we also take it as unreal, never having happened, never to happen in the future. Thus, shining ranges from spatial to a sort of temporal liberation, Jung's "synchronicity," toward imaginative transcendences—images that never have been and never will be in the actual events but that nevertheless impinge on them.

The essential shining reiterates images cut loose from time, images that leave "traces" from which we interpolate connections and values.[7] They are the ones that, like the movie's events, provide a basis for our engaged understanding. Halloran explains the shining image as having come from an event that can "leave a trace of itself behind." For the inexperienced Danny, who needs Tony to reveal those images, they do not mean anything, except as a vague anxiety, until he begins to understand them and their terrible referents. Tony "shows" him "things," but when he wakes up, he "can't remember."

We receive the "traces" or "appearances" of art, let them appear, as Danny receives images of shining. We need the "text," but we need also the imaginative understanding. We not only reflect but also reflect upon possible correlations and significances. If we accept not only our complicity and responsibility in such involvements but also our limitations—in life, in art—we go as far as we can and at the same time let be: for the appearances always appear out of the darkness. We cannot finally control the ultimate meanings of the appearances, the artist's intention, the total structure as mimetically reflecting our world, or the work's own coherence as *Gestalt*. We can, however, stand open to the appearances that are lit up out of the darkness. That darkness involves the "untruth" as concealment as well as the "falling away" of all beings into spatial and temporal absence. Consequently, that darkness provokes our anxiety in our apprehension of loss, nothingness, meaninglessness, chaos. But to name the nothing brings to light the structures of light and dark, and the dark is necessary to the lighting (or Heidegger's clearing, *lichtung*). The supernatural beings that appear in the horror film bring those very structures to light. Heidegger's *lichtung* is, after all, a shining. The "more simply and essentially" we apprehend in Van Gogh's painting the peasant's shoes "engrossed in their essence, the more directly and engagingly do all beings attain a greater degree of being along with them [*for us*]. That is how self-concealing Being is illuminated [in art]. Light of this kind joins its shining [*Scheinen*] to and into the work. This *shining*, joined in the work, is the beautiful" (my italics).[8] The beauty in life and in art appears at the threshold of horror. The simple, inconsequential peasant's shoes, like ironic art, can set us forth into beauty, into the shining forth of being—in the work and in the world. Designs, structures of reality, are neither illusion within the nothing nor totally apprehensible by us. We have to interpret, for engagement and transcendence, but we have to respond as well to the mystery into which the forms of being continually fall away. Being is "duplicitous. . . . Its unfolding is finite. . . . As mortals shatter against death and so first open themselves to the unconcealment of beings, as the revelation of Being remains essentially lethal, so does the clearing of Being find and lose itself among the thickening shades."[9]

Shining is *Lichtung*.

NOTES

1. Heidegger's argument against "logocentricity" is explored in William V. Spanos, "Breaking the Circle: Hermeneutics as Dis-closure," *Boundary 2* 5 (1977): 421–57.

2. Pauline Kael, review of *The Shining, The New Yorker* (June 9, 1980): 130. Kael follows this potentially fruitful criticism toward judgmental rejection rather than the opening up of reflexiveness in art and audience. Her final complaint is that the movie itself produces for the audience the "cabin fever" that the characters feel, being locked away in the hotel (p. 147). Bill Warren, in "Warren's News & Reviews," *Fantasy Newsletter* vol. 3, no. 8 (August 1980): 14–15, reads the action in psychological terms, but pays Kubrick the respect of having "reshaped another genre." My brief citations from *The Shining* are based on viewing the film rather than on reading a script.

3. An abbreviated version of Albert Hofstadter's translation of *Der Ursprung des Kunstwerkes* is printed in Martin Heidegger, *Basic Writings*, ed. David Farrell Krell (New York: Harper and Row, 1977). This essay and "What Is Metaphysics?" are cited parenthetically from Krell's text. In quotations from *Being and Time*, trans. John Macquarrie and Edward Robinson (New York: Harper and Row, 1962), page numbers refer to the marginal numbers in this edition.

4. Heidegger's treatment of the Being–Nothingness antithesis would undermine the implicitly discrete categories. See his discussion of "anxiety" in "What Is Metaphysics?", *Basic Writings*, 95–112.

5. The mirror metaphor is essential to Platonic *mimesis*. For a discussion that tries to open up the metaphor in Heideggerian terms, see Howard D. Pearce, "Stage as Mirror: Tom Stoppard's *Travesties*," *MLN* 94 (1979): 1139–58.

6. "Warren's News & Reviews," *Fantasy Newsletter*, 14.

7. Heidegger's concern with "traces" is taken up by Jacques Derrida in his pursuit of paradoxes in "difference-differance" and "presence-absence." See, for instance, *Speech and Phenomena*, trans. David B. Allison (Evanston, IL: Northwestern University Press, 1973), 154–58. Derrida's ruthless "de-constructing" leaves us in the paradoxical presence of paradox that absences its objects. The way I have put that one-sentence explanation explains my resistance to Derrida's absencing, even of "traces": "Whoever believes that he tracks down some *thing*?—one tracks down tracks" (p. 158).

8. Heidegger, *Basic Writings*, 178. See the editors' note in Heidegger, *Being and Time*, 28–29, for a discussion of *Erscheinung* that reveals the connection between "shining" and "appearances."

9. David Farrell Krell, "Art and Truth in Raging Discord: Heidegger and Nietzsche on the Will to Power," in *Martin Heidegger and the Question of Literature*, ed. William V. Spanos (Bloomington: Indiana University Press, 1979), 50.

ECHOES OF MYTH AND EPIC

Hawthorne and Delany use the fantastic to show that myth and epic fail in America, just as in various texts the fisher king waits in varying moral climates. Attention to mythic and epic aspects of the fantastic may, as in the following essays, illuminate deep layers of the social context.

Intimations of Epic in *The Scarlet Letter*

Chester Wolford

Hawthorne was well acquainted with the epic and its traditions. Not widely read for a member of the *literati*, he was nevertheless well educated, loved Spenser, and knew the works of Milton and Dante. As a student he must have read several times the epics of Homer and Virgil. Whether he wanted to be so knowledgeable is not recorded. In addition, he read Mather's *Magnalia Christi*, Bunyan's *Pilgrim's Progress*, and Pope's *Dunciad*.

Had he chosen to write an epic in 1850, Hawthorne could have looked back with much satisfaction upon a substantial apprenticeship, which, said the ancients, is required of anyone attempting this most difficult of genres. In addition to his long Horatian seclusion, Hawthorne would have been prepared by a deep and abiding concern for history and culture, which his acquaintance with such luminaries of Transcendentalism as Emerson, who almost daily discussed America's "place" in literature and the world, would have fostered. Most importantly, much of his fiction demonstrates that he was a user and maker of myths of the first order far beyond his retelling of classical myths in *Tanglewood Tales*.

The trappings of epic are ubiquitous in *The Scarlet Letter*. Like formal epics, *The Scarlet Letter* is based on a single action. It begins *in medias res. Dei ex machina* are everywhere, but most spectacularly in the brilliantly meteoric "A" traced in Boston's night sky. There are rumors and demons, flashes back and forward, and even outward manifestations of inward conditions such as Chillingworth's progressive physical deformity matching his growing inward perversity so reminiscent of Spenser's Malbecco.

On the other hand, Hawthorne insisted upon calling his longer pieces "romances," and romance is so tightly bound with epic that unless one can show that *The Scarlet Letter* goes beyond the trappings of epic, those trappings could be said to be subsumed by romance. Although Hawthorne did not care much for William Gilmore Simms's politics, he would have agreed with the Southerner that "modern Romance is the substitute which people today offer for the ancient epic."[1]

While romances of the period involve heroic elements, few if any partake so completely of epic conventions as *The Scarlet Letter*. Even "The Custom-House" section that Hawthorne later appended to the novel serves an epical function. It establishes the author, if only by way of a pun, as being what all epic poets must be: a Surveyor of the Customs.

It serves as well to place the author and the story in time. Epic deals with time, with history. And, contra Aristotle, this concern allies epic with tragedy, and, in some cases, makes epic tragical: Achilles dies young after discovering a genuine manhood; Aeneas becomes a headless, unburied corpse after founding the Roman nation; Adam and Eve are cast out from Eden. The tragic sense is increased by a heightened sense of inevitability lent by the pastness of things: the more remote in time, the more tragic.

Hawthorne's announced purpose, to take revenge upon his political enemies, is also part of the epic tradition, for more than any other genre the epic is political. Virgil, for example, is careful to include in *The Aeneid* the names of politically powerful families. Dante had at everyone he disliked, as did numerous other epic poets, although since Pope's *Dunciad* the mock-epic has largely assumed that function.

The most serious of the less important imitations of epic undertaken by "The Custom-House" has been identified by Daniel Hoffman in *Form and Fable in American Literature*:

Although invocation of the Muse was out of fashion when Hawthorne wrote his romances, in his prefaces he performed a somewhat similar rite. In each he attempts to define the nature of his imaginative faculty. . . . What Hawthorne seeks is "a neutral territory, somewhere between the real world and fairy-land, where the Actual and the Imaginary may meet, and each imbue itself with the other.[2]

The actual and imaginary meet at the very beginning of *The Scarlet Letter* with the historically accurate placement of the prison, cemetary, marketplace, and scaffold. While Hawthorne's imagination infuses these places with extraordinary meaning, he also takes a scene that no doubt occurred numerous times in early Boston and lends it epic significance by harking back to the opening lines of *The Iliad*, *The Aeneid*, and perhaps even *Paradise Lost*. As in these works, a debate occurs among "divines" as to the disposition of certain cases involving unruly mortals. Hawthorne places his representatives of authority and law—Governor Bellingham ("chief ruler"), the "reverend and famous" John Wilson, Dimmesdale, and others—on a "balcony" over Hester's platform, where, like gods, they may look down upon the doings of mortals.[3] The debate between "divines" occurs offstage and must be reported to the populace by Wilson: "I have striven with [Dimmesdale] . . . that he should deal with you. . . . But he opposes me" (p. 65).

While Hawthorne rarely alludes directly to anything, this scene may be taken as indirectly allusive. The debate among common folk, which in epic often parallels that of the divines, occurs among the women who stand firmly on the ground looking up at Hester on her platform and the others on the balcony. Most debate whether Hester should be executed or let off more lightly with a brand seared into her forehead. One young woman thinks Hester's punishment already sufficiently severe, but she is decidedly in the minority.

Hawthorne's narrator could be playing Homer's Nestor when he describes these women in the same way that Nestor repeatedly contrasts the amazing strength of men he knew as a youth with the comparative weakness of men as they now are. Hawthorne describes these women as morally and physically "coarser" than women of his day, stronger, broader shouldered, more sturdy, but also less refined (pp. 50–51).

Yet because the narrator is describing women here, there remains Hawthorne's characteristic ambiguity as to whether he is undercutting early Puritan women or their descendants; that is, is he mocking himself or Nestor? Hawthorne's own work or Homer's? Human nature and the epic tradition of competition, which demands denigration of former epics, perhaps provide an answer. Virgil, for example, was forced to compete with Homer and with Homer's notion of heroism. The *arete*—the ruthless pursuit of excellence and glory—of Greek heroes had to be replaced by the Roman notion of *pietas*—the idea that man's duty is to the gods, the empire, and the family. Later, Milton was forced to replace both *arete* and *pietas* with Christian "true patience and heroic martyrdom." This is one way that all epics denigrate and mock their predecessors.

Hester, too, takes on epic qualities, especially in her excessive pride (which every Christian epic poet after Homer has identified with *hubris* and *arete*), her noble lineage, and her emotional if not physical retirement from society (she is isolated in a "sphere"). Each of these qualities Hester holds in common with Achilles. Later, we learn that Hester's hut, like Achilles's on the Aegean, faces west (p. 81).

Since Virgil imitated *The Odyssey*'s first half, epic has required that a protagonist visit hell. While *The Scarlet Letter*, like Dante's *Inferno*, may be seen as a prolonged journey through hell, most epics include such a journey only as an episode. The original, of course, is Odysseus's descent into Hades. There he is visited by herds of shades, among whom are his mother and an old friend, Elpenor. Similarly, Aeneas's journey includes visits from the shades of old friends and his father, Anchises, as well as Dido, who refuses to forgive his leaving her a fallen woman.

In *The Scarlet Letter*, Dimmesdale is driven by Chillingworth to vigils that become increasingly hallucinatory. His dark nights of the soul then become hellish, and that hell is classical rather than Christian. First, Dimmesdale sees a "herd of diabolical shapes," then the "dead friends of his youth," "his white-bearded father," "his mother," who like Dido is seen "turning her face away as she passed" (p. 145). Finally, and in direct contrast to Dido, whose situation is otherwise not unlike Hester's, comes "Hester Prynne, leading along little Pearl, in her scarlet garb, and pointing her forefinger, first, at the scarlet letter on her bosom, and then at the clergyman's own breast."

It had been foretold that Odysseus could not reach Ithaca before journeying through hell, nor could Aeneas reach Italy. Such journeys are prerequisite to fulfilling the heroes' destinies. To the degree that *The Scarlet Letter* imitates the epic, such a journey is required of Arthur Dimmesdale before he can hold again the hand of his Penelope, or found a new Rome.

The narrative placement of journeys through hell is important to epic structure. *The Iliad, The Odyssey*, and *The Scarlet Letter* all have twenty-four sections. As Odysseus journeys to hell in Book 11, Dimmesdale's hellish vision occurs in Chapter 11. *The Aeneid*, with twelve books, takes Aeneas to hell in Book 6. Precisely at the end of the first half, Aeneas is ready to enter Italy and Odysseus to sail to Ithaca.

The first half of formal epics is taken up with preparing for the second half. Odysseus wanders for half the epic and sets his house in order in the other half; Aeneas wanders for the first half and conquers Italy in the second. Furthermore, Aeneas is purged in the first half of his *arete* (he was a minor hero in *The Iliad*) and assumes Roman *pietas*. The first half is essentially internal; that is, Aeneas fights an internal battle with his Homeric values. In the second half, the battle is external; that is, he fights Turnus, a manifestation of Homeric *arete*.

The middle of the epic, then, is a landmark in the development of the hero. In every formal epic, the end of the first half forms a high point for the enemy and a low one for the hero and the values he represents, as well as a beginning of the upward swing of the second half. Halfway through *The Iliad*, the Trojans are storming the walls of the Greek encampment. By the middle of *The Odyssey*, Odysseus seems as far from home as ever. Arthur Dimmesdale, in Chapter 12, is driven by despair to the scaffold in the marketplace, by "remorse which dogged him everywhere," and by "Cowardice" (p. 148). Once there, Dimmesdale "shrieked aloud," and the ensuing hubbub nearly gives Chillingworth his victory: Dimmesdale is almost discovered. For the first time, too, the reader knows that while Chillingworth is its embodiment, the real enemy is the culture he represents.

Hearing the cry are Bellingham (earthly power), Mistress Hibbins (diabolical power), and Reverend Wilson (heavenly power). Hearing also is Chillingworth. "It is done," says Dimmesdale, and probably all would have been done had not Hester and Pearl also heard. When Hester, Pearl, and Arthur hold hands on the scaffold, Dimmesdale is conferred the inner strength to fight the external battle of the second half. The moment that he holds their hands in his, Dimmesdale receives a "tumultuous rush of new life, other life than his own" (p. 153). Chillingworth, too, becomes the external embodiment of evil in this chapter. And since he was "no great distance" away, he may be assumed to have overheard the conversation. For the first time, he knows for sure. He is now clearly on the outside what he had become on the inside: "To his features

...the meteoric light imparted a new expression...malevolence." He looks like "the arch-fiend" (p. 156). As the later scaffold scene in Chapter 23 provides a culmination to the battle between the old evil and Dimmesdale (and Hester, since she and Arthur are, in this scene, united as one), so the scaffold scene in Chapter 12 concludes Dimmesdale's internal battle.

The task of the hero in the second half of an epic is to conquer. Achilles kills Hector; Odysseus massacres Penelope's suitors; Aeneas defeats Turnus. The job is to set one's house in order, whether it be a battlefield, a kingdom, or, like this Puritan colony, an empire *in potentia*. In the end, by acknowledging Hester and Pearl, if only to Hester and Pearl and the heavens, Dimmesdale defeats Chillingworth. Dimmesdale, like epic and tragic heroes, rises as he falls. He dies. Like Moses at the gates of the promised land, having shown his people the way, Dimmesdale is denied entrance in this life.

If *The Scarlet Letter* went no further than this in imitating epic, it could be said that the novel remains solidly in the genre of romance. It may use heroic conventions a bit more than most novels of the period, but it does not differ generically from romance.

But epic goes much further than romance, and *The Scarlet Letter* goes further. For example, epic does more than imitate. Defeating a particular cultural view, even a way of life such as that of Puritan New England—and neither is normally part of romance—is only half the job of the epic. Each formal epic must replace former world views, or "Supreme Fictions" as Wallace Stevens called them, with a new one.

The Scarlet Letter repudiates the Puritan view of the world. Chillingworth is a caricature of all that is evil in that culture: its probing into the heart of individuals (the unforgivable sin); the exaggerated quest for Truth in its foulest aspects; and even its sense of allegory epitomized by Dante, Spenser, and Milton.

Spenser's and Dante's works are clearly allegorical, and Milton, although less so, retains much Christian allegory in *Paradise Lost*. Allegory involves a one-to-one correspondence of meaning, and, in spite of much criticism to the contrary, Hawthorne's style is anti-allegorical. As Hoffman says, "Hawthorne's allegorical method is to use allegory to destroy the absolute certitude of the allegorical mind: by offering several certainties which any given phenomenon, wonder, or providence may be believed to represent, and by attributing to each of these alternatives a tenable claim to absolute belief, Hawthorne undermines the dogmatic monism of allegory itself."[4]

In addition, these "alternatives," which include a myriad of interpretations of Hester's "A" (and Dimmesdale's), of the meteor, of Hester's seeming humility and Arthur's divinity, extend beyond destroying the certainty of belief in a Puritan way of life. They also mock a way of looking at the world that stretches back to Homer and before, for the epic is fundamentally about ways of looking at the world. For Homer, man's task was to shine, however briefly, in the encompassing darkness of the universe. For Virgil, time and space extend outward to include devotion to an empire whose existence would span millennia and cover the world. For Milton, "true patience and heroic martyrdom" meant partaking of a creation covering the universe and spanning time.

With Hawthorne and Melville, the process begins to reverse itself. Democracy, new findings in science, the doctrine of self-reliance ironically attributed almost as much to the Puritans as to the American frontier, began to drive man back into himself, and such efforts were to be felt in the Naturalism, Impressionism, and Modernism of later generations of Americans.

Hawthorne's relativism and his astounding ambiguity make any final interpretation of *The Scarlet Letter* incomplete. Only within the framework of an epic structure could the work have produced so many reasonable interpretations. Finally, *The Scarlet Letter* becomes more epical than romantic not so much because of the epic trappings, although these are considerable, but because of its insistence on something new to replace the old ways, in its mystical, puzzling attempt to provide an epic transcendence for Arthur Dimmesdale, in the possible effects upon the inheritor of that transcendence: Pearl.

All epic heroes must come to full consciousness, to an awareness and acceptance of mortality. By willing his own death, as it were, by denying Hester and himself the solace of life together, by sacrificing himself to the good of the people, Dimmesdale reaches toward transcendence.

To be completely epical, a work must include a transcendence of death. False transcendence is presented to Dimmesdale by Hester. Escape to the wilderness would be to escape from time; to return to Europe would be to return to that that had already failed. Moreover, Chillingworth, having lived with Indian and European alike, would dog them. Dimmesdale is fooled by neither offer.

Both the key to the mystery of Dimmesdale's transcendence and the mystery itself lie perhaps with the Election Sermon. Like other epic and mythic heroes, Dimmesdale had been "there" and returned to tell the people what all myth is designed to do—explain the relationship between gods and mankind: "His subject, it appeared, had been the relation between the deity and communities of mankind, with a special reference to the New England which they were here planting in the wilderness" (p. 249). And Arthur's transcendent heroism is expressed soon after: "It was as if an angel in his passage to the skies, had shaken his bright wings over the people for an instant,—at once a shadow and a splendor,—and had shed down a shower of golden truths upon them" (p. 249).

Zeus had once appeared as a shower of gold to one he was seducing, but the reference to Greek mythology is pointedly used to denigrate that mythology when Hawthorne writes that his hero has "shed down a shower of golden truths." As readers, however, we are both awed by the revelation and denied its particulars. The same thing happens in *The Divine Comedy*. When Dante approaches heaven after having described all details leading up to the moment, he is rendered speechless, for "no words can describe" what was seen there.[5] Similarly, not a word of Dimmesdale's sermon reaches us, nor, it would seem, were the revelatory aspects of the sermon written down: "According to their testimony, never had a man spoken in so wise, so high, and so holy a spirit more evidently than it did through his. Its influence could be seen, as it were, descending upon him, and possessing him, and continually lifting him out of the written discourse that lay before him'' (pp. 248–49).

In short, Dimmesdale had learned the way for New England, and, by the lights of a mid-nineteenth-century New Englander, for America. We are still searching for Arthur Dimmesdale's words.

There remains only the problem of the legacy, the purpose of Pearl. If Hawthorne had written a straightforward, formal epic in *The Scarlet Letter*, the last chapter of the novel would include much of her new life in a new society destined, because of her, for greatness. This does not happen. Hawthorne was incapable of joining wholeheartedly the Transcendental movement that ultimately spawned the country's one acknowledged epic, *Leaves of Grass*, five years later in 1855.

He was able, nevertheless, to point in the direction of a national epic in Chapter 24. Pearl, who in all other chapters has been interpreted as symbolic of everything, is said by some to have been redeemed by her father's confession and death, and to have become at that point human. It is also true that she becomes symbolic of the other major characters. Given patrimony by her father, an independent spirit by her mother, and wealth—with all of its ambiguous connotations—by Chillingworth, Pearl matures and moves away.

Pearl is, in terms of an American epic, a literary Virginia Dare: the first truly American child, her parents and benefactors having been born in England, she, however, born in America outside all the old laws.

It is generally accepted that Pearl marries into European nobility, thus denying her American heritage. But even that interpretation is less than certain, for ''letters came [to Hester], with armorial seals upon them, though of bearings unknown to English heraldry'' (p. 262). Since English heraldry from the time of William the Conqueror became inextricably bound with that of other European nations, it must be that Pearl did not marry into a Western culture. The question for *The Scarlet Letter*, and for its Americanness, is ''Where did Pearl go?''

If America could be found neither west of the Puritan settlements nor east of them, and if Pearl did not settle in one of those morose towns, where did she go? It is a question that should plague American literature. Even Huck Finn, who, at the end of his book, plans to ''light out for the territories,'' would find civilization's duplicities anywhere.[6] Henry Fleming will not find ''an existence of soft and eternal peace'' at the end of *The Red Badge of Courage*.[7] Where does Frederic Henry go? Yossarian? No American hero finds what he thinks he is looking for. All he can do is escape.

If Pearl cannot enter a society in or east or west of America, it may be that her legacy from Arthur Dimmesdale, Hester Prynne, and Roger Chillingworth is an America of the mind. A legacy of guilt from the physician who could not heal himself, of freedom from the mother who could not be free, of responsibility from the father who could not accept responsibility is the America engendered by Dimmesdale, nurtured by Prynne, and provided for by Chillingworth. More likely, as with others who inherit America, she escaped.

Unlike Whitman's eternal "Yes" and Melville's thunderous "No," Hawthorne's is a realistic, yet marginally hopeful cry for limited potential: "Maybe." The epic of America seems to have failed in *The Scarlet Letter*, as it has failed ever since in our literature. Still, if the American epic is coming, it will owe much to Hawthorne's hell-fired tale, as much as his tale owes to the epic tradition.

NOTES

1. William Gilmore Simms, *The Yemassee* (New York: Harper and Brothers, 1835), vi-vii.

2. Daniel Hoffman, *Form and Fable in American Fiction* (New York: Oxford University Press, 1965), 169.

3. Nathaniel Hawthorne, *The Centenary Edition of the Works of Nathaniel Hawthorne* (Columbus: Ohio State University Press, 1962), vol. 1, p. 64. Further references appear in the text.

4. Hoffman, *Form and Fable*, 173.

5. Dante Alighieri, *The Divine Comedy*, trans. Charles S. Singleton (Princeton: Princeton University Press, 1975), canto 33, lines 55–57.

6. Samuel Clemens, *Huckleberry Finn*, Norton Critical Edition, ed. Sculley Bradley, Richmond Croom Beatty, and E. Hudson Long (New York: W. W. Norton, 1961), 229.

7. Stephen Crane, *The Red Badge of Courage*, ed. Fredson Bowers (Charlottesville: University Press of Virginia, 1975), 135.

Wasteland Myth in C. S. Lewis's
That Hideous Strength

Jeannette Hume Lutton

In C. S. Lewis's *That Hideous Strength*, Jane Studdock's first reaction is understandably negative, when Camilla and Arthur Denniston approach her about joining the company at St. Anne's: they begin by telling her that they "belong to" a Mr. Fisher-King, an invalid with a wound that will not heal. The name by which they call him is not, they explain, his original one but has been recently assumed, as the condition of a legacy, from a sister in India whose married name it was. Along with a large fortune, this sister has bequeathed him an immense responsibility. An Indian friend of hers, the Christian mystic known as the Sura, has foretold a danger to the human race that will manifest itself first in England. The new Mr. Fisher-King is charged with heading up a company that will gather to watch for this danger and strike it down when it appears. He is, Arthur tells Jane, "really a Head," to whom she must give certain promises, including the promise of obedience, if she is to join.[1] Is it any wonder that Jane, proffered a story like this one, resolves to keep her distance? Though she is attracted, in spite of everything, to the Dennistons, she declines to join their company and devoutly hopes she can have their friendship "without meeting this Fisher-King man and getting drawn into his orbit."

But such immunity is not, of course, granted her. She has been selected, though not by the Dennistons, their Head, herself, or any other human agent, to be the company's Seer, and she is inevitably drawn, in due course, to St. Anne's. There, Miss Ironwood, the company's doctor, instructs her in what to expect: The man she is about to meet looks young but is nearly fifty years old, has traveled widely and mixed in unimaginable societies, is often in great pain. Jane seizes upon the possible excuse: "If Mr. Fisher-King is not well enough to see visitors . . . " (p. 141). But she is allowed no escape and conducted forthwith to the invalid's room, where all her resistance is instantly swept away at sight of the golden-haired, wounded boy–man in his blue tower above the mist. She has meant to say, "Good morning, Mr. Fisher-King," to put their relations on an easy social basis, but she finds herself actually saying only, "Yes, sir."

With the collapse of Jane's plan to offer a conventional greeting, the name "Fisher-King" disappears for good from *That Hideous Strength*. It has occurred fewer than a dozen times in all and is, in any case, only one of a number of suggestive names and titles by which this character is known: Pendragon, Head, Director, and, of course, Ransom, since he is none other than the protagonist of the two earlier volumes of C. S. Lewis's space trilogy, here simply transferred to a presiding role and succeeded in his adventurous one by Jane and Mark Studdock. But although the name "Fisher-King" is confined to that part of the story in which Jane first resists, then yields to her calling to St. Anne's (suggesting that we are to understand the first element in the sense "Fisher of Men"), its potential application is much broader. It invites us to bring to bear upon the last book of the space trilogy not only those medieval romances about the search for the Holy Grail in which the Fisher King is a prominent character, but at the very least the most influential of their twentieth-century progeny, Jessie Weston's *From Ritual to Romance* and T. S. Eliot's *Waste Land*.[2]

The last mentioned is especially relevant because Lewis is, in one respect, clearly following Eliot's footsteps—introducing an allusion to the Grail romances into a twentieth-century work in such a way as to make a comment on trends in the modern world. Perceiving this relationship, the reader naturally asks how far the similarity extends—how closely, that is to say, Lewis resembles Eliot in his adaptation of the medieval stories to their modern use. If the answer is not immediately obvious, differences in genre are largely responsible. It is, in fact, very difficult to think in one set of terms about a poem (organized rather like a musical composition) and a prose fantasy. What makes it possible at all is that Eliot's work, in spite of its distinctive form, does have some elements in common with prose fiction: a setting, characters of sorts, even a peculiar kind of story. Taking advantage of this common ground, we can explore the ways in which Eliot and Lewis draw upon the Grail tradition in shaping these three elements of their respective works. It seems most natural to begin with setting—in fact, with that very Waste Land that provides Eliot's poem with its title.

Venturing into the modern world of Eliot's *Waste Land*, the reader may need a little time to get his or her bearings—to learn to take in stride, for example, the brief, unheralded excursions into history or vegetation myth—but soon recognizes basically familiar ground. This is, the reader quickly realizes, a postwar world, post–World War I to be exact, stamped by the colloquial expressions like "got demobbed . . . " and by street encounters between old naval buddies (lines 139, 69). Geographically, it is London, an Unreal City perhaps, but certainly not an unrecognizable one, sprinkled as it is with place names like St. Mary Woolnoth, the Cannon Street Hotel, the Strand, and Queen Victoria Street. By extension, the reader senses, it is any large modern city, or, by a different extension, Western civilization as defined by the cities, ancient and modern, that have shaped it. This is the setting on which Eliot superimposes the image of a desert, thereby identifying it with the wasteland traversed by the Grail Knight of the romances, and thereby also indicting the culture it represents.

As though to document his charge, Eliot goes on to explore the sterility of the culture on three levels that were presumably suggested to him by Weston's theory of the evolution of the Grail story. In tracing the medieval romances back to ancient ritual, Weston dwells upon the connection made by primitive man between vegetable and human fertility, a connection by which the prosperity of an agricultural society might be felt to depend upon the sexual vigor of its ruler. She also explores the dual nature of certain life cults of antiquity—their exoteric rites concerned with the secrets of physical life and their esoteric rites concerned with the secrets of spiritual life. In analyzing the symbols carried in the Grail procession, a question about which would restore both King and land to fertility, Weston argues that the chalice was a symbol of female reproductive energy "long ages" before it was identified as the cup of the Last Supper. All in all, her discussion suggests an intimate association among environmental, human sexual, and spiritual vitality, and Eliot evidently has this analysis in mind as he demonstrates how, in the postwar world, vitality has failed on all three levels. Environmentally, his London is a permanent dead land, where the vegetation is mostly paved over, the air is polluted with "the sound of horns and motors," and the river, the sweet Thames, "sweats" modern wastes, "oil and tar" and in summer bears an unlovely freight of mass-produced litter (lines 197, 266–67). The sexual atmosphere of the city is hardly more appealing. The state of passionate relations between Waste Land men and women is memorably crystallized in the Typist's comment on sexual intercourse: "Well now that's done: and I'm glad it's over" (line 252); and the only report we get on the offspring of Waste Land unions is the one about Lil's abortion. Lastly, the spiritual life of the inhabitants is characterized by denial, refusal, and willful blindness. As though taking their cue from Madame Sosostris, the fortune-teller, they stubbornly "do not find / The Hanged Man" (lines 54–55) even when He is encountered, risen, on the road to Emmaus. This highest level on which fertility has failed is the key to all the rest. Secularism and the resultant decay of meaning and value are just what have made this desert a desert, a place where the waters of civilized life have simply dried up.

For this catastrophe, everyone and no one is responsible. Eliot's Waste Land, in spite of its spatial range and the variety of economic and social classes represented, is a rather undifferentiated place because of its moral sameness. Since the loss of faith and direction is general, everyone is victim as well as perpetrator of the crime against civilization. As a result, the poem has no villains or strongholds of villainy—just a diffused degradation and pathos. It has no heroes either. One character in the poem who seems troubled by a vague sense that something is amiss and, according to his lights, explores it might be called the Quester but can hardly be called the Pure Knight. Brief glimpses of vital-sounding persons like the Hyacinth Girl and Ferdinand, Prince of Naples, or of inspiriting places like the Hyacinth Garden and the interior of St. Magnus Martyr suggest unrealized possibilities or limited survivals, rather than sources of rescue. There is no Grail Castle and no Grail Company.

Lewis's story also has a postwar setting, in this case post–World War II, a point he troubles to mention in his Preface and keeps before the reader by means of occasional allusions: "He was killed in a blitz, wasn't he?" (p. 41); "It's almost as if we'd lost the war" (p. 76). The place is the university town of Edgestow and its environs, which include not only St. Anne's but the ancient and beautiful village of Cure Hardy, and Belbury, where the National Institute of Coordinated Experiments (N.I.C.E.) has its temporary headquarters. Like Eliot's London, Lewis's local setting epitomizes a much larger one—the whole of England, of the West, even perhaps of the world. Thus, when it is suggested to Ransom that he get outside help in dealing with the local crisis, he replies that things are much the same everywhere:

However far you went you would find the machines, the crowded cities, the empty thrones, the false writings, the barren beds: men maddened with false promises and soured with true miseries, worshipping the iron works of their own hands, cut off from Earth their mother and from the Father in Heaven. (p. 293)

The huge but indefinite extent of the blighted area is suggested in Lewis's principal image for it, found in his epigraph, which is taken from a description of the Tower of Babel:

The shadow of that Hyddeous Strength
Sax myle and more it is of length.

(Epigraph, title page)

This Wasteland, in other words, is coextensive with the shadow cast by the Tower, however long one imagines that to be.

And in what way does the Tower of Babel manifest itself in the twentieth century? Generally and chronically, no doubt, it appears in all sorts of impious and misguided practices such as have produced the conditions Ransom says are worldwide. Specifically and acutely, however, it appears in the program of the N.I.C.E., that is, the corrupt use of science to enable man "to shake off that limitation of his powers which mercy had imposed upon him as a protection from the full results of his fall" (p. 204). And of this program, which is the modern equivalent of building a tower to reach heaven, Belbury is both the seat and the symbol. As he surveys the Wasteland that lies in its shadow, Lewis focuses on the same three levels of infertility that Eliot found in postwar London. On the environmental level, the N.I.C.E., led by men with names like Frost and Wither, spreads its ruin over the once-lovely countryside. The worst of these violations is the assault on Bragden, "the conversion of an ancient woodland into an inferno of mud and noise and steel and concrete" (p. 90), but the wreck of the Dimbles' garden, the planned riot at Edgestow, and the plot to destroy Cure Hardy are similar projects. On the human sexual level, the story focuses on the failing marriage of the Studdocks, which is not initially the fault of Belbury but of that chronic condition of infertility in modern life that has paved the way for Belbury. Mark's association with the N.I.C.E. does manage to make things worse between the couple, however, and the presence on its staff of the mannish, sadistic Fairy Hardcastle and of Filostrato, "the love-vanquished" [or "that Italian eunuch" (p. 70)], shows clearly enough which way its influence will go. Similarly, on the spiritual level, the merely secular society of the neighborhood is to be transformed into a truly diabolical one by the Institute, where members of the inner circle literally serve devils—bent eldila whom they call "macrobes."

Obviously, it cannot be said of Lewis's setting, as of Eliot's, that it is characterized by moral sameness and that everyone and no one is at fault. The Edgestow Wasteland is the result not just of general cultural decay but of the quite purposeful activity of the aforementioned devils, with evil men as their agents and Belbury as their stronghold. Opposing Belbury and contrasting with it point for point is St. Anne's, where the garden [an archetypal affair that recalls "all walled gardens" (p. 62)], the ongoing informal seminar on love and marriage, and the general commitment to Maleldil represent statements of fertility to counter the extreme statements of infertility emanating from Belbury. The characters who produce these contrasting statements are Ransom-as-Fisher-King and the company that has gathered around him, assisted by the eldila and obedient to Maleldil. So Lewis's story does contain a Grail Castle and a Grail Company. In *That Hideous Strength* we have, in fact, a Tale of Two Citadels: the Tower of Babel, home of sterility and presumption; and the Grail Castle, home of fertility and faith.

Turning to character, we at once encounter the problem posed by the fluidity of Eliot's personages, the tendency, which he mentions himself in his notes, of one figure to melt into another, who is "not wholly distinct" from a third (p. 52). The situation might, indeed, prove hopeless for analysis were there not indications of some system at work in the merging and disjoining of personalities. Eliot points to it in writing that "all the women are one woman," in saying that the sexes "meet" in Tiresias, and in describing Tiresias as "uniting all the rest." What we have is a single comprehensive character built up out of categorical characters (for example, "woman"), which are themselves built up out of smaller categories or of individuals ("all the women"). The comprehensive character peoples the poem by separating into his or her larger or smaller components, which interact as autonomous personages, not mere projections of inner life. The story that Eliot quotes from Ovid about Tiresias shows this suitably inclusive figure to have experienced life both as a man and as a woman and to have been made a seer in compensation for physical blindness. Not surprisingly, then, Eliot's Tiresias divides at the first level into three categorical characters: Man, Woman, and Prophet (see Figure 1).

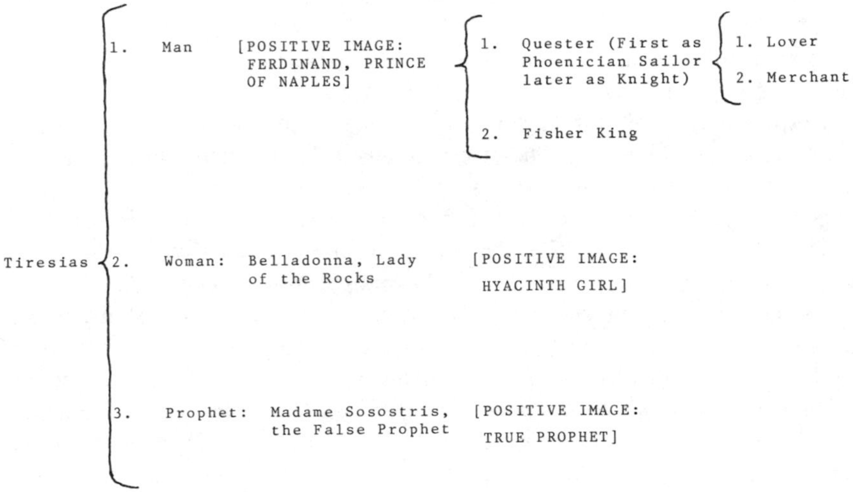

```
        ┌  1.  Man     [POSITIVE IMAGE:     ┌ 1.  Quester (First as  ┌ 1. Lover
        │              FERDINAND, PRINCE    │     Phoenician Sailor  │
        │              OF NAPLES]           ┤     later as Knight)   ┤ 2. Merchant
        │                                   │                        └
        │                                   │ 2.  Fisher King
        │                                   └
        │
Tiresias ┤ 2.  Woman:  Belladonna, Lady    [POSITIVE IMAGE:
        │             of the Rocks
        │                                   HYACINTH GIRL]
        │
        │
        │  3.  Prophet:  Madame Sosostris,  [POSITIVE IMAGE:
        │               the False Prophet
        │                                   TRUE PROPHET]
        └
```

Figure 1. Tiresias and the Categorical Characters in *The Waste Land*

Since they are Waste Landers, these characters display the same sterility as the land. The Prophet is a false prophet: Madame Sosostris, the fortune-teller, whose card-images of things and people to come are accurate but whose advice, warning against "death by water," is exactly wrong for a desert-dweller (line 55). The Woman is a siren, seductive but barren: Belladonna, Lady of the Rocks, to call her by her name in the Tarot cards. The Man has no name until he subdivides into the active male Waste Lander (or Quester), whom Madame Sosostris refers to as the Drowned Phoenician Sailor, and the passive male Waste Lander (or Fisher King), who appears in the pack as the Man with Three Staves. Though each of these categorical characters makes a generally negative impression, all three are given a positive association—an image suggestive of what they might have been or could be. Set against the False Prophet is a True Prophet, the Old Testament voice that identifies the modern city as a desert and issues the crucial invitation to look upon "fear in a handful of dust" (line 30). Set against Belladonna is that fertility goddess, or Grail Bearer, the Hyacinth Girl, economically characterized by her full arms and wet hair. And set against the male Waste Lander, either in his active role as Phoenician Sailor or his passive one as Fisher King, is Ferdinand, Prince of Naples. Act 1 of *The Tempest* provides the basis for this last association. There, Ferdinand embodies an ideal unattained by the Sailor, in that he undergoes symbolic death by water and is "resurrected" to a new life and a pure love. He also embodies an ideal unattained by the Fisher King, in that he experiences rescue (by Ariel) as he sits disconsolate upon the bank "weeping again the King (his) father's wreck."[3] It is only in this positive image of Ferdinand, the negative of which Sailor and King must combine to create, that we actually meet in unified form the third categorical character, the Man.

The Prophet has no subdivisions, but both the other main aspects of the Tiresias personality, the Woman and Man, do (see Figure 2). Belladonna is encountered as a number of individual Waste Landers: as Marie, the rootless cosmopolite of the opening stanza, who reads much of the night; as the Nervous Lady who sits at her dressing table brushing her vocal hair that actually "speaks" her staccato lines; as Lil, the thirty-one-year-old "antique" whose marital problems are under discussion in the pub scene; as the Typist who entertains the Young Man Carbuncular; as the Thames Maidens who mourn their lost treasure. The Man, whose division into active Phoenician Sailor and passive Fisher King has just been noted, undergoes further division in the former role, into aspects as Lover and Merchant (or Businessman). The Waste Land lover, always in some sense a sailor and in some sense unsuccessful, is met in such figures as the Hyacinth Girl's lover, the Nervous Lady's lover, the Thames Maidens' lovers, and the Young Man Carbuncular. Similarly, the Businessman is seen in Stetson's War Buddy, who is among the office workers in the rush hour crowd, in Bill the Barman who overhears the pub conversation between May and Lou, and in Mr. Eugenides, the Smyrna Merchant. Lover and Merchant drown together in Part 4, in the person of Phlebas the Phoenician, and when we meet the active male

Woman: Marie

Belladonna, Lady of the Rocks   Nervous Lady

                                                    Lil

                                                    Typist

                                                    Thames Maidens

Man (Active):   Man at Fortune-Teller's

Drowned Phoenician Sailor   Phlebas the Phoenician

                                                    Hyacinth Girl's Lover
Man (Active):
                                                    Nervous Lady's Lover
Phoenician Sailor as Lover   Young Man Carbuncular

                                                    Thames Maidens' Lovers

Man (Active):   Stetson's War Buddy

Phoenician Sailor as Merchant   Bill, the Barman

                                                    Mr. Eugenides, the
                                                        Smyrna Merchant

Figure 2. Categorical and Individual Characters in *The Waste Land*

Waste Lander in Part V, he has assumed a new questing role, that of Knight.
As for his passive counterpart, the Fisher King, we know him only as a man
who sits fishing in singularly unfavorable surroundings. His three staves, evidently supports, hint at the wound that keeps his kingdom a Waste Land, and
when last seen he is still waiting for rescue. Thus, his characterization, though
brief, contains all the elements traditionally associated with Fisher Kings—the
fishing, the wound, and the waiting.[4]

Lewis's more realistic mode naturally does not allow for a comprehensive
personage who divides and subdivides, but his three main characters do correspond, in a general way, to the three basic components of the Tiresias figure:
Man, Woman, and Prophet. Or, more accurately, they correspond to the four
basic components arrived at when Man is subdivided into Quester (Mark) and
Fisher King (Ransom). Jane, it will be noticed, is the counterpart of not one but
two of Eliot's categorical characters, since she is not only the principal Woman
of Lewis's Wasteland but also its Seer.

Without, fortunately, being very much like Madame Sosostris, Jane does resemble her in a few limited ways. She, too, has accurate images of people and events outside her normal ken, receiving her images through dreams as the fortune-teller receives hers through the Tarot. She, too, is heir to a distinguished tradition, deriving her gift from a Tudor ancestor as the fortune-teller derives hers from prophets and sibyls of the ancient world. Finally, she, too, is something of a modern "comedown" from an exalted past. Although her gift is not tainted with charlatanism like the fortune-teller's, it is blocked by her own superficial rationalism and dislike of commitment. Only gradually does she grow to accept it and dedicate it to the high purpose for which it was intended, thus becoming a True Prophet.

When we turn from Jane as Seer to Jane as Woman, we find reminiscences also of Belladonna, as Eliot saw fit to particularize her. During one period, Jane "kept herself awake reading in bed, as long as she could, each night" (p. 112), reminding us of Marie. She can be moody and difficult like the Nervous Lady, whom she recalls especially in the tense scene at her dressing table, where she sits doing her hair while she and Mark argue about her "nerves."[5] Like Lil, she has refused pregnancy, and with far more serious consequences: the loss of a child by whom, Merlin says, "the enemies should have been put out of Logres for a thousand years" (p. 278). Because Jane is, as Ransom assures Merlin, "chaste," she does not undergo the degrading sexual adventures experienced by Eliot's Typist and Thames Maidens. But Mark's failings as a lover, her own failings as a wife, and the "laboratory" attitude toward marriage that they share have brought some of the characteristics of casual sex into what is supposed to be a committed relationship. What distinguishes Jane most sharply from Belladonna, as from Madame Sosostris, is her capacity to change—to evolve in the direction of Hyacinth Girl as she evolves in the direction of True Prophet, to become, in other words, a full citizen of the Grail Castle and member of the Grail Company.

Of Mark, Lewis's Quester, only two points need be made just here. One is that we are caused to follow his misguided quest, as we were Eliot's Sailor's, in the fields of both love and work—as failing husband and aspiring social scientist. The other is that for Mark, Jane is always a Hyacinth Girl, or Grail Bearer, even in her most sterile days, before she takes her initial step toward St. Anne's:

When she first crossed the dry and dusty world which his mind inhabited, she had been like a spring shower. (p. 360)

This experience of her is possible to him because of their relative positions, at the outset, on the scale of fertility–sterility. Mark is, by far, the more thorough-going Wastelander, as he eventually realizes:

He was aware that it was he himself . . . that had chosen the dust and broken bottles, the heap of old tin cans, the dry and choking places. (p. 247)

As for Jane,

she seemed to him . . . to have in herself deep wells and knee-deep meadows of happiness, rivers of freshness, enchanted gardens of leisure, which he could not enter but could have spoiled. (p. 247)

It is not, of course, by chance that Jane is first attracted to the Grail Castle, Mark to the Tower of Babel.

Ransom, Lewis's Fisher King, does not fish, except metaphorically for his company, and even that ingathering he does not deliberately engineer. His chief physical resemblance to other Fisher Kings lies in his wound, but this characteristic is also, paradoxically, the main one by which Lewis differentiates him from the rest. Ransom's wound is in the foot, not the reproductive organs, and it is not a punishment for sin or a misfortune of ordinary warfare but (as readers of the space trilogy in its proper sequence know) the result of combat with the devil on the planet Perelandra. In that battle, Ransom had been not only Maleldil's representative but also his imitator. He had offered himself to save Perelandra by preventing its Fall, as Maleldil offered Himself to save Tellus after it was fallen. The relation of the later act to the earlier is emphasized by its epigonous fulfillment of a scriptural prophecy, the one directed at the serpent in Genesis 3:15: "[The woman's] seed . . . shall bruise thy head, and thou shalt bruise his heel." From early Christian times, these words have been interpreted as a prophecy of the Redemption, in which the serpent is made to stand for Satan, its presumed master during the temptation of Eve, and the seed of woman is identified with Christ in particular. But these same words might also apply to the contest on Perelandra, in which the serpent's role as vehicle for the devil was reenacted by Dr. Weston, and Ransom, another seed of woman, literally smashed the physicist's head with a rock, to frustrate the designs of the bent eldil within him. The wound in the heel that Ransom received on this occasion and continues to suffer is not, therefore, a defect but a distinction, similar in meaning to the stigmata on the bodies of some of the saints. It is further differentiated from the wounds of earlier Fisher Kings in that it *must not* be cured. Merlin, who offers treatment, has it roundly refused:

God's glory, do you think you were dug out of the earth to give me a plaster for my heel? (p. 288)

It is his "business," Ransom says, to bear the pain of the wound to the end. We already know that Ransom's business, otherwise stated, is to save the earth from the threat posed by Belbury. The conclusion is inescapable: This Fisher King's wound is indeed related to the sterility of his land, but inversely. Only by continuing to endure it can he restore the land, even partially, to health. Clearly, where character is concerned, it is in Lewis's conception of this personage that he differs most markedly from Eliot, as well as from the romance writers on whom both twentieth-century authors have drawn.

To speak of "story" in reference to Eliot's poem is to speak of the barely traceable career of the Quester—a career by no means subject to the conventions of realistic prose fiction, yet governed by a certain logic of its own.[6] Like his literary forebears, this Quester is traveling through a Waste Land—but one not easily known for what it is, since it looks, sounds, and smells like twentieth-century London. The nature of the quest is not clear to the reader or even, it appears, to the hero, but perhaps we are to infer that it has the traditional dual aim of spiritual benefit to him and restoration of the King and land. In any case, this hero's story follows a common, though not invariable, pattern of the Grail romances, in which an initial mistake leading to failure is followed by a correction that leads to a degree of success. For convenience, I will summarize his special variation on this pattern in six steps.

Step 1: Refusal of a correct interpretation of the environment and acceptance of an incorrect one. Eliot's Quester makes his original mistake in the very process of emerging as a character. He, presumably, is the person addressed by the prophetic voice in the first half of stanza 2—the "Son of man" who is informed that he is in a Waste Land and is invited to look upon "fear in a handful of dust" (line 30). To do so would be to recognize the reality of his situation and thereby perhaps to take a first step on the road to a better one. Instead, he seems to contradict the Prophet by affirming, in his sailor's song, the presence of water and by responding to the image of the desert with the counterimage of a garden. This denial of the Waste Land is the beginning of failure, for the episode in the garden ends unsatisfactorily and drives the young adventurer to seek help. Unfortunately, he does not turn to the Prophet, who has told him the truth; instead, he visits Madame Sosostris, who substitutes the warning against drowning for the invitation to experience "fear" in "dust" and seemingly wins his acquiescence in her view of the environment and its dangers.

Step 2: Pursuit of an incorrect course. In accepting Madame Sosostris's advice instead of the Prophet's invitation, the Quester cuts himself off from the kind of baptismal death that brings a "sea change" and enters upon a series of self-defeating adventures, amorous and mercantile, that lead, in the last lines of Part 3, to a flaming progress down the Thames. As he goes burning along the river like a human fire ship, to be extinguished in the ocean, the Quester must pass the wounded King, who sits fishing on the bank. Naturally enough, though, under these circumstances, the encounter does neither any good, and no sign, even, of recognition passes between them.

Step 3: Death as a logical outcome of the incorrect course, and emergence of a "new man." When Phlebas the Phoenician drowns in Part 4, the sterile burning of both his love life and his business life is over, and the Quester has reached a dead-end indeed, in an ocean that puts out his fire without causing a sea change. But, "Now I'm a new man," as the children say after enacting some Wild West fatality. The Quester is back in Part 5 and is now accepting the Prophet's once-rejected invitation to look at "fear in a handful of dust" (line 30). This choice requires experiencing the environment for what it is—desert—

and taking on the role of Knight in the sense of actively seeking the causes and solutions of the prevailing barrenness.

Step 4: A nightmarish struggle in the now correctly perceived environment. Knight and Prophet pursue a dreadful journey in a world of sand, rock, and the acutely felt absence of water. Tantalizingly, the "third" that walks beside them is the Hanged God, now risen, whose resurrection is the real key to renewal. His presence brings no relief to the stricken land or the travelers, however, because He is, as long before on the road to Emmaus, unrecognized. Thus, it is in the last extremity of thirst and hallucination that the Knight and his companions reach their destination, the Perilous Chapel in the heart of the Waste Land.

Step 5: Climax of the struggle in an initiation ordeal. Weston thinks that the adventure of the haunted Chapel, as it appears in the romances, is the reminiscence of an initiation rite, an ordeal whereby a candidate for admission to a life cult proved his worthiness to learn its secrets. For the modern Knight, whose skepticism has emptied the Chapel of its supernatural terrors, the ordeal is an insipid yet somehow frightening one. His flat pronouncement about the harmlessness of "dry bones" (line 391) combines contempt for a credulous past and disappointment that nothing more perilous (or more interesting) is in store for him. Yet it must be at this moment that he sees fear in a handful of dust, experiencing with full force the threat of meaninglessness when belief in the supernatural has failed. Just then, the cock crows, calling his attention, as it once called St. Peter's, to his denial. Does the accompanying flash of lightning stand for momentary insight? If so, perhaps he realizes, however fleetingly, that the denial is willful and unnecessary, that it alone maintains the Waste Land after the Hanged God has been resurrected and even encountered on the road.

Step 6: Aftermath of the ordeal and results. Some partial success, at any rate, has been achieved by the Quester, because the Chapel experience ends with the approach of rain (lines 394–95) and is followed by the thunder's instruction in the life secrets of ancient India. What the Knight has won, he has evidently won for the Fisher King as well as for himself, for the passage in which the thunder speaks is followed by a return to the perspective of the King, suggesting that he has received its teaching. Perhaps we are to imagine the three precepts ("Give," "Sympathize," "Control") as the three staves of his Tarot card, which he is only just now acquiring and which will henceforth support him.[7] If so, the benefits of the quest, as in the romances, are divided between Knight and King. It is noticeable, however, that these two personages never meet face to face in the poem. Just as the Quester as Sailor missed the King by flaming past him, the Quester as Knight is kept apart from him by the intermediary role of the thunder. And neither Knight nor King ever comes face to face with the Hanged God, by whom alone the land might be not just "set in order" but restored.

In starting out to trace Mark's career in *That Hideous Strength*, as I have the Quester's in *The Waste Land*, I do not, of course, equate it with "the story."

Lewis is very evenhanded in treating the experiences of his two young adventurers, and Jane's career is every bit as important as Mark's. But there is a significant difference between them: Jane at St. Anne's is answering a call, however reluctantly at first; Mark at Belbury is pursuing a quest and is thus the true counterpart of Eliot's Quester. In Mark's career, furthermore, it is possible to discern six phases that correspond, in a general way, to the six steps of *The Waste Land* quest.

Step 1: Refusal of a correct interpretation of the environment and acceptance of an incorrect one. Like Phlebas, Mark begins by making a mistake, or rather a whole constellation of mistakes. The most obvious is to go to the wrong address, the Tower of Babel instead of the Grail Castle. But once there, he recalls Eliot's Quester more precisely by his misperception of his environment— an especially gross misperception, since he is not just in the Wasteland but in the Dark Tower that governs it. Mark's ruling passion, to be an insider, induces him to listen to false prophets—"knowing" men like Curry and Feverstone in the early stages of his adventures and members of the inner circle like Wither and Miss Hardcastle after he has taken up residence at Belbury. These all assure him that he is in a garden spot of professional opportunity. He is given access to the truth by William Hingest, who correctly interprets his new environment and offers to take him out of it; but with a stubborn blindness worthy of Phlebas, he refuses to admit the accuracy of the description, and stays.

Step 2: Pursuit of an incorrect course. Acting on his false perception of his surroundings, Mark, too, enters upon a series of self-defeating adventures. These compose the bulk of his half of the story, are motivated by his wish to find acceptance and recognition at Belbury, and culminate, after a series of ups and downs, in his arrest for Hingest's murder.

Step 3: Death as the logical outcome of the incorrect course, and emergence of a "new man." Mark's absolute conviction that he will be hanged for the murder provides a realistic foretaste of the experience—a "choking, smothering sensation" and a vision of his hand as the hand of a corpse and then a skeleton. This "death" affects him somewhat as drowning affects Phlebas. For one thing, it gives rise to a correct perception of his environment, which he now sees clearly as "the world of plot within plot, crossing and double-crossing, of lies and graft and stabbing in the back" (p. 245). For another, it conquers an old resistance to self-examination, rooted in the intuition that this would mean "really beginning over again as though he were an infant" (p. 246). Now he can afford to acknowledge the futility of his life, since he is as good as dead already and starting over seems out of the question. Thus, with Mark as with Phlebas, "death" prepares the way for the emergence of a "new man."

Step 4: A nightmarish struggle in the now correctly perceived environment. Mark's trial is by no means over. Merely knowing that one is in a Dark Tower does not automatically get one out. His hunger to be an insider brought Mark to the Tower in the first place; and even when he recognizes it for what it is, he finds himself unable to cease experiencing that hunger. Frost and Wither, understanding his weakness, have decided to play upon it by telling him he is a candidate for admission to the "Circle" (p. 255) and letting him in on the secret of the macrobes, the true shapers of the Institute's policy. Mark's desperate struggle at this time thus has three aspects: the effort to hold on to his new and correct perception of where he is and what sort of people he is associated with; the effort to prevent their realizing that he has attained this perception; and the effort to avoid surrendering to the temptation they put before him, even as he realizes how horrible it and they are. The dream-like agony of this struggle renders it atmospherically comparable to Eliot's Knight's progress on his thirst-tormented journey. And as Eliot's Knight arrives at the ultimate trial of the Perilous Chapel, Mark arrives at the ultimate trial of the Objective Room.

Step 5: Climax of the struggle in an initiation ordeal. The training in "objectivity" that Mark is to undergo is succinctly explained by Frost, who is the sponsor of Mark's candidacy for admission to the Circle. It is a program to prepare him for association with the macrobes by killing in him all the values, "ethical, aesthetic, or logical," on which his life has hitherto been based. It is, in short, a pinpoint "abolition of man," its purpose being to eliminate in Mark just those characteristics that make him a human being. The place where his training will occur, he discovers, is a room inside Belbury, entered by a Gothic-sounding "little door with a pointed arch" (p. 297).

To sit in the room was the first step towards what Frost called objectivity. . . . Higher degrees in the asceticism of anti-Nature would doubtless follow: the eating of abominable food, the dabbling in dirt and blood, the ritual performance of calculated obscenities. They were, in a sense, playing quite fair with him—offering him the very same initiation through which they themselves had passed and which had divided them from humanity. (p. 299)

The language of this passage—its reference to "asceticism," "ritual," "initiation"—makes nearly explicit what is taking place. Mark is being prepared to learn the secrets of an anti-life cult, and the Objective Room is his Chapel Perilous. As he has anticipated, the ordeal has several phases; but the climactic one is reached when Frost orders Mark to trample upon and otherwise insult a crucifix, a nearly life-size carving of appalling realism. It is too much, and Mark finds himself responding, with unconscious double meaning, "It's all bloody nonsense, and I'm damned if I do any such thing" (p. 337).

Step 6: Aftermath of the ordeal and results. Obviously, Mark, too, has achieved a modest success at the Chapel Perilous. In *That Hideous Strength*, as one might expect, this structure is not, as in *The Waste Land*, merely a place of failed belief; it is a place of misbelief sponsored by devils. In its practices, the Hanged God is not just ignored; He is savagely attacked. Success in the personal sense—that is, spiritual survival—thus means refusal of initiation, and this refusal, in the incident of the crucifix, Mark just manages to supply. He does nothing thereby for the Wasteland; but in this story, as we have seen, its return to relative well-being has quite a different instrument, the Fisher King himself.

In insisting upon this point, I do not forget that the destruction of the N.I.C.E. and its haunts is accomplished by the eldila working through Merlin and that Ransom meanwhile sits at home. Lewis, I think, permits no failure to understand that, whoever may be acting, Ransom, who simply waits, is the key figure in the destruction of Belbury. This insight leads in turn to the recognition that Ransom's waiting, like his wound, while it puts him in the tradition of Fisher Kings including Eliot's, at the same time sharply distinguishes him from the rest. It is neither passive nor pathetic but a positive redemptive act. Camilla interprets it in what is clearly the correct way by her quotation from Charles Williams's *Taliessin Through Logres*: "All lies in a passion of patience."[8] Ransom, who has already reenacted the Passion of Maleldil once before, in *Perelandra*, where it was represented as victorious combat with the devil, reenacts it again in *That Hideous Strength*, where it is represented as suffering, prolonged and willingly endured: a Passion of patience. The persistence and increasing mastery of his imitation of Maleldil doubtless explain the iconography with which he is surrounded in the latter story. He has what can be perceived only as a halo: "All the light in the room seemed to run towards the gold hair and the gold beard of the wounded man" (p. 142). His ordinary lunch sounds like the institution of the Eucharist: " 'It is a surprisingly pleasant diet.' With these words he broke the bread and poured himself out a glass of wine" (p. 149). He even harrows hell in one of Jane's visionary dreams:

If only someone would come quickly and let her out. And immediately she had a picture of someone, someone bearded but (it was odd) divinely young, someone all golden and strong and warm coming with a mighty earth-shaking tread down into that black place. (p. 136)

Eliot has two different cards of the Tarot pack to represent the Fisher King and the Hanged God and distinguishes between the two personages at all times. The latter, indeed, never appears except as that shadowy and unrecognized third presence on the road to the Perilous Chapel. Weston's study suggests, however, that the Fisher King of the romances had just such dying and reviving gods as his ritual forebears. Under the circumstances, it is neither surprising nor inappropriate that Lewis's Fisher King and Hanged God figures are one and the same person.

We have noticed that Eliot's Quester never meets either of these personages face to face, and it is likewise true that Mark never meets Ransom. But the experience of Frost's "Perilous Chapel" has brought Mark far enough along to be a beneficiary, at one remove, of Ransom's "rule"—and not only by escaping the Belbury holocaust. Instead of causing this Fisher King to be presented with three "staves," Mark, it appears, will indirectly receive three (and roughly the same three) from him. The transmitter of these life secrets will be Jane, who is about to be reunited with Mark as the story closes and who approaches that reunion with the three staves of Ransom's counsel, given her on a series of occasions when she has raised questions about her relations with Mark and about marriage in general. The life secrets expressed in this counsel—perhaps they should remind us that Mr. Fisher-King's legacy comes from India—are essentially those found in "What the Thunder Said." They are appropriate to Wastelanders in general and Mark in particular, but especially appropriate to their recipient, Jane. "Give" addresses her dislike of commitment, her fear of entanglements, so strong that Camilla nearly loses her forever by using the expression "Give yourself to us." "Sympathize" speaks to her *daungier* and "inarticulate sense of grievance against Mark," bringing her "a novel sense of her own injustice and even of pity for her husband" (p. 147). "Control" is raised for Jane as that form of self-control called obedience, in which she and Mark have both failed, she as wife and he as lover. Eliot described such obedience as the heart's responding "gaily" to "controlling hands." In a similar vein, Ransom tells Jane at their parting, "Go in obedience and you will find love" (pp. 379–80).

Thus, Jane and through her Mark are left with an opportunity to experience human love in a higher form than they, as ordinary Wastelanders, have yet known. The place of their reunion is a lodge situated in that archetypal garden at St. Anne's, the garden where Jane has earlier committed her life to Maleldil and where a temporary summer, caused by the nearness of Perelandra, now prevails. The combination of environmental, human sexual, and spiritual fertility associated with this setting reminds us that both of our adventurers end within the precincts of the Grail Castle. Mark's arrival occurs after the destruction of Belbury and more or less coincides with Ransom's departure for Perelandra, so that he has no part in the contest between the two citadels, no meeting (as has been noted) with the Fisher King, and no acquaintance with the Grail Company, as such. But at least he has finally come to the right castle and in the right— that is, the appropriately humble—frame of mind. And as the story ends, he is about to meet an important member of the Grail Company—Jane—whose experiences since he last saw her have made her in the fullest sense a Grail Bearer and Hyacinth Girl.

As for the more general effects of Ransom's "rule," they are considerable but at the same time limited. He has carried out his mission of striking down Belbury and destroying the hopelessly infected Edgestow, and the Wasteland in its most intense form has thus been defeated in the immediate neighborhood and averted from the world at large. But the chronic Wasteland, the general condition of sterility that Ransom has earlier described, remains. Its return to health is the responsibility not of one man but of entire nations:

The whole work of healing Tellus depends on nursing that little spark, on incarnating that ghost, which is still alive in every real people, and different in each. When Logres really dominates Britain, when the goddess Reason, the divine clearness, is really enthroned in France, when the order of Heaven is really followed in China—why, then it will be spring. (pp. 370–71)

Meanwhile, the winter, the season in which the story has been set and which has been only briefly interrupted by the visit of Perelandra, will continue. In that sense, at least, Lewis's fantasy, like Eliot's poem, ends with the Wasteland still a reality.

How much is Lewis's use of the Grail material like Eliot's? When we return to this question after surveying the comparative settings, characters, and stories, we can only answer "very much indeed." Rather surprisingly, in view of Lewis's avowed distaste for Modernist poetry, it appears that *The Waste Land* is a pervasive allusion in *That Hideous Strength* in nearly the same way that *Paradise Lost* is in *Perelandra*. Yet among the many correspondents of Lewis's design to Eliot's, two pointed differences obtrude. One is in the moral climate—the polarization of good and evil forces in the fantasy as opposed to the generalized moral squalor in the poem. The other is in the divergent values assigned to the Fisher King's wound and his waiting. Are these differences to be construed as dissents? Is Lewis, in other words, criticizing certain aspects of Eliot's vision in *The Waste Land*, even while wittily adapting so many of its elements to his own uses? That would be like Lewis. Anyone familiar with a representative sample of his work, scholarly and imaginative, will have noticed his habit of challenging Eliot in a variety of contexts—a policy he frankly confirmed in a letter to Dorothy Sayers:

Oh Eliot! How can a man who is neither a knave nor a fool write so like both? Well he can't complain that I haven't done my best to put him right. I hardly ever write a book without showing him one of his errors.[9]

Is Lewis, in *That Hideous Strength*, showing Eliot one (or more) of his "errors"? Where the moral climate is concerned, the answer is probably "yes." Lewis's insistence upon his two citadels, besides implying a strong preference for heroism to squalor as a literary subject, asserts his dissenting view of the twentieth-century predicament: What he sees is not just cultural decline but an assault by demonic forces calling for determined counterattack. Where Ransom's wound and waiting are concerned, however, the answer is probably "no." Lewis's treatment of them is best explained not as a shaft aimed at Eliot but as an interpretation required by the larger plan of the trilogy. Ransom's role has, in reality, been consistent from the start, though an evolution has occurred both in its outward circumstances and in his understanding of it. Throughout the trilogy, Ransom has been a sacrifice. In the first volume, he was an unwilling sacrifice, a kidnap victim whose only thought was to escape being "offered"; in the second, he was a reluctant but finally voluntary sacrifice; and in the third, he is a willing and continuing sacrifice, a ransom for many, who has finally actualized the full potential implied in his name. His complete acceptance of his role in the last volume is, we come to realize, the basis of his Kingship. What Camilla has articulated, the reader is gradually brought to understand: "All lies in a passion of patience, my lord's rule."

NOTES

1. C. S. Lewis, *That Hideous Strength* (New York: Macmillan Paperbacks, 1965), 124. Further references appear in the text.

2. Jessie L. Weston, *From Ritual to Romance* (Garden City, NY: Doubleday Anchor Books, 1957); and T. S. Eliot, *The Waste Land*, in *The Complete Poems and Plays, 1909–1950* (New York: Harcourt Brace, 1952), 37–55. Further references appear in the text.

3. William Shakespeare, *The Tempest*, in *The Complete Plays and Poems of William Shakespeare*, New Cambridge Edition (Cambridge, MA: Riverside Press, 1942), Act 1, scene 2, line 390.

4. Weston calls the Fisher King's habit of fishing "an obviously *post hoc* addition" (*From Ritual*, 116) and, setting it aside, connects his title with the long tradition of the fish as a life symbol. But the romances have created a tradition of their own on this point. The many readers whose earliest acquaintance with the story came through Chrétien de Troyes or Wolfram von Eschenbach tend to remember the King as first glimpsed in a boat on river or lake with his line in the water. Eliot's King, though he fishes from the bank, is of this ancestry.

5. In *That Hideous Strength*, the positions of the disputants are, in one sense, the reverse of those found in Part 2 of *The Waste Land*. It is Mark, not Jane, who says that Jane's nerves are bad and suggests that he ought to stay with her (pp. 46–47).

6. My understanding of *The Waste Land* is different enough from any with which I am familiar to require that I write out the "story" at some length. Yet I am conscious of beginning from a high plateau of criticism and of owing more to earlier readings of the poem than I can fully know, much less properly acknowledge. I can name only those to whom I am most aware of my indebtedness: Elizabeth Drew, *T. S. Eliot: The Design of His Poetry* (New York: Scribner, 1949), 58–90; *Modern Poetry, American and British*, ed. Kimon Friar and John Malcolm Brinnin (New York: Appleton-Century-Crofts, 1951), 472–97; Grover Smith, *T. S. Eliot's Poetry and Plays: A Study in Sources and Meaning* (Chicago: University of Chicago Press, 1956), 72–98; George Williamson, *A Reader's Guide to T. S. Eliot*, 2nd ed. (London: Thames and Hudson, 1967), 115–54; Derek Traversi, *T. S. Eliot: The Longer Poems* (New York: Harcourt Brace Jovanovich, 1976), 11–54; Eloise Knapp Hay, *T. S. Eliot's Negative Way* (Cambridge, MA: Harvard University Press, 1982), 48–68.

7. Such, at any rate, is the reading of Williamson in *Reader's Guide*, 152.

8. Charles Williams, "Mount Badon," in *Taliessin Through Logres* (London: Oxford University Press, 1938), 17. In their original context, these words are spoken in defense of Taliessin's "waiting" policy at Mount Badon. Lewis makes Camilla use them in a similar way in defense of Ransom's "waiting" policy toward the N.I.C.E. But because of Ransom's wound and his history, the word "passion" necessarily takes on additional meaning as she speaks it (p. 194).

9. Letter from C. S. Lewis dated 23 October 1945, quoted by James Barbazon in *Dorothy L. Sayers: A Biography* (New York: Scribner's, 1981), 235.

Allegory in Delany's *Einstein Intersection*

Robert A. Collins

In an epigraph to one of the late chapters of *The Einstein Intersection* (they are not numbered), Samuel Delany quotes a bit of conversation recorded in his journal: "What's a spade writer like you doing all caught up with the Great White Bitch?" Gregory Corso says to him, and then adds an afterthought, "I guess it's pretty obvious."[1] Both the content and the tone of these epigraphs, mostly from his journal, suggest that the writing of *The Einstein Intersection* was for its author a sort of ritual exorcism of old demons. At the head of the next chapter, for instance, Delany remarks, "The images of youth plague me. . . . By the end of TEI I hope to have excised them. Billy the Kid is the last to go" (p. 118). Like those of all good writers, Delany's narratives may be read on several levels. The various kinds of myth in the novel have been explored by Stephen Scobie,[2] and parallels with T. S. Eliot's "Waste Land imagery" have been outlined by H. Jane Gardiner.[3] But it is my purpose to suggest here that the American black's struggle for a cultural identity, a prominent theme of the 1960s when the novel was written, was at least one of the demons that occupied a corner of Delany's mind.

My inference is based on a series of analogies, applied to images and events that seem transparently sociopolitical. Taken together, these analogies suggest an allegorical message: Blacks in the West must discard the "borrowed" culture of their adopted land, including the Christian religion, which dominates Western myth, before they can achieve a genuine sense of themselves.

Ostensibly, of course, Delany's protagonists belong to a future race. They are alien beings who have inherited man's planet after mankind has abandoned it and who have uneasily adopted man's form (his body) as well as the myths that shaped his "racial memory" (a Jungian concept). But members of this new race find the old forms difficult to maintain, and the rebellious spirits among them chafe against such limitations.

Since the point of view is first person, Delany's principal alter ego in the narrative is Lo Lobey, a villager whose knowledge of his own world is limited, and who thus undergoes a series of epiphanies that make up the inward plot. The science fictional premise of the novel is implied in its title: an "intersection" of the knowledge based on Einsteinian physics (knowledge that has apparently enabled the old human race to extrapolate itself physically throughout the universe) with a growing knowledge of the irrational principles present (though unproven) within any logical system according to Goedel's law. Lobey's world is changing: The irrational (apprehended only pragmatically through experience since it cannot be logically or "scientifically" demonstrated) is beginning to dominate this new race. The various psychic phenomena that make Delany's principal characters "different" may thus be explained.

The mathematical paradox involved in the intersection, however, is not the main burden of the narrative. The novel is about myth, as Delany tells us in another of the many excerpts from his journal. And its basic metaphor concerns another equation, in which the myths of mankind become the symbols of Western culture, while the alien spirits locked uneasily into foreign bodies represent the black consciousness, alienated and dispossessed by its immersion in Western culture. Essentially, Lobey's (Delany's) racial quest is to free himself from the straightjacket of man's (whitey's) culture, first by exorcising it through the reenactment of myth, and then by discarding these myths as they are seen to have no relevance to the "new reality" emerging in the consciousness of his race.

Lobey's epiphany is shared, to some extent, by other principal figures in the novel, all of whom carry the burden of mankind's myths on their backs. "What do you know about mythology?" Spider asks Lobey.

And I want a Goedelian, not an Einsteinian answer. I don't want to know what's inside the myths. . . . I want their shape, their texture, how they feel when you brush by them on a dark road, when you see them receding into the fog, their weight as they leap your shoulder from behind. (pp. 126, 130)

Like Jung's "shadow personalities," these myths are real and parasitic—they "leap" you "from behind." Lobey carries on his back Ringo Starr, Orpheus, and Theseus seeking the Minotaur. Spider has Judas Iscariot, Pat Garret, and King Minos to bear, but with a "difference." Knowing one's burden gives options to the "beast" thereof. "It's fixed!" Lobey cries at first, "I'll fail! La Dire said that Orpheus failed" (p. 131). But it is not fixed. As Spider reminds him, "Everything changes: the labyrinth today does not follow the same path it did at Knossos fifty thousand years ago."

Lobey's proof of the possibility of change is most strikingly demonstrated not in the search for the lost Friza (his Eurydice), which he ultimately abandons, or in his confrontation with Kid Death (Billy the Kid, Pluto, Satan), but in his ambivalent rejection of the Christ figure (Green-eye), which has dominated Western culture for the last two thousand years.

Green-eye's parallel with Christ is complete, even to the "virgin birth" (parthenogenesis) that sets him apart from his peers. As Spider describes him, he has the ability not only to change matter (shared by Kid Death) but to create it out of nothing (a power attributed in the Bible only to God the Creator and his only begotten son). Lobey's association with Green-eye reveals the pattern that a contemporary observer would recognize in witnessing the gospel story. In a parody of the famous Christian temptation scene, in which Satan taunts Christ in the desert, tempting him with riches, power, and pleasures, Lobey watches Kid Death fail in a parallel attempt to corrupt Green-eye. He sees the mob then come to usher "Christ into Jerusalem" (Green-eye into Branning-at-Sea). Betrayed by the illusory appearance of Friza conjured by the Great White Bitch ("Le Dove," Jean Harlow, Helen of Troy), he gets a glimpse of hell ("the Kage" beneath the floors of The Pearl) and finally a glimpse of the crucifixion (Green-eye hanging from a tree in the square).

Phaedra (the computerized "kage-keeper," but also in myth the wife of Theseus) gives Lobey the word on his Orpheus quest:

It's still the wrong maze, baby. You can find another illusion down there [in hell]. She'll follow you all the way to the door, but when you turn around to make sure she's there, you'll see through it all again, and you'll leave alone. Why even bother to go through with it? . . . You're a bunch of psychic manifestations, multi-sexed and incorporeal, and you—you're all trying to put on the limiting mask of humanity. Turn again, Lobey. Seek somewhere outside the frame of the mirror. (p. 148)

"Have you begged at the tree?" she asks, sending him to his final confrontation with the central image of Christian myth. Lobey prays, but Green-eye, like the Christian god, is unresponsive. Beginning humbly, Lobey's prayer ends in outrage. He grabs his knife–flute (called an "ax," punning on the musician's word for his musical instrument), symbol of the ordering principle in his psyche, and plunges it into the crucified Green-eye's thigh.

The blow proves to be the mortal one. As Spider says, "You killed him. It was that last stroke of your [ax]" (p. 154). But by this time, having witnessed the demise of Kid Death at Spider's hand (Lobey, by mesmerizing the Kid with his "ax," is an accomplice), Lobey has discovered that he, too, has the power to bring back those he has killed.

Lobey has thus discovered that gods and mythic heroes are under the power of their believers, who shape them, make them, destroy them. Will he, then, revive Christ, fulfilling the resurrection myth central to Western culture? "Not now," he says, in answer to Spider's urgings. Rejection of the Christ figure (now metaphorically dependent on the will of the alien hero for its existence) implies a rejection of the martyr–hero archetype as the exemplum of black racial consciousness. The figure of passive resistance and suffering, applicable to Martin Luther King and the Southern Christian Leadership Conference, is symbolically thrust into limbo.

"Green-eye will . . . wait, I suppose," Spider responds (p. 155), more caught up in his role of Judas than Lobey is in the Orpheus routine. Meanwhile, Lobey turns away from the cultural imperatives of Western myth, abandons his Eurydice and his Christ, and begins a new voyage of self-discovery, following the "darkness . . . [as it falls] away at the far side of the beach." As a representative of black consciousness, Delany's alter ego is still in search of himself, but freed at last of the need to follow alien archetypes.

NOTES

1. Samuel R. Delany, *The Einstein Intersection* (New York: Ace, 1967), 107. Further references appear in the text.

2. Stephen Scobie, "Different Mazes: Mythology in Samuel R. Delany's *The Einstein Intersection*," *Riverside Quarterly* 5 (1971): 12–18.

3. H. Jane Gardiner, "Images of *The Waste Land* in *The Einstein Intersection*," *Extrapolation* 8 (1977): 116–23.

LINGUISTIC ARCHAISM
AND INVENTION

Language is the object examined in the following essays on Victorian, Christian Modernist, and contemporary deconstructionist texts. Disruption of apparent narrative strategies gives the reader an uncanny feeling of otherness in the language itself. The fantastic may recover the primal potency of language.

William Morris's Anti-Books: The Kelmscott Press and the Late Prose Romances

Frederick Kirchhoff

William Morris embarked on two enterprises in 1890 that were to occupy him for the last six years of his life: He founded the Kelmscott Press and he began writing the series of works known collectively as the "late romances." He had written prose romances before 1890—much shorter ones at the very beginning of his literary career and, more recently, the two Germanic romances, *The House of the Wolfings* and *The Roots of the Mountains*, and the Marxist dream-visions *A Dream of John Ball* and *News from Nowhere*—and these works are not un-related to those he wrote in the 1890s. But the late romances—*The Story of the Glittering Plain*, *The Wood beyond the World*, *The Well at the World's End*, *The Water of the Wondrous Isles*, *The Sundering Flood*—have a thematic co-herence that argues they should be read as aspects of a single literary project; and it is as such that I wish to consider them.

The coincidence of this project with the "adventure" of the Kelmscott Press is significant. The first of the late romances was also the first book published by the Press. It was not written for that purpose—the romance had already appeared serially in the *English Illustrated Magazine*—nor was it the book Morris had originally planned to initiate the Press. And so, although it might strengthen my argument if I could show that the romances were written specifically for the Kelmscott Press, I cannot. Instead, I offer the simpler—and in the long run, I think, more useful—observation that the romances and the Press are analogous efforts, and that what they most significantly share is a concern with the act of reading.

Morris insisted that even though the chief purpose of the Kelmscott Press was "to produce books which it would be a pleasure to look upon as pieces of printing and arrangement of type," there was no conflict between this aim and the aim of "readableness." Indeed, one of his reasons for disliking "ordinary modern type" was that it was "difficult to read"; and in determining to design a Gothic typeface for the Press, he set himself the task "to redeem the Gothic character from the charge of unreadableness."[1]

Critics like Paul Thompson have argued that Morris was fooling himself about the legibility of the books he printed, and "that the Kelmscott volumes were books to be collected, not to be read."[2] But Morris rarely fooled himself. There are, it seems to me, two problematic assumptions behind Thompson's judgment. First, he implies that the speed with which a book is read is the index of its typographical legibility; second, he implies that "reading" is simply a matter of ingesting the words on a page. It is doubtless true that the Kelmscott books are not legible if one tries to speed-read them, and that their overall appearance— typeface, layout, paper, and binding—suggests a purpose other than the mere conveyance of information. They are in this sense "Anti-Books"—deliberate frustrations of what Thompson and almost everyone else take to be the function of the printed page. But, conversely, they *are* legible if read slowly; and ugly type, because it discourages the reader from lingering over words and sentences by making any pause an unpleasant experience for the eye, may render a text that requires lingering and pause unreadable. Moreover, because Morris's books are beautiful in addition to being slowly readable does not necessarily mean they have a primary purpose other than being read. It simply redefines reading as an act in which the physical qualities of the book play a major role.

Morris's comments on the act of writing complement this point: "There's a pleasant feel in the paper under one's hand and the pen between one's fingers that has its own part in the work done. . . . I always write with a quill because it's fuller in the hand for its weight, and carries ink better—good ink—than a steel pen. . . . I don't like the typewriter or the pneumatic brush . . . because they come between the hand and its work . . . and again beause they make things too easy. The minute you make the executive part of the work too easy, the less thought there is in the result. And you can't have art without resistance in the material. No! The very slowness with which the brush moves over the paper, or the graver goes through the wood, has its value."[3]

This notion of resistance applies as readily to the act of reading a text—or, more generally, apprehending any work of art—as it does to the artist's creativity. Resistance can, of course, take the form of obscurity in the diction or syntax of a text. The Kelmscott Press locates resistance in the physical format of the book itself, not only in its appearance to the eye, but in the size, weight, and feel of the volume and also—although here a new consideration is raised—in its monetary value. These are not books to carry on the train or peruse in the doctor's office. The consciousness that the materials of a book are the best available and therefore precious and that the time and effort of skilled craftsmen have shaped these materials into a work of what Morris would have called one of the "lesser arts" makes reading a special event. Thompson's belief that such books exist primarily to be collected defeats their most important purpose: to rehabilitate the act of reading. Morris's fine printing was not, in other words, merely a challenge to Victorian typography. As a reaction against the "plague of book-making" that Bob the weaver complains of in *News from Nowhere*[4] and that we now refer to as "the information explosion," it restores to reading its significance as a special experience, set apart from the confusion of day-to-day life.

Morris's 1890 concern with the special nature of reading was more than a response to the proliferation of mass-produced books and the sloppy reading habits it encouraged. The concern had antecedents in the notion of literature implicit in his earlier experiments with narrative form, and this notion clarifies the intent behind both the Kelmscott Press and the late romances.

Two related efforts characterize the poetry Morris wrote from *The Defence of Guenevere* (1858) through *The Story of Sigurd the Volsung* (1876): an effort to remove or distance the subjective voice of the poet from his narrative poetry, through the use of dramatic monologues and substitute narrators; and an effort to distance or dissociate the narrative itself from its audience through the use of narrative frames, archaic diction, and non-developmental plot structure. The first can be explained as a typically Victorian attempt to overcome Romantic self-consciousness. It has a further purpose, however, when the absence of the poet and, especially, the presence of a substitute voice are perceived as a means of limiting the reader's response. For the Romantic, first person is not only a representative of the poet; it is also a recognizable human voice—in Words-worth's terms, "a man speaking to men"—with whom the reader can form a human bond, no matter how alien the subject matter of his narrative. By dis-solving this bond, Morris prevents the reader from using the assumed humanity of the narrator as a grounds for naturalizing the text.

Underlying these efforts is, I believe, Morris's sense or feeling that art must be experienced as an alterity and that its real power is understood only when its limitations are recognized. The Apology that opens *The Earthly Paradise* ex-presses this paradox in two mutually referent metaphors:

> Folk say, a wizard to a northern king
> At Christmas-tide such wondrous things did show,
> That through one window men beheld the spring,
> And through another saw the summer glow,
> And through a third the fruited vines a-row,
> While still, unheard, but in its wonted way,
> Piped the drear wind of that December day.
>
> So with this Earthly Paradise it is,
> If ye will read aright, and pardon me,
> Who strive to build a shadowy isle of bliss
> Midmost the beating of the steely sea,
> Where tossed about all hearts of men must be.

(Vol. 3, p. 2)

The wizard's magic is "wondrous" not because he erases winter, but because he never allows his audience to lose consciousness of "the drear wind of that

December day.'' The poet's ''shadowy isle of bliss'' is a significant achievement
not because it escapes from but because it is placed ''midmost the beating of
the steely sea.'' An awareness of the limits of art is necessary if we are to
understand its strength.[5]

This recognition of limits is analogous to the resistance embodied in the
Kelmscott Press editions. Consider the alternative: An art without resistance
seduces us into confusing it with reality. The nineteenth-century realist novel
exemplifies such art. If, as Patrick Brantlinger argues, Morris's *News from
Nowhere* is an ''Anti-Novel,'' then its implied criticism of Victorian fiction
confirms the view that it was realism—or naturalism—against which Morris was
opposing his own fictions.[6] Such art gains credibility by linking itself to our
preconceived notions of what is real; yet, by so doing, it forfeits the ability to
contrast itself with reality: to create a tension between the real and the imaginary,
the possible and the impossible. This tension is an aim of Morris's art, and it
explains his turn to fantasy in the late romances.

The first of the romances is itself a parable of the misuse of literature—or, in
this case, literary illustration. Hallblithe in *The Story of the Glittering Plain* is
lured from his home to satisfy the desire of a King's Daughter who has fallen
in love with his picture in ''a book covered with gold and set with gems'' (vol.
14, p. 265). He loves another woman, and the only result of the King's efforts
to assist his Daughter is to increase her unhappiness and cause trouble for
Hallblithe and his betrothed. No good, it seems, can come of confusing an
artistic representation with actuality. The search for a real equivalent to the
portrait in a book is a gesture appropriate to tyrants and their spoiled children—
persons who seek to relate themselves to the world through dominance rather
than fellow-feeling. What the very ornateness of her book should have taught
the King's Daughter was that its pictures represent persons and places she could
never experience directly. She eventually meets Hallblithe, but, unlike his picture, he resists her control.

In contrast, Ralph in *The Well at the World's End* is prepared to be skeptical
about the book that pretends to tell the story of his mistress's life. The volume
is ''sweet poison'' to him, because he is not sure how much of it is true, and
this uncertainty is borne out by the Lady, who tells him ''there are matters written
wrong in the book'' (vol. 18, p. 147) and gives him an alternative version of
her story in her own words. The book, it turns out, is partly reliable, partly not.
It resembles the truth, but it is not the truth—and is in some ways misleading.
And it is because its relationship to the real world is uncertain that it is able to
transform the consciousness of the reader. Ralph allows himself to be moved
by his reading, but not to accept what he reads at face value. He thus distances
himself from his own desire, questioning its relationship to his real circumstances;
as a result, ''his manhood seemed changed'' (vol. 18, p. 110).

The book and the place at which Ralph reads it—the Little Land of Abundance—are a halting place in the narrative. He reads, but the content of his
reading is not proved or disproved by any immediate experience. Nothing hap-

pens here. He waits for his mistress to appear, but she fails to arrive. It is a place, like the intellectual space of reading itself, outside time and the flow of events. Yet it is for Ralph a place of limited but nevertheless significant human growth. Such, it would seem, is the space of the late romances themselves.

It is easy to assert that the fantasy mode of the late romances functions as resistance to naturalization, but less easy to demonstrate this function. An experiment in reader-response criticism might hold the answer. How, on the average, do readers react to a work of fiction, like *The Water of the Wondrous Isles*, that opens with these three paragraphs:

> Whilom, as tells the tale was a walled cheaping-town hight Utterhay, which was builded in a bight of the land a little off the great highway which went over the mountains to the sea.
>
> The said town was hard on the borders of a wood, which men held to be mighty great, or maybe measureless; though few indeed had entered it, and they that had, brought back tales wild and confused thereof.
>
> Therein was neither highway nor byway, nor wood-reeve nor way-warden; never came chapman thence unto Utterhay; no man of Utterhay was so poor or so bold that he durst raise the hunt therein; no outlaw durst flee thereto; no man of God had such trust in the saints that he durst build him a cell in that wood. (Vol. 20, p. 1)

A sense that this language is not the language of everyday life—either in the 1890s or the 1980s—is inescapable. Yet just how the prose of the late romances achieves its unique effect is difficult to explain. One can point to archaisms—words like "hight" and "durst" and "cheaping-town"—but the vocabulary is less archaic than it may at first seem, and the feeling we may want to call "archaism" is more a result of sentence structure and idiom than of diction. Subordination is minimal; sentences develop by compounding clauses. The essential syntactic relationships are equivalence and opposition. If prose is the formal expression of a way of thinking, then the implications of this incremental syntax may be central to the romances. Like the figures in a medieval tapestry, the events of the narrative stand side by side, without the subordination to a dominant point of view explicit in visual perspective. The paratactic prose of the romances suggests a way of thought that should strike the reader as markedly different from that of other nineteenth-century fiction, with its careful subordination of events to a law of cause and effect. An adjectival phrase like "mighty great," which takes the form of an idiom, but is, in fact, unidiomatic, confirms this feeling of otherness.

The formal structure of Morris's prose is not, however, the only element of this passage that resists naturalization. The very opening phrase—"Whilom, as tells the tale"—defines "the tale" as an entity prior to and other than the story we are reading. Like the framing devices of Morris's earlier verse narratives, it discourages us from identifying the text we read with the events it recounts, and thus from reacting to the text as we would to a realistic narrative.

Finally, the geography of the passage offers a special case of defamiliarization.

Morris uses indefinite articles in his first reference to Utterhay ("*a* walled cheap-ing-town") and its location on "*a* bight of the land," but it is "*the* land a little off from *the* great highway which went from over *the* mountains to *the* sea." These definite articles modifying nouns in what would otherwise be a "Once upon a time there was *a* . . . " construction suggest a consciousness for which what is indefinite for the reader is perceived as definite—a consciousness familiar with the great highway that goes over the mountains to the sea, but not with the specific location of Utterhay. The effect is analogous to that of free indirect style, in which we infer the presence of a point of view other than the present reader. Subtly, we ought to get the feeling that this story was not written for us.

This account of the reader's response is, of course, hypothetical. However, my contention that the late romances offer resistance to the reader is borne out by the curious antagonism they have elicited from persons otherwise sympathetic to Morris. For Paul Thompson, "The shallowness of character, the frequent use of magic, and the general feeling of purposelessness makes the longer stories almost unreadable. . . . The unreality of the later romances was intentionally increased by their style, which combines a relatively simple syntax with a strange archaic vocabulary, which only Morris could easily understand. . . . The later prose romances were never popular and Morris probably did not think of an audience when he wrote them. They were Gothic fancies of his old age, created for his own pleasure, like the Kelmscott Press where he had most of them printed."[7] If Thompson bothers to write about them at all, it is because "they exaggerate to absurdity tendencies which are present in most of Morris's writing; and . . . because they must be grouped with" Morris's two Marxist romances, *A Dream of John Ball* and *News from Nowhere*, which succeed where the other romances fail "because reality breaks through into the dream."

"Reality breaks through" quite literally in *A Dream of John Ball* and *News from Nowhere*: Both end with the narrator's waking up from a dream. But I do not think this is what Thompson, despite his metaphor, has in mind. He is referring, I believe, to the fact that both romances direct our attention to events in the real world, by way of either historical reference or utopian prediction. That this happens is certainly part of the effectiveness of the two works, and I would not argue with the point that they are among Morris's most important literary achievements. But this direction of attention to the real world is not a matter of fantasy being resuscitated by a healthy dose of the real; rather, the opposite is the case. It is fantasy in both instances that rescues reality. In both romances, fantasy is the route to reality by which the real is reconstructed or transformed. It is in this respect a mode of resistance that defamiliarizes reality and so forces the reader to a new apprehension of human potentialities. And so *A Dream of John Ball* and *News from Nowhere* are not radically dissimilar to the late romances. The late romances simply leave up to the reader what the Marxist romances had already spelled out.

The late romances are not escapist, because they never let us forget their essential unreality. In this respect, they offer a sharp contrast to fantasies written in a naturalistic style, which use conventions of "ordinary" human behavior borrowed from realistic fiction to overcome the resistance inherent in their literary mode. Like the wizard's Christmas-tide magic in *The Earthly Paradise*, the power of Morris's late romances derives from our recognition of the difference between the illusion they temporarily offer and the real world against which it is cast. If they pose a threat to the reader, it is not the threat of forgetting the real world but of the dissatisfaction with it that may arise out of the contrast between the world of the romances and the day-to-day reality he has taken for granted.

The error of the King's Daughter in *The Story of the Glittering Plain* is not that she responds too strongly to the portrait of Hallblithe in her book, but that she wishes to possess the vision of life embodied in a literary text without transforming her own consciousness. Ideally, the book should have made her dissatisfied with the Glittering Plain. She should have sought, like Hallblithe, to leave the Plain and by this positive act create a world, if not identical to that depicted in her book, at least closer to it than the world in which she has lived.

Ralph's heartsickness over the book he reads in the Little Land of Abundance exemplifies this dissatisfaction; however, it is not the only account of reading in *The Well at the World's End*. Later in the narrative, Ralph and Ursula pause in their journey to the Well to study a book of lore in the possession of a wise man. The book, which is kept in an ark and "wrapped in a piece of precious web of silk and gold, and bound in cuirbouilly wrought in strange devices" (vol. 19, p. 27), is taken out of doors and opened on an ancient stone altar, where it is read aloud by the Sage. To hear it, Ralph and Ursula must dress in white linen albs, a precaution necessary because the lore in the book is that of the "ancient folk" who "in these wastes and wilds . . . of old time . . . did worship to the Gods of the Earth as they imagined them" (vol. 19, p. 29). To enter into its spirit, they must put off modern dress and assume the clothing of innocence. The lore of the "ancient folk" cannot be integrated with the modern world—in the way that the King's Daughter would have integrated Hallblithe with her life on the Glittering Plain. Moreover, the power of this book is of a kind with that of the Well itself—an identification confirmed by the fact that Ralph and Ursula wear similar garments when they reach the Well and drink of its waters. (There is also a related episode before they reach the Well, in which they read another book of lore, again out of doors, again dressed in white albs.) The power of the book, like that of the Well—which, significantly, is itself inscribed with a text—is that of the natural world: of the natural forces worshipped by primitive man. To drink of the Well is to recapture that power and thus reinvest an enervated civilization with primitive energy. To put on this power without a transformation of vision—to devote it to a predetermined purpose— is wasteful or destructive.

The books that lead to the Well are thus an analogue to the late romances. Morris's archaisms are not only more than a form of Victorian nostalgia; they are also an attempt to recover the primal potency of language and its capacity to disturb and transform. Creating a world other than the one we have known, they remind us that any "reality" is a function of words and sentences. Creating a world that is patently unreal, they teach us that human desire is more than a function of its preconditioning. Like the manuscript Ralph studies in the Little Land of Abundance, and unlike the romantic fiction of the supermarket, they awaken desire but do not in themselves offer a vicarious fulfillment of desire. Thus, like the books that direct Ralph and Ursula on their quest from civilization to the origins of civilization, they lead beyond themselves to a new view of reality. The barriers to the Well are geological—mountains, wastelands, distance itself. Like the resistance we noted in the style of the romances, these barriers discourage the fainthearted and single out the "strong of heart" capable of participating in the primitive energy of Morris's vision. They are, in that respect, dangerous texts. We read them at our peril: that, having read, we may never return quite the same persons with quite the same complacency to quite the same world we had known before.

NOTES

1. William Morris, "A Note by William Morris on His Aims in Founding the Kelmscott Press," in H. Halliday Sparling, *The Kelmscott Press and William Morris Master-Craftsman* (1924; reprint Folkeston, England: Dawson, 1975), 135–36.

2. Paul Thompson, *The Work of William Morris* (New York: Viking, 1967), 143.

3. Quoted in Sparling, *Kelmscott Press*, 13–14.

4. *The Collected Works of William Morris*, ed. May Morris, 24 vols. (1936; reprint New York: Russell and Russell, 1966), vol. 16, p. 20. Further references appear in the text.

5. This interpretation is developed in my "Aesthetic Discipline of *The Earthly Paradise*," *Victorian Poetry* 18 (1980): 229–40.

6. Patrick Brantlinger, " 'News from Nowhere': William Morris's Socialist Anti-Novel," *Victorian Poetry* 19 (1975): 35–50.

7. Thompson, *Work of William Morris*, 158–59.

"Jesperson on Toast": Language Acquisition in C. S. Lewis

Michael R. Collings

One of the few studies of C. S. Lewis's use of language in his space trilogy, Myra Barnes's *Linguistics and Languages in Science Fiction/Fantasy*, asserts that *Out of the Silent Planet* is "a religious allegory that is, on several levels, a book about communication."[1] It is to Lewis's credit that he does not simply sidestep the issue of *how* his characters are able to establish communication with an alien race; he does not merely comment that Ransom "learned the language." Instead, he carefully defines a character proficient with languages, chiefly (as he later wrote in "A Reply to Professor Haldane") to "render his rapid mastery of Old Solar more plausible."[2]

Lewis emphasizes the non-human in the language; he is not going to settle for anything as easy as "The whole galaxy operated on an English basis," or "It was a curiously slurred English that I could barely understand," both variants on science fiction stereotyping of language acquisition.[3] Lewis insists that Malacandrian is essentially alien, with no ties to any earthly language.

In presenting the process by which Ransom learns Malacandrian, Lewis incorporates the alien vocabulary into his own narrative, then allows Ransom to discover the meanings of the words. In a sense, Ransom—and the reader—actually learn the language.[4] But this chore is made easier by the fact that the reader can easily recognize the grammatical structures of the language. Logic and rudimentary awareness of prefixes and suffixes in English tell the reader that "thulc" means "quiet, silent," for example. Barnes emphasizes the logical relationships between English and Malacandrian but fails to ask the more essential question of whether this similarity is a flaw on Lewis's part—that is, whether his Malacandrian is too much like English, allowing Ransom to learn it too easily to be convincing. There is no inherent reason why the prefix "thulc" should follow the form and function of English prefixes; yet it does. There is no reason why "hross" should take a Latinate plural; yet it does.

Barnes approaches a reason, however, when, in speaking of a carved representation of the Solar System Ransom describes, she writes:

The stone carving itself is an interesting medium of communication; even with no knowledge of the Greek mythology on our planet, the Malacandrian impression of planets as gods, with gender and special interest, parallel those of our mythology.[5]

There is indeed a relationship, one fundamental to and inherent in *Out of the Silent Planet*. The foundation of that relationship is one of the keys to Lewis's treatment of language acquisition and to his overall Christian conception of the universe.

In general, the seeming linguistic flaws in *Out of the Silent Planet* have three possible sources: Lewis's ineptitude as a linguist and/or craftsman, leading to an overly simplistic model of language; his vanity as a philologist, which might impel him to create an Anglo–Latin shadow-language; or a third, less obvious artistic impulse that might, for the moment, overwhelm the more immediately apparent dangers. This third possibility does emerge, not from an isolated discussion of Old Solar, but rather from the relationships between the language and the universe Lewis imagines.

Initially, however, one *is* tempted to see Lewis's language as stereotypically science fiction—that is, as slovenly and inept. After all, both Devine and Weston understand some Malacandrian, limited primarily by their disinclination to accept the Malacandrians as rational beings and only partially by their inability to assimilate the structures of the language. That Weston in particular becomes even marginally familiar with Malacandrian says little for the intrinsic "alienness" of the language, since he is almost anti-linguistic, rejecting the word in all of its forms.[6] Yet even Weston learns enough Malacandrian to become peripherally functional.

Ransom, of course, learns far more quickly. He is introduced to the language with the single word "Malacandra," and is prepared for a new language, one as alien as the landscape, a "new, extra-terrestrial, a non-human language" (p. 55). Arriving on Mars, he is subjected to an abrupt wrenching of senses and perceptions. He cannot define anything; naming is roughly a function of understanding, and without familiar parameters, Ransom is at first unable to make sense of his physical surroundings. He recognizes at this early stage that words are essential in defining the reality underlying perception—and that until the words are known perceptions remain unidentified. As far as Ransom's reactions to the physical environment are concerned, Lewis builds a convincing case for the essential "otherness" of Malacandra.

Ransom goes beyond his physical sensations, however, and begins to people the planet with imaginary, nightmare-inspired aliens: monstrous, insectile, amorphous, or—even worse, from his perspective—things so alien, so "other," as to be literally unimaginable (p. 35). He allows his imagination, prodded by fear and dread, to conjure fantastic versions of sorns before he understands what the word refers to; and when he first sees a *sorn* in the distance, he reacts to his imagined definition, panicking in response to something beyond his imagination and uniquely non-human (pp. 45–46).

Nothing Ransom had ever encountered had prepared him for the landscape or his first sight of alien life forms. And to this extent, Lewis satisfies the reader's desire for something non-human, extra-human, and alien. Yet when Lewis discusses the language, he retreats to common ground.

Ransom recognizes immediately that the creature he has met is speaking; yet Lewis seems to commit a flaw in suggesting that articulate sounds would be identifiable "almost at once," even when those sounds are part of a communication system the auditor would presumably have no knowledge of. Lewis seems to argue that *all* articulations in *all* languages—human and alien—share certain characteristics, an assumption justified only if one assumes simultaneously psychological or physiological connections between all speakers of all possible languages. To so assume would be to retreat to the level of Lewis's contemporary Stanley Weinbaum, whose "Martian Odyssey,"[7] while a turning point of sorts in science fiction, away from Wellsian horrors and toward a gentler sort of alien, fails to move forward in terms of linguistic credibility. Weinbaum describes first contact between human and Martian in the most rudimentary of terms and actions: Human points to himself and speaks his name; alien points to human and speaks (as closely as alien physiology permits) the name in return. Then they reverse the procedure.[8] To this point, Lewis parallels Weinbaum. The creature Ransom sees slaps its chest and makes what Ransom interprets eventually not only as language but as the species name it associated with itself (p. 57). For Lewis and Weinbaum, speech is immediately recognizable, leading to almost identical hand-to-chest movements and an exchange of names.[9] But this action begins to strain the reader's credibility. A gesture and a sound, associated with an entirely non-human culture and expressing a concept definable only within the parameters of an alien language, should not be so immediately decipherable.

Lewis compounds the problem by making the earliest stages of linguistic interchange instantly successful. With far fewer credentials in language than Lewis had, Weinbaum at least introduces a degree of complication. Dick points to the Tweel and repeats its sound; and there his attempts at communicating stall. The alien does not respond to Dick's use of the name it had given itself; instead it produces an entirely different series of sounds. Dick was always "Tick," but the alien responded to "sixteen other noises" in addition to the first two. Dick concludes that either there were unknown and unidentifiable subtleties in the alien language, or the two—human and Martian—simply thought so differently that speech was largely impossible. Later episodes confirm Weinbaum's hypothesis—human and Tweel never really understand each other.

Yet Lewis fails even to suggest such difficulties. Instead, the language lessons progress unimpeded.[10] Ransom does all of the right things, learning first the names of nouns and then the functions of affixes. Everything proceeds easily—too easily, even allowing for Ransom's training as a philologist. In fact, the sequence almost requires that the two species share essential presuppositions about the structure and functions of language that, given the restrictions of science fiction and first-contact narratives, simply should not be shared.

Lewis further complicates his narrative by describing the two "alien" creatures' responses to each other, both physical and emotional. Hross and human initially hesitate to move closer to each other, but there are suggestions of more than mere caution and fear. Both human and alien respond to the same need to move nearer to each other, an impulse Lewis calls "foolish, frightening, ecstatic and unbearable all in one moment" (p. 56). Beyond that, it resembles almost a mating ritual. Lewis immediately notes that the experience transcends the first meeting of male and female, however; it must, in fact, transcend all of the ingrained fear and hesitance implicit in first contact between alien species. The rather stunning implication of the episode, in fact, is that communication is not only easy, but virtually inevitable, as sexual intercourse is inevitable between an Adam and an Eve. Lewis suggests an intimacy between species that parallels the ease with which Ransom becomes proficient in Malacandrian.

Ransom is, of course, aware of his tendency to evaluate Malacandra in human terms. When the hross invites him to enter a boat, he is impressed by the craft—that it was "really very like an earthly boat; only later did he set himself the question, 'what else could a boat be like?' " (pp. 58–59). He is aware of the curious drawing power the hross exerts; he is aware of his tendency to think in human terms, and struggles against both. Yet with all of his linguistic experience, Ransom never asks himself why Malacandrian is so like human languages in form and structure, in phonetics, in the loss of certain sounds in specific linguistic contexts.

At this point in the novel, it is difficult to define precisely what Lewis is doing with language and language acquisition. On the one hand, he makes Ransom's task incredibly easy; the process is too quick, too immediate, with virtually no missteps by teacher or pupil. On the other hand, however, it is hard to accuse Lewis of outright ineptitude. Since he was, above all, a careful craftsman, especially in matters of language, it seems inconceivable that he would settle for anything as transparently amateurish as this Anglo–Martian, without an overwhelming artistic or philosophical reason.

Nor does it seem likely that Lewis would have created the language purely to show off his linguistic abilities. He would not have needed to, since his scholarly and critical works were sufficient evidence of his skill. Nor did he usually incorporate such intensely personal—and artistically destructive—elements into works designed to transcend their author as individual.[11] Finally, it is even unusual that Lewis has his hero learn the alien language. Frequently in science fiction, the alien shows unusual propensities for language and learns English out of courtesy to the less-gifted human. More commonly, humans chauvinistically assume that the aliens will learn English. But Lewis's humans—including Weston and Devine, who can hardly be accused of undue consideration for or civility toward other life forms—learn Malacandrian.

The explanation for this rather confusing series of issues emerges as Ransom understands Malacandrian culture more deeply, and as Lewis simultaneously moves closer to the central theme of the space trilogy, first hinted at early in *Out of the Silent Planet*, when Ransom describes his responses to the sorns in terms reminiscent of childhood nightmares. The alien is not utterly unknowable, he realizes, but instead—and ironically—reflects Ransom's own childhood nightmares: "Giants—ogres—ghosts—skeletons: those were its key words" (p. 47). Lewis removes his characters from the normal environment of science fiction and Wells's "bug-eyed monsters" to suggest that the sorns affect Ransom subconsciously, intuitively. In a sense, the sorns are oddly human-like; they stir archetypes embedded within human consciousness. This element in Ransom's description of his experience implies an unusual mutual intelligibility that Lewis builds into his fiction—overtly through the deceptively simple and human-like structure of Malacandrian language, and less overtly through the theological presuppositions of the novel.

In Lewis's theology, Creator and creation are linked. Leanne Payne writes:

For himself and for many others, Lewis recovered the vision of an immanent God—a God who indwells His people—Who is yet sovereign over, and beyond, His creatures. Knowing well that Christians had for the most part lost this understanding, and that the non-Christian of the twentieth century had not even an inkling of it, Lewis proclaimed in philosophical, theological, and imaginative terms that the creature is linked—and can be absolutely linked—to the creator.[12]

One of the most critical functions of Lewis's alien creatures is to show that all rational life within the universe—or the solar system, at least—do indeed touch each other through their relationship with the Creator. Ransom, and by extension all humans, shares sufficient common ground with the Malacandrians that it becomes not merely acceptable but virtually required that they be linguistically compatible. What seems on a first reading to be a near-fatal science fictional stereotype becomes, in fact, a tool with which Lewis combats the "scientism" he defines as opposing Christian belief.

Humans and aliens are compatible because both are rational and, by virtue of their rationality, parallel each other. All *hnau*—be they human, hrossa, sorn, Perelandrian, or talking beasts of Narnia—have reason. Even the guiding "angel" of Malacandra, Oyarsa, assures Ransom that in spite of obvious differences between them (Oyarsa can barely see Ransom, for instance), they are fundamentally linked and alike in that both reflect the creative power of Maleldil; both are "copies" of Maleldil (pp. 119–120).

Here is the final explanation for Lewis's unusual treatment of language in the earlier chapters. Ransom understands Malacandrian, as do Devine and Weston, precisely because the Malacandrians are *not* true aliens, "bug-eyed monsters," or other Wellsian horrors. They are instead previous creations, older brothers, if you will, of humankind. This is the point toward which Lewis has been driving

since Ransom's first ill-perceived vision of Malacandra and his unusually successful first attempts at communicating with the hross. Lewis is neither inept
nor unnecessarily involved with his own ego enhancement; instead, *Out of the
Silent Planet* is a treatise on the universality of creation, and on the intrinsic
relationships existing between superficially unlike life forms, for the simple
reason that they are all creations of the Old One through Maleldil–Aslan–Christ.

Once Ransom reaches this awareness, puzzling elements in the novel no longer
puzzle. In *Perelandra*, standing before the spirit entities who are Malacandra
and Perelandra, Ransom realizes that the universe is, in fact, a single entity. He
uses the dual images of spider's web and whispering gallery in which "no news
travels unchanged yet no secret can be rigorously kept."[13]

In such a universe, language signals relationships and moral development. On
Malacandra the three species speak a single tongue, yet each has its own variant,
based upon physical, psychological, emotional, and temperamental differences.
Unity underlies all; but since Malacandra was created before the Incarnation,
rationality could be inherent in different forms and expressed in different languages. On Perelandra, on the other hand, there is a single rational form, based
on the Incarnational form of Maleldil, and concurrently a single language, which
both Ransom and the Un-man–Weston easily understand.

The extent to which language parallels meaning equally ties in with Lewis's
conception of a Christian universe. Weston and Devine enter Malacandra as
predators and destroyers—as forces of the Bent Eldil of Thulcandra. Significantly, they have great difficulty understanding Old Solar, the language of unity.
Weston, in fact, systematically reduces language to near babble at the end of
Out of the Silent Planet, speaking an Old Solar characterized by idiotic, childish
simplicity. At the end of the trilogy, at the final confrontation of good and evil,
Lewis returns to this technique as the languages at Belbury are literally confounded; and out of the destruction of evil, a refined and purified good arises.[14]
In the final scenes of *That Hideous Strength*, Mark Studdock thinks consciously
about language:

The word *Lady* had made no part of his vocabulary save as a pure form or else in mockery.
He had laughed too soon. (p. 381)

Within a few lines, however, he experiences the Otherworldly:

Suddenly the diffuse light brightened and flushed. He looked up and perceived a great
lady standing by a doorway in a wall. It was not Jane, not like Jane. It was larger, almost
gigantic. It was not human, though it was like a woman divinely tall, part naked, part
wrapped in a flame-coloured robe. Light came from it. (pp. 381–82)

He penetrates language sufficiently to participate in the unity of creation. He
not only understands at last the proper referent of *Lady* in his own language,
but also easily applies that word to another entity, something beyond his imag-

ining, something that defines (as Lewis has already established) ultimate femininity, not only for all humans but for all creation.

There are, then, particular connections between Earth and Malacandra that allow Lewis to construct Old Solar along the lines that he did. He is neither inept nor self-obsessive; rather, language becomes a metaphor for the relationship between various creations within a Christian universe. The Malacandrian language is "unhuman" but still functions within the same framework as Ransom's Latin or English or any other human tongue. Lewis notes explicitly that no contemporary human languages are descended directly from Hressa-hlab, his Ur-language. But by virtue of the shared "creaturehood" of rational beings, and by virtue of their direct relationship to the same Creator and their concomitant indirect relationship with alien but related creations inhabiting Mars and Venus, humans can understand the aliens' language. What seems on the surface a flaw in Lewis's performance becomes evidence for the care with which he constructed his fictions. The reader—and particularly the reader who is overly critical of Lewis's treatment of language at the beginning of *Out of the Silent Planet*— might easily find the justice in applying Ransom's comment about Malacandrians to himself: It is not the "alien" who is ultimately unknowable, but Ransom's own species (p. 74). It may seem conspicuously easy for Lewis's characters to learn Old Solar; but the critical theological point is that they are the only species who do not already *know* it. They are the only ones divorced from the influence of Maleldil and the Old One.

NOTES

1. Myra Barnes, *Linguistics and Languages in Science Fiction/Fantasy* (New York: Arno Press, 1975), 98. Related materials, discussing communication in science fiction in general, also occur in Robert Plank, "Communication in Science Fiction," in *The Use and Misuse of Language*, ed. S. I. Hayakawa (Greenwich, CT: Fawcett Publications, 1962); and Walter E. Meyers, *Aliens and Linguists: Language Study and Science Fiction* (Athens: University of Georgia Press, 1980).

2. Cited in Donald E. Glover, *C. S. Lewis: The Art of Enchantment* (Athens: Ohio University Press, 1981), 77.

3. Beverly Friend, science fiction editor of the *Chicago Daily News*, has compiled a list of common devices to substitute for rigidly defined language acquisition in science fiction. The list is reproduced in Meyers, *Aliens and Linguists*, 105.

4. Barnes, *Linguistics and Languages*, 100–01.

5. Ibid., 98n.

6. C. S. Lewis, *Out of the Silent Planet* (New York: Macmillan Paperbacks, 1965), 29. Further references appear in the text.

7. Stanley Weinbaum, "Martian Odyssey," in James Gunn, ed., *The Road to Science Fiction #2: From Wells to Heinlein* (New York: New American Library, 1979), 238–63. The story originally appeared in 1939.

8. Weinbaum, "Martian Odyssey," 244.

9. Ibid.

10. Here I am discussing basic vocabulary building and understanding of grammatical

structures, not the artistic nuances of poetry, which Ransom acknowledges often eluded him entirely.

11. Chad Walsh, "C. S. Lewis: Critic, Creator and Cult Figure," *Seven* 2 (March 1981): 74.

12. Leanne Payne, *Real Presence: The Holy Spirit in the Works of C. S. Lewis* (Westchester, IL: Cornerstone Books, 1979), 14.

13. C. S. Lewis, *Perelandra* (New York: Macmillan Paperbacks, 1968), 201.

14. C. S. Lewis, *That Hideous Strength* (New York: Macmillan Paperbacks, 1965), 343 ff. Further references appear in the text.

Vulcan Revisited: Kenneth Patchen's *Journal of Albion Moonlight*

Stephen J. Robitaille

What perverse pleasure finds me returning to Kenneth Patchen's *Journal of Albion Moonlight*? Each page is a palimpsest, a violent disruption of sense and form, a flagrant shattering of meaning. And how to view *The Journal* in the context of a critical biography—of a life? One begins with the notion of "journal" as trope. Journal, from the French *journal*: day book; *jour*: light, day-light . . . a book of days, of shedding light on days. I follow, impulsively, the Derridian urge to explore the *signature* of the author of this text, to explore the interpenetration of subject and object in *Journal of Albion Moonlight*.

Patchen: "Patch (pach) a piece of material used to mend a hole, rent, etc., a covering for a small wound; v.t. to mend with a patch, to repair clumsily; — work n. made by sewing together pieces of cloth of different material and color (O.F. pieche, a piece)."[1] But the converse is also true: The patch is no whole cloth, there are seams ("seems"?), discontinuities. As with a journal, there is the matter of where the pieces come together, and of the process of selection: of what gets left out.

My own thoughts feel their way along the seams of Patchen's *Journal*, and there I detect the traces of tiny folds, fragments of patches, of other texts . . . and of other signatures. Anaïs Nin, during the period that Patchen was attempting to piece together his *Journal*, sent Henry Miller a copy of an essay on Patchen's strange manuscript in which she stated:

What I see in this book, what cries behind windows, haunting every scene, sightless, voiceless, throughout this drama of violent acts, what is murdered each time anew, what passes from one man to another, is a soul dispossessed by violence, crying to be born, *a soul not yet born.*[2]

Miller, on his way across America in search of material for his forthcoming book *The Air Conditioned Nightmare*, arrived in Warren, Ohio, birthplace of the poet, where he wrote Nin the following:

I passed through Warren, Ohio where Patchen came from. If you could see it, you'd understand Patchen even more. The whole journey today thru Pennsylvania and Ohio was like a ride through an Inferno.... It's almost beyond words ... so glum, so black, so terrible. Like the planet Vulcan if there is one.[3]

Patchen ... patch ... covering for a wound ... to mend ... drama of violent events ... crying to be born ... Warren ... Vulcan ... so black ... beyond words. To describe with words what is beyond words to describe: a hint, perhaps, to what *Journal* critics have called unreadable, chaotic. For, ever since its private publication by the author in 1941, *The Journal of Albion Moonlight* has defied attempts by critics and literary historians to be categorized. William Carlos Williams called Moonlight's "allegorical" (a missed-reading here?) journal "order lost" and suggested that "the chief defect of such a work lies in the very plan and method of it, one is locked up in the other."[4] David Gascoyne called Patchen "the lone one-man Dada of contemporary America" and viewed Patchen's *Journal* as "giving vent to poignantly incoherent, fragmentary utterances."[5] Charles Glicksberg agreed that "it is practically impossible to suggest the substance and structure of a work like *The Journal of Albion Moonlight*, which has no logical structure, no determinate principle of continuity from beginning to denouement to conclusion.... It is surrealism run amok."[6]

This critical view, that Patchen's fantastic journey through "the plague summer of 1941" lacks any discernible structure, plot, or theme, has resulted in its being, in the words of Ronald Sukenick, "elbowed out by the novel."[7] However, recent deconstructionist critics such as J. Hillis Miller have provided us a possible key for reevaluating works such as Patchen's *Journal*. Miller states that certain texts possess the "ability to devalue all values, making traditional modes of interpretation impossible."[8] And Jacques Derrida, in his own discursive analysis of certain deconstructive elements in Shelley's "Triumph of Life," provides us with another clue when he offers the following alternative "approach" toward understanding a text:

If we are to approach a text, it must have an edge. The question of the text, as it has been elaborated and transformed in the last dozen or so years, has not merely "touched" "shore" *le bord* (scandalously tampering, changing, as in Mallarmé's declaration, "on a touché au vers"), all those boundaries that form the running border of what used to be called a text, of what we once thought this word could identify, i.e., the supposed end and beginning of a work, the unity of a corpus, the title, the margins, the signatures, the referential realm outside the frame, and so forth.[9]

Patchen's *Journal* is a tale told from its borders; it is, in essence, a tale told from a borderland in which content and language are, to borrow a term from

Harold Bloom, "shattered," and in their shattering create a meaning. For it would seem that beneath the chaos that earlier critics have suggested overwhelms the text, there exists a level of meaning dependent, in fact, upon the violent disruption of whatever might appear, at any given moment in the work, to be an authorial strategy. Consider the following, from Chapter 5 in a short novel that begins on page 290 of *The Journal*:

V. *Moonlight explains that the journal is not a literary form at all . . .*
An interruption:
There are two kinds of writers: those who *speak*, and those who talk about something.
It may be an exaggeration to say that there are five writers in the world at this hour.
THE LITTLE JOURNAL OF ALBION MOONLIGHT
An introduction:
   The journal, whether real or imaginary, must conform to only one law: it must be at any given moment what the journal-keeper wants it to be at any given moment. It is easily seen from this that time is of the greatest importance in the journal; indeed, there must be as many journals as there are days being covered. The true journal can have no plan for the simple reason that no man can plan his days.[10]

This entry announces what *The Journal* has been illustrating throughout: the dubious attempt at enframing an event (the pilgrimage to Galen), a text (*The Journal*), and a life (Albion's–Patchen's). In the case of *The Journal of Albion Moonlight*, the "realm outside the frame," the text that repeatedly directs attention away from itself is a patchwork of traces biographical, literary, historical, etc.: traces of Vulcan, Percy Bysshe Shelley, Walt Whitman, Guillaume Apollinaire, Franz Kafka, and Mickey Spillane, newsreels and news real. My own research into Patchen's life has revealed what Miller and Nin could only intuit from their brief encounter with the author, what new modes of critical inquiry seem to confirm: that the radically shifting, discontinuous moods, point of view, and subject matter, the use of language to call into question the value of language, of the text itself, *is the meaning of The Journal*. Since it is my contention that Patchen, like other innovators of the narrative mode, was not purposefully "experimenting" with language and form, that he had to, in fact, express himself as he did, I have speculated as to the primordial events that may have shaped such a sensibility, created such a text. My thoughts return to planet Vulcan, and consequently to traces of Vulcan in the text—that constitute a text beneath, behind, in the margins of *The Journal of Albion Moonlight*. It is here that a *meaning* is made. For even a shattered vision is a vision—a marginal position from which the reader is able to glimpse what is being shown.

   About midway through *The Journal*, Patchen's narrator, who has been continually disrupting Albion's journal entries concerning the bizarre pilgrimage to Galen in search of the anti-Christ, Roivas, begins to rage at the impossibility of keeping such a text under control:

There is nothing stupider than books which attempt to follow a human being through childhood into manhood. I say that the thread breaks, that the man does not come out of the child—God knows where the man comes from or where the child goes. All our damn sense of continuity. (p. 151)

Critical readers may wonder what this seemingly personal commentary has to do with Moonlight's journal of the impending war and its terrible, surreal manifestations. It might profit us to know that as Patchen was handing these pages to Robert Duncan, a young poet–friend who was then typing the manuscript for the author, he confessed: "Everything that I ever needed to know about life, I knew by the age of eight."[11] In light of the narrator's query into his origins cited in the passage above, it may be of some significance that Patchen suffered, at this time, a debilitating childhood illness, one accompanied by fever and delirium, and followed by a pattern of disabling illnesses that would leave him bedridden half the years of his life. It is from this bed as a child that Patchen began his journal making and fantastic drawings.[12] It was from his bed in a Greenwich Village apartment that Patchen scrawled Moonlight's journal in his large, child-like hand.

Earlier, in the June 30 entry, which follows a section entitled "The novel begins . . . " the narrator states:

However much we desire to remember, there is something which pulls our minds up short when we attempt to recapture the sensations of childhood. Our stomachs grow weary of food; our eyes ache to view new objects; the old, never changing sounds finally grate our ears; but we never tire of contemplating the world we knew as children. That is always fresh, pure, sweet. No matter how wretched and hungry we were. (p. 57)

To a certain extent, this passage, another disruption by the narrator of the fantastic journey to Galen, ought not to be confused with Patchen's "real" childhood in Warren, Ohio. That is to say, the Patchen family never wanted for food, clothing, or shelter. But it would appear that following his brush with serious illness, Patchen's sensitivity to the dark side of planet Vulcan was heightened. Some aspects of the Vulcan–Warren experience may be pertinent here. Accounts of relatives and childhood friends suggest that the author was, as Nin implied in her essay on *The Journal*, a soul "crying to be born"—trying, that is, to recreate a self that had been lost in the fissures that marked the edges of the borderland between Vulcan–Warren. Patchen, for example, lived in a series of unfinished houses, patchworks if you will, built and then sold by the father, before they were completed. The houses were drab, gray, unfinished boxes, covered by coal dust from the nearby mills.[13] But images of the American mill town inform the text, as in the sudden disruption of the July 5 entry in *The Journal*, where our gaze is directed from the fantasy landscape of the novel to the following observations: "America's face is smiling. A new blood quickens her step; her mills and foundries are pouring out black smoke in a frenzy of exultation—but do not be deceived: it is the false, painted bloom on the face of a corpse" (p. 91).

Two pages later it is Moonlight himself who speaks the following dialogue:

"I'm the grandson of a man who was killed in a coal mine because the owners saved a few dollars" (p. 93). There is little mistaking the thinly veiled autobiographical nature of such a line. What is particularly relevant to our discussion is the conflation of politics, violence, and childhood memory. These are the stories, the texts, that shape the meaning of *The Journal*. Such scenes were common to the young Patchen and were the subject of numerous poems and prose works. In *The Journal*, they move in and out of the frame of the novel, the fiction, until it would seem the narrator realizes the folly of the form, the futility of shaping with words the text that would enframe a life, the text that would remain unnarratable. It is as if the eruptions of the Vulcanic landscape, its harsh atmosphere, might break the spirit of a sensitive young poet, even as it would crush the limbs of the unwary millworker. Consequently, it would appear that the violent, surreal landscape of Patchen's anti-war journal is, to a significant extent, the planet Vulcan revisited.

There are two other major Vulcanic events that seem to have preoccupied the author, that move in and out of the narrative frame, disrupting the continuity of the text and thus further shaping its meaning. In correspondence and interviews with the poet's widow, Miriam, to whom *The Journal* was dedicated, there appeared yet another episode, one concerning the killing of a deer while Patchen was on a hunting trip with his father and brother. Patchen's brother, Hugh, confirmed this fact, and more than fifty years later still recalled how the enraged youth returned to his room, rejecting what he considered to be the barbaric behavior of the Patchen men. This event would not be particularly interesting were it not for the repeated images of wounded animals, the wounded green deer, the blood-hungry hounds that haunt the corpus (the corpse?) of Patchen's prose and poetry and appear repeatedly throughout the gothic episodes of *The Journal*.

Conversely, we are presented with the idealized and fantastic forms of various creatures, such as the "baby rabbit asleep in a thicket" (p. 5) and "the orange bear" (p. 161). In the May 29 entry, one of a great flock of parrots says, "The painter will strive to exclude all living images from the canvas. He will paint only that which cannot be seen." Albion responds to those "delightful parrots": "How are you settled on the little matter of death? I know . . . contained in the skin!" (p. 162).

This passage, one of pure fantasy, represents an adumbration, as it were, of the attempts throughout the novel to delete certain material from the canvas, the text, only to discover, as if it were completely out of his control, that certain events will violently disrupt certain authorial maneuvers to impose a given order on the material. It is not simply the impending war that shapes Patchen's shattered vision here; but quite obviously it is a fusion of fantasy and fact as seen through the Vulcanic mists of the author's imagination.

Finally, there is one other pattern of haunting images that I would like to consider as disruptive interpenetrations of the Galen–Vulcan worlds. These are the images of women deceased, mutilated, or sexually violated. In an autobiographical short story entitled "Bury Them in God" published in 1939, just months before Patchen began work on *The Journal of Albion Moonlight*, the author recounted the traumatic events surrounding the accidental death of his younger sister, Kathleen, at a time when he was obviously preoccupied with the notions of violence and death, as well as with the mysteries of his own emerging sexual desires, which the narrator confirms were initially directed toward the sister. The story bears a striking resemblance to Patchen's *self*-conscious *Journal*, and concludes with the narrator traveling back and forth between the present (Boston, 1936) and the past (the occurrence in the 1920s of the sister's death). The narrator considers the possibility of changing the ending of the story he is writing, as if somehow the act of writing is, paradoxically, one of erasure. Numerous letters and interviews confirmed that the sudden loss of the sister triggered an already hypersensitive reaction to life's violent discontinuities. This moment intrudes on Patchen's *Journal*, and in so doing further shapes its meaning.

In the June 30 entry, Albion, just prior to asking Jackeen to sleep with him, thinks to himself, *"You're so beautiful, but you gotta die some day"* (p. 62). Later, in Chapter 7 of a novel within the novel, Albion considers that he has "lived many years in the summer of 1929. Some years in our lives are as minutes, possessed of a woeful frailty in time—time, that is human, not of the clock" (p. 69). And turning to the enchanting Leah, he laments, "We did not know what the world would be; there was no warning from anywhere. . . . Leah, they had no right not to prepare us for what was to come."

The scene becomes increasingly more erotic until it reaches a curious pitch of sexual ambiguity. Albion

could think of nothing to tell her. His hunger for her was a tiger; he did not so much want her as he wanted to be her; he wanted never to leave her; he did not want his desire to part him from her; he did not want to place himself in a lover's position upon her; he wanted to breathe her; he wanted to find a sexless body somewhere and take both of them into it. (p. 72)

Critics have pointed to the juxtaposition of violent sex and idealized love as one of the chaotic elements that renders the work untranslatable. Given the numerous sources, subtexts, that shape Patchen's *Journal*, these Vulcanic eruptions, aftershocks, serve as a code that signals the meaning of a text that can be read on the edges, borders, margins of *The Journal*. The occasion of such violent episodes no doubt invites a psychological interpretation; however, such textual details as "rents" in the patchwork would seem to predate news *real* events "of the plague summer of 1941."

I began with the impulse to play off the author's name—make a whole cloth of the patchwork—to see in a life and in art a patching together of what has been torn. I arrive, finally, at my own patchwork of moments in *The Journal* that serve as codes of violence, and the flight from violence, throughout *The Journal*, the journée. One senses in these "fragments" that discontinuity, and the ultimate failure of form to create form, *are* the story here:

Albion: Something in me is wise. It knows when I labor to make people talk in my
    journal—the complete fraud of this; it is I who speak. (p. 22) . . . I never learned to
    cry properly as a child. (p. 28) . . . I want to take a club and go into the house and
    break them down. (p. 31) . . . There is no danger from the world; all that is dangerous
    lives in us. (p. 83) . . . Behind the world another world, stretching away into the
    wailing shadows, awaited the crumbling of that curious wall which would free all
    of us. (p. 111)

A drawing by Albion Moonlight is of a "man trying to attach an umbilical
cord to his navel. The cord is withered and thready" (p. 119). "The novel is
being written as it happens, not what happened yesterday, or what will happen
tomorrow, but what is happening now, *at this moment*" (p. 145). "Much has
been omitted in this tale: some things should not be known" (p. 187). And
finally, "I will heal the child which the devouring night-horror has fed on"
(p. 271).

There are, in addition, the seemingly endless surreal happenings of Moonlight's pilgrimage to Galen, the numerous "endings" of the novel, the text of
another fantasy written in the margin of *The Journal*, the newsreel announcements
of troop advances in Europe, the passage where type gives way to the handwritten
scrawl of the narrator's urgent message to his readers, the crude drawing of the
hanged man on page 245, and the prayers, poems, and incantations that shape
this patchwork. As such, *The Journal of Albion Moonlight* belongs, argues
Ronald Sukenick, to a tradition of narrative innovation that begins as early as
Laurence Sterne's "multifaceted, anti-sequential, surrational" *Tristram Shandy*,
and arrives, more recently, in the fantastic wordscapes of Jean Genet, Donald
Barthelme, John Hawkes, and numerous others.[14] It is not surprising, therefore,
that new critical modes of inquiry have offered us a means to make a thrust
toward discovering what often remains unnarratable in such works.

Patchen concludes *The Journal* with the following:

> There is no way to end this book.
> No way to begin (p. 313)

Derrida speaks of endings, or nonendings:

Survival and *revenance*; living on and returning from the dead: living on goes beyond
both living and dying, supplementing each with a sudden surge and a certain reprieve,
deciding [*arrêtant*] life *and* death, ending them in a decisive *arrêt*, the *arrêt* that puts an
end to something, a sentence, a statement, a spoken word or a word that goes on
speaking.[15]

Because Patchen did not end with a sentence, the final utterance being *periodless*,
he did not *sentence*, to use the French sense of the word, himself to the confines
of a narrative form. If Patchen renders himself unreadable, it is in order to
survive. There would follow only a few long prose works. Verbal expression

would give way to the painted poems that seem to mirror a child's nighttime imaginings, filled with weird and incredible creatures, the poet's brief poems no longer page bound, but suspended in a strange atmosphere of the author's own making. But this is the subject of another essay, another patch in the patchwork.

NOTES

1. *Webster's Dictionary*, ed. John Allee (New York: Ottenheimer Publishers, 1978), s.v.

2. Anaïs Nin to Henry Miller, in *The Diary of Anaïs Nin* (New York: Harcourt Brace Jovanovich, 1969), 64.

3. Henry Miller, *Henry Miller's Letters to Anaïs Nin* (New York: G. P. Putnam's Sons, 1965), 237–38.

4. William Carlos Williams, "A Counsel of Madness," in *Kenneth Patchen: A Collection of Essays*, ed. Richard Morgan (New York: AMS Press, 1977), 5.

5. David Gascoyne, "Introducing Kenneth Patchen," in Morgan, *Kenneth Patchen*, 146.

6. Charles I. Glicksberg, "The World of Kenneth Patchen," in Morgan, *Kenneth Patchen*, 184.

7. Ronald Sukenick, "The New Tradition in Fiction," in *Surfiction: Fiction Now and Tomorrow*, ed. Raymond Federman (Chicago: Swallow Press, 1975), 41.

8. J. Hillis Miller, "The Critic as Host," in *Deconstruction and Criticism*, ed. Harold Bloom, Paul de Man, Jacques Derrida, Geoffrey Hartman, & J. Hillis Miller (New York: Seabury Press, 1979), 226.

9. Jacques Derrida, "Living On," in Bloom, *Deconstruction and Criticism*, 83.

10. Kenneth Patchen, *The Journal of Albion Moonlight* (New York: New Directions, 1961), 304–5. Further references appear in the text. The book was published privately by the author in 1941 when James Laughlin refused to publish the manuscript unless, as he urged Patchen in a series of as-yet unpublished letters, he "put more structure into it and discipline it." Laughlin further advised the author to create "a more formal pattern, which would be reasonably apparent. Naturally, it does not have to be a logical pattern, it could be a dream." Laughlin then outlined four "levels" into which Patchen could organize the novel. Patchen responded defiantly: "I had no intention of writing either a murder-mystery or a love-story, and even less to write a novel of ideas—it was my task to keep inviolate my intention of writing a journal of this summer—a summer when all codes and ethics which men lived by for centuries was subjected to the acid test of general war and universal disillusionment. . . . It has been my weapon against the false and sterile reality of the story books—I have satirized the creaking framework of the who-did-it and what's-to-happen-next fairy tale. . . . The meaning of this book? It means a thousand and a thousand things. What's the meaning of this summer?" The letter is dated 9 August, 1940.

11. Stephen Robitaille interview with Robert Duncan in San Francisco, California, 3 May 1980.

12. From interviews with Miriam Patchen, 2 May 1980, and Hugh Patchen, 7 November 1979.

13. From correspondence with Miriam Patchen and with Isabel Stein, a high school

friend, dated 17 November 1979. Further information from an interview with Patchen's brother, Hugh, 7 November 1979.

14. Sukenick, "New Tradition," 40.

15. Derrida, "Living On," 108.

FREEDOMS IN THE FANTASTIC

The fantastic opens and accentuates many kinds of freedom: in allegory's imprecise equivalencies, in the play-within-the-play's ironic commentaries, in the intercalated tale's possibilities for disjuncture and collage. The following essays explore such instances in Spenser, Shakespeare, and the film *Thief*, describing the effects as, respectively, political, phenomenological, and psychological liberation.

Spenser's Order, Spenser's Ireland: Competing Fantasies

Paul L. Gaston

No other work of fantasy shows a concern with social issues more sustained and more systematic than that evident in Edmund Spenser's *Faerie Queene*. In the six completed books of the lengthy epic poem, Spenser addresses questions of land management, of taxation, of social welfare, of education, of public health, of bureaucratic management, of crime and punishment, of transportation, and of resources allocation. These issues arise appropriately in a work of fantasy intended "to fashion a gentleman or noble person in vertuous and gentle discipline," for the public welfare was regarded in the sixteenth century as a gentleman's proper concern.[1]

Readers who enjoy and admire *The Faerie Queene* agree, moreover, that Spenser characteristically shows exemplary objectivity as he uses the subjects and methods of fantasy to raise social issues that concern him. *The Faerie Queene* demonstrates just how flexible an instrument fantasy can be for dealing with complex questions of legal equity, of theology, of diplomacy. He shows us, almost without fail, how the resources of fantasy can function to clarify the obscure and objectify the highly personal.

However, my concern in this essay is with Spenser's signal lapse as a fantasist in the one book of *The Faerie Queene* that reveals failures of the imagination and of the heart. If *The Faerie Queene* characteristically illustrates the analytical and descriptive applications of fantasy, it also, in Book 5, provides a startling reminder that fantasy can be exploited through a variety of means to subvert and misdirect the imagination. Specifically, the book shows how fantasy can camouflage the flaws in an argument; its narrative coherence can conceal logical inconsistencies. Book 5 shows as well how fantasy can distort complex issues by oversimplifying them. Further, when it is peopled by allegorical characters, fantasy can encourage and justify characterizations that may dehumanize and degrade particular persons or entire populations. Finally, by virtue of the popular appeals it offers, fantasy can discourage scrutiny of means proposed for the securing of desired objectives. All in all, Book 5 of Spenser's *Faerie Queene* can supply an efficient short course in fantasy as propaganda. It supplies much else, of course. Though deservedly the least admired of the completed books of the poem, it serves an essential purpose by portraying the most austere of the virtues celebrated in the poem, that of justice. Still, as it pursues this purpose, those interested in the uses of fantasy will observe how Spenser attempts to persuade his audience to his point of view by subliminal means, even as he discourages clear-headed consideration of the positions he seeks to promote.

His point of view, that of an English landlord occupying a grant of land in occupied Ireland, appears clearly enough in his prose tract *A Veue of the Present State of Ireland*, completed in 1596.[2] There, he argues for severe military repression and enforced famine as the only workable solution to continued unrest among the Irish. Laws and ordinances will help little. Only the sword will suffice, "for all those evills muste firste be Cutt awaie by a stronge hande before anie good Cane be planted, like as the Corrupte braunches and vnholsome boughes are firste to be pruned and the foule mosse clensed and scraped away before the tree cane bringe forthe anye good fruite" (lines 2956–60).

As the practical means for this "good husbandrie" (line 3031), Spenser recommends that English forces garrison the country and starve its native people into submission. "By this harde restrainte they [the Irish] woulde quicklye Consume themselves and devour one another" (lines 3252–53). Spenser knows that a policy of enforced famine can work, for he has observed its results during a limited campaign in Munster:

Out of euerie Corner of the woods and glinnes they Came Crepinge forthe vppon theire handes for theire Leggs Coulde not beare them, they loked like Anotomies of deathe, they spake like ghostes Cryinge out of theire graues, they did eate the dead Carrions, happie wheare they Coulde finde them, Yea and one another sone after, in so muche as the verye carkasses they spared not to scrape out of theire graves. (lines 3259–64)

Leniency has proved a present danger, Spenser believes. English policy must be reformed and made consistent—consistently firm and unforgiving—if the English hold on Ireland is to be preserved.

Spenser's personal circumstances provide some explanation for these views, of course. Book 5 of *The Faerie Queene*, which in various ways promotes the suggestions Spenser advances in *A Veue*, reflects as well the profound personal fears that generated them. As an occupying landlord in an oppressed and destitute land, Spenser knew that his life, his family, and his property were terribly insecure. His occupancy in Ireland may at times have seemed an exile, but his lands there were his chief possession. They were at constant peril. Even as Spenser worked on Book 5, he thought the outbreak of active resistance inevitable. All around him were his enemies, and he could but wait, with them, for the critical moment. The Irish, he says in *A Veue*, "all haue theire eares vprighte waytinge when the watchwords shall Come That they shoulde all rise generallye into Rebellion and Caste awaye the Englishe subieccion, To which theare nowe little wantethe for I thinke the worde be all readie given and theare wanteth nothinge but oportunitye" (lines 2939–43).

Events proved Spenser right. In 1598 an uprising of the Irish Kerns drove him and his family away from Kilcolman to the garrison in Cork. His castle was razed, his fields spoiled, his unpublished manuscripts burned.[3] In *A breife note of Ireland*, which Spenser addressed to the Queen "out of the ashes of disolacon and wastnes of this your wretched Realme of Ireland," we can read of the English rout that Tyrone and his forces created. Spenser's worst fears had come true.[4]

The historical context in which Spenser wrote Book 5 of *The Faerie Queene* may provide some extenuation, then, for the harsh views that the book reveals. At any rate, knowledge of Spenser's circumstances discourages facile judgment of his political morality. In his views on the Irish situation, Spenser was, unfortunately, a man of his time. But if we do not condemn him for his opinions, we may nevertheless consider his use of fantasy to promote them. Indeed, Book 5 has much to tell us about the darker side of fantasy. When Spenser places the most important social issue of his time in a world of the fantastic, he exploits the resources of his imagination but exposes the limitations of his heart.

In order to examine the ways in which Spenser uses fantasy to serve his particular ideological ends, we should first recall the book's main characters and the principal features of its plot. When Irena (i.e., Ireland) complains to the Fairy Queene that she is oppressed by the powerful criminal, Grantorto (i.e., "great wrong"), the Fairy Queene assigns a knight to impose justice on Irena's dominion.[5]

> That soueraine Queene, that mightie Emperesse,
> Whose glorie is to aide all suppliants poore,
> And of weake Princes to be Patronesse,
> Chose *Artegall* to right her to restore;
> For that to her he seem'd best skild in righteous lore.
>
> (1.4.5–9)

On his way to render this service, Artegall meets various lesser malefactors, most of whom embody varieties of villainy attributed to the rebellious Irish. He learns through his encounters with them that justice, if it is to be effective, must be swift and instinctive. His assistant, an "iron man" named Talus, ensures that such justice is brutally efficient as well. Both learn the dangers of leniency when Artegall fails to pursue a temporary advantage over a woman warrior, Radigund, and finds himself her captive.

For though that he first victorie obtayned,
Yet after by abandoning his sword,
He wilfull lost, that he before attayned.

(5.17.6–8)

Finally, after a timely rescue and several other intermediate adventures, Artegall and Talus arrive in Irena's land, apply what they have learned, defeat Grantorto, and restore Irena to her possessions. Artegall even remains for a time, attempting "to reforme that ragged common-weale" (12.26.4), but he is recalled (like Spenser's former master, Lord Grey) before he can complete the job to his satisfaction.

It is within the context of this tale that Spenser finds opportunity to exploit the conventions of fantasy for essentially propagandistic purposes. Several episodes, in particular, illustrate those exploitations of fantasy described above— the use of fantasy to distort, to dehumanize, to distract.

First, by developing a fantastic tale in which an idealized public servant liberates a beleaguered "Irena," Spenser camouflages the glaring logical problem implicit in his poem and explicit in his prose tract: He proposes nothing less than the liberation of Ireland by means of the suppression of its entire native population. In A Veue, Spenser's careful arguments from history and natural law founder on the absurdities of imperialistic bigotry. The native population constitutes a "Contagion" in the occupied land;[6] native initiatives to recover occupied native lands threaten "justice";[7] and the longing for "libertye and naturall fredome" by the native population requires an externally administered "reformacion."[8] Only in his fantasy, which embodies Ireland's distress in a beautiful but weak maiden, can Spenser juxtapose the deliverance of Ireland and the suppression of its people. Only there can Artegall's mission make sense. In the prose tract, Spenser cannot or will not designate precisely who or what is to be saved by means of the harsh strategies he recommends. In The Faerie Queene, he avoids the problem by his resort to fantasy. He need never admit that his concern for Ireland expresses by and large the economic interests of foreign landlords. Perhaps, by the fantasy of the lovely Irena, he avoided admitting it to himself. Spenser was undoubtedly sincere in his professions of love for Ireland. But that sincerity is part of the problem with Book 5, as it reflects Spenser's inclination to camouflage the inconsistencies in his feelings about Ireland and the Irish, an inclination expressed in the inventions of fantasy.

Moreover, by setting his characters in narrative fantasy, Spenser can evoke allegorical relationships without having to respect the responsibility for consistent equivalence that allegory imposes. The Lady Irena, then, represents Ireland, but not the interests of the native Irish population. The trial of Duessa recovers much of the indictment against Mary Stuart, but little of the defense she offered. In victory, Artegall stands for Lord Grey; in subjection to Radigund, he stands as an example of the dangers attendant upon leniency, dangers that Lord Grey rarely courted. In the world of fantasy, equivalents need not be precise. So, we can accept Irena's plight, rejoice in her timely liberation, and, not incidentally, accept the methods Artegall employs—methods strikingly similar to those Spenser recommends elsewhere as English policy. In short, the fantasy becomes an apology for specific policy recommendations even as it distracts us from the flaws in the reasoning behind those recommendations.

Second, Spenser uses fantasy to simplify and thereby distort particular conflicts of interest in which he takes a personal concern. Proposals by Anabaptist sects for the limited redistribution of excess wealth Spenser ridicules, by embodying them in a simple-minded giant who attracts great crowds of the greedy poor by promising generous gifts for all. Artegall enjoys a brief debate with the giant. Neither countenances the arguments of the other. So Artegall summons Talus:

> Approching nigh vnto him cheeke by cheeke,
> He shouldered him from off the higher ground,
> And down the rock him throwing, in the sea him dround.
>
> (2.49.6–8)

Thus, Artegall wins the argument. Inequity is God's will: "The hils doe not the lowly dales disdaine; / The dales doe not the lofty hils enuy" (2.41.2–4). Those who disagree must pay the price.

Another lively contemporary issue, that regarding the status of women, emerges in Spenser's fantasy as an Amazon's campaign to overthrow and emasculate all worthy men. She defeats men in battle, then humiliates them by dressing them in women's clothes and setting them to women's work: "A sordid office for a mind so braue. / So hard it is to be a womans slaue" (5.23.4–5). Such remarkable behavior threatens the order of the universe itself, in Spenser's view, for "vertuous women wisely vnderstand, / That they were borne to base humilitie" (5.25.7–8). Radigund, who has captured Artegall, must learn humility at the point of Britomart's sword. And like most others in this book who disagree on some point with Artegall and his comrades, she must pay for her error with her life.

Similarly, complex international confrontations become in Spenser's fantasy simple contests between right and wrong. England's perennial enemy, Spain, stood ready as a potential ally for an independent Ireland. In the fantasy, Spain becomes a "proud Souldan" seeking "onely slaughter and auengement" (8.30.5). England, however, as figured in "the braue Prince," fights only "for honour and for right" (8.30.6). Such reductivism rarely produces even interesting fantasy. In this instance, it serves to obscure a fascinating struggle between rival personalities, religions, and economic and territorial imperatives.

Third, Spenser uses the resources of fantasy to dehumanize and degrade those on the wrong side of his argument. The Irish Kerns scamper through the hills of Ireland: "liky wyld Goates them chaced all about, / Flying from place to place with cowheard shame" (8.1.7–8). The Irish people, the common people, appear "like a swarme of flyes" (2.53.6). When Talus bends his iron arm against the "lawless multitude," his opponents *fly* away and hide "in holes and bushes" (2.53.9). Having accepted the fantasy Spenser creates, we regard such local irritants as temporary impediments to heroic success. Only when we observe that in this "swarme of flyes" Spenser figures the men, women, and children of Ireland do we glimpse his exploitation of the fantastic in his designated "legend of justice."

No less disturbing than these depictions of the Irish people is that of the recently executed Mary Stuart as Duessa, the whorish witch from several previous books in *The Faerie Queene*. While it is true that in Book 5 Duessa stands before Mercilla's court only as an "vntitled queen" brought to justice as a traitor, she necessarily brings with her to the dock the record of murder and sexual promiscuity she has established in earlier episodes. We can understand in reading the account of her trial why James VI of Scotland protested. Spenser was not content with depicting James's royal mother as a traitor. He would intimate a far more scurrilous indictment. But by imposing an oblique allegorical link between Duessa and the Queen of Scots long after the characterization of Duessa has been established in the fantasy, Spenser can evade and then reject the necessity of justifying the connection.

The clearest example of dehumanization lies, perhaps, in the picture of Malengin. With Malengin, Spenser's contempt for the Irish breaks into the open. Malengin's crime, cattle rustling, is one endemic to occupied Ireland, and his outlaw's gifts are those Spenser thought innately Irish: craftiness, deceptiveness, and courage born of desperation. He lives deep within the rocks. He dresses in rags. He knows the landscape and is swift of foot. Most important, however, he is inhuman. He may appear a man, but his essential nature is that of a fox, a bird, a hedgehog. Trying to escape the remorseless fist of Talus, he assumes each of these identities, but in vain. Such a creature deserves no humane considerations, so when Artegall and Arthur finally apprehend him, they slaughter him at once and leave his body "a carrion outcast; / For beasts and foules to feede vpon for their repast" (9.14.8–9). As it is embedded in a carefully articulated fantasy, this account repels few readers, however repellent the practical premises it embodies. Indeed, to the extent that we concede Spenser's perception of the Irish people as treacherous creatures of the caves, we consider the necessity of their brutal suppression. Fantasy can work in this way.

Finally, by describing the situation in Ireland as a simple juxtaposition of divinely sanctioned order and criminal disorder, Spenser attempts to persuade us (and, I believe, himself) that his interests must eventually prevail. Resistance by the wild and disorganized Irish, in the service of "great wrong," must inevitably dissolve before English force and English law. Or so Spenser would like to believe. As Book 5 ends, then, Irena rejoices in her liberation. Though Artegall may have been recalled prematurely, Ireland at last is free. "Great wrong" has fallen in defeat.

In short, I have proposed that Spenser uses fantasy in Book 5 of *The Faerie Queene* to serve priorities that are more political than artistic. Yet that is not quite right, for we perceive, finally, that there are two fantasies at work in Book 5, not one. The first concerns a lovely land and a people oppressed by powerful but contemptible rebels. With its fertile meadows, well-stocked rivers, and picturesque mountains, the land of Ireland welcomes English order. So, too, will its people, once they gain their freedom from the Kerns. This is a domestic fantasy, the dream of one who wishes to believe the best of the land he has taken as his own. The alternative fantasy is militaristic. The path to glory leads through territories inhabited by wild creatures who obey uncivilized outlaws. But the English will prevail in one encounter after another, exterminate surviving remnants of the mutinous rabble, and achieve at last a permanent mastery.

Both fantasies reflect understandable motives. Each sustains memorable episodes. But the two are, finally, irreconcilable. The book's logical problem appears somewhat more clearly in *A Veue*, where Spenser argues that a people starved into submission will welcome as liberators those who have starved them. But while the problem may be less obvious in Book 5, it finally emerges there as well, as I have tried to suggest.

Though we might speculate that the problems inherent in the book reflect unresolved conflicts in Spenser himself, we will still regret, I believe, Spenser's exploitation of fantasy in the service of interests and prejudices that would corrupt the most enlightened imagination. He is a great fantasist, undeniably. He shows us how splendidly fantasy can entertain and instruct. But in this instance, he also shows us how insidiously fantasy can work upon the unwary when the motives that sustain it are dark.

NOTES

1. Edmund Spenser, "A Letter of the Authors expounding his whole intention," in *Spenser's Faerie Queene*, ed. J. C. Smith (Oxford: Oxford University Press, 1909), vol. 2, p. 485.

2. Line number indications for *A Veue of the Present State of Ireland* refer to Edmund Spenser, *Spenser's Prose Works*, ed. Rodolf Gottfried (Baltimore: Johns Hopkins University Press, 1949), 43–231.

3. Still the standard work on the episode is Pauline Henley, *Spenser in Ireland* (Cork: Cork University Press, 1928). See especially pp. 146–67.

4. Edmund Spenser, *A breife note of Ireland*, in Gottfried, *Spenser's Prose Works*, 235–45.

5. Line indications in parentheses refer to Smith, *Spenser's Faerie Queene*, by canto, stanza, and line number. All references are to Book 5.

6. Spenser, *A Veue*, 63.

7. Ibid., 146.

8. Ibid.

Shakespeare, Freedom, and the Fantastic

Peter Malekin

The difficulty of dealing with literature is that it forces us to deal with ourselves. An object, say a bridge, has a defined status—it exists for an end, to enable us to get from one side of the river to the other. If that end is fulfilled, more fundamental problems can be ignored as irrelevant. Not so with art. The bridge, once regarded as architecture, becomes an experience that raises the question of value, which in turn raises the question of the self. Simply to cross the bridge from one side of the river to the other is to function as an object, a physical body transported in space–time. To experience the bridge as architecture involves an experiencing mind, the arbiter of values to which practical considerations of transportation may well in their turn be irrelevant, for an experience can be of value in itself, not merely as a means to some other end. Objectivity in the appreciation of literature is encouraged in universities within our objectivity-oriented culture; but total objectivity is possible only with total subjectivity, for literature is the point where literary object and experiencing mind meet.

Awareness of this quality in the visual arts, triggered by Ludwig Wittgenstein, led to the investigation of visual perception in the work of Rudolf Arnheim and E. H. Gombrich. In the study of literature, the process has gone further to take in the whole nature of the mind, and of the subject–object relationship, in phenomenological criticism. While criticism without some sense of values is impossible, older literary criticism tended to be primarily utilitarian in its approach, extracting ideas—often moral ideas—from literature and holding that these could then be "applied to " ordinary life. This approach is, up to a point, legitimate; but used as a basis for the evaluation of great literature, and specifically the great plays of Shakespeare, it has never been adequate. To return from the criticism to the play is to leave the ideas behind in a direct experience. It is this experience, the play as mental process, that I wish to investigate here, and in particular the function of the fantastic and the play-within-the-play in shaping this experience and making it an experience in freedom. In order to do this, two preliminaries are necessary: the production of a paradigm of the mind, and some notion of the range and effect of stage technique. The latter, stage technique, is the simpler of the two factors, and I will consider that first.

The fundamentals of stage technique are second nature to any director or actor, but not always to any literary critic. They are polarity and rhythm, rhythm being polarity extended in time. In the case of Shakespeare's platform stage, these come into being through the physical presence of the actors and through the actors' voices. The physical presence involves posture, relative speed and violence of movement, and the grouping of actors on stage. Speed of action gains meaning from its relationship to a baseline: The mere constant hurtling of actors about the stage would become meaningless, tedious. The nearest to an absolute in terms of movement is rest, and the movement of the actors therefore emerges from and returns to rest. Similarly, the scattering of a stage group has most meaning if it emerges from a tight-knit grouping, and the meaning of an isolated figure is gained, at its simplest, from his or her being separated on stage from a coherent group. These are the principles that function, for instance, in the first scene of *Hamlet*. Thus, the wording of the speeches makes it clear that Marcellus and Bernardo form a group slightly apart from Horatio, who enters after Marcellus. They then all sit together with Bernardo's "sit down a while" and Horatio's reply:

> Well, sit we down,
> And let us hear Bernardo speak of this.[1]

They rise and push Horatio forward on the first entry of the ghost, once more sit down together with Marcellus's line "Good now, sit down" (1.2.70), and remain seated for the next forty lines until the ghost's second entry, then explode outward and scatter about the stage with the lines:

Ber. 'Tis here!
Hor. 'Tis here!
Marc. 'Tis gone!

                              (1.1. 141–42)

Finally they come together again as a group for the exit. This stage movement constitutes a physical language, part inborn, part culturally conditioned, whose recognition is instinctive on the part of the audience. Coupled with the similar use of the voice—speed, pitch, and volume growing out of and returning to silence—it creates a physiological rhythm that is powerfully emotive quite independently of the meaning of the words spoken. The words then build on this, the passage on Christmas at the end of the first scene of *Hamlet* muting the sense of alarm and strain, this muted sense then being introduced as an undercurrent into the second scene with the opening lines

> Though yet of Hamlet our dear brother's death
> The memory be green.
>
> (1.2.1–2)

Thus, the emotional modulation of the scene sequence starts with physical movement and physical sound; the play breathes and the audience breathes with it,
an obvious point, but one to be remembered as the basis of the more extreme
uses of stage technique in the fantastic scenes in plays like *King Lear*.

Besides stage technique, the other preliminary factor is some paradigm for
the mind, and among Western paradigms the most adequate is to be found in
the later writings of Martin Heidegger. In his *Discourse on Thinking*, Heidegger
distinguishes between man and man's nature, and he sets out "to behold man's
nature without looking at man," for

if thinking is what distinguishes man's nature, then surely the essence of this nature,
namely the nature of thinking, can be seen only by looking away from thinking.[2]

As John M. Anderson, the editor of *Discourse on Thinking*, points out, the claim
that man's nature can be "found in relation to something else" suggests that
"to comprehend man one must transcend the specifically and merely human,
the subjective."[3] Heidegger goes on to draw a distinction between two types of
thought: calculative thought, ratiocination moving stepwise from premise to
conclusion or some end, and *Gesinnliches Denken*, or meditative thought. The
latter requires what he calls *Gelassenheit*, a term borrowed from Meister Eckhart.
Usually translated "releasement," it means a letting-go-ness, a non-willed thinking beyond the dichotomy of active and passive, an openness to the field of
thought itself, which leads to an awareness of the horizon of the field of thought
as the expression, or, so to say, the turned-toward-usness of what lies beyond
that field. What lies beyond he names the *Gegend*, the region, or the *Gegnet*
(an older form of the same German word, probably containing a pun on *gegen*,
"opposite," and usually translated as "that-which-regions," since Heidegger
also uses "region" as a verb): It is to this that man belongs by nature, for it is
"the prior of which we really can not think . . . because the nature of thinking
begins there";[4] and it is this that in meditative awareness itself comes toward
us in the objects that emerge within the field of thinking, "so that things which
appear in that-which-regions no longer have the character of objects . . . no longer
stand opposite us."[5] In other words, as Heidegger puts it when reformulating
the problems of traditional metaphysics in "The End of Philosophy":

The questions are paths to an answer. If the answer could be given, the answer would
consist in a transformation of thinking, not in a propositional statement about a matter
at stake.[6]

Through this transformation of thinking, the object is found to contain within
itself its own meaning; and its "history," a word Heidegger uses in a special

sense, is the mode or changing modes of its emergence into space–time knowing. The object emerges into consciousness–time and is determined by what lies beyond time, hence its "meaning," a word no longer understood merely as a reference to something else in the field of knowing outside the object itself.

These ideas have obvious advantages when applied to art. They relate even to the subject matter of much Romantic and modern literature. It is impossible to get far in Blake's prophetic books, for instance, without grasping the possibility that space–time is an aspect of consciousness, instead of consciousness being an aspect of space–time; they obviate the crude extraction of ideas and "messages" from literature; and they relate to another very positive idea of Heidegger's, which is directly relevant to the appreciation of the greater Shakespearean plays, the idea of freedom. In his "Memorial Address," Heidegger speaks of freedom as the alternative to our own domination by technology, a domination that affects our relationship with all other things, including works of art and literature:

The power concealed in modern technology determines the relation of man to that which exists. . . . [Nevertheless] we can use technical devices, and yet with proper use also keep ourselves so free of them, that we may let go of them any time. We can use technical devices as they ought to be used, and also let them alone as something which does not affect our inner and real core. We can affirm the unavoidable use of technical devices, and also deny them the right to dominate us, and so to warp, confuse, and lay waste our nature.[7]

It is freedom in this inner sense that lies very near to the heart of Shakespearean drama; indeed, Shakespeare's great dramas are objects designed to be experienced in freedom. And the creative realization of that freedom, which already exists as our true nature, depends largely on Shakespeare's use of the fantastic.

At the beginning of Shakespeare's career, the fantastic element in his drama is subdued, hidden beneath but appearing through inherited conventions. In an early play like *The Comedy of Errors*, his gothic imagination luxuriates around Plautus's single pair of twins, doubling it in a typical Shakespearean mirror effect, then producing a further reflection or echo in the relationship between the main and secondary plots. Within this highly improbable setup, he launches on a major theme that runs throughout his dramas: the relationship between social role and individual identity. As the Antipholus and Dromio of Syracuse are locked up as madmen in an Ephesus that seems to them to have gone mad, the vulnerability of the external role is underscored; while this social condition is balanced by a search for personal fulfillment modulated through the myth-like framing plot of the family torn asunder, only to be reunited in the banquet at the end. The myth-like elements are, however, an outgrowth of the plot; the comedy is situational comedy, conventional in kind, the humor of people being unexpectedly forced "out of role." When the roles are restored, the individuals fit comfortably back into them; their roles are even reinforced by the family reunion at the end. In consequence, the play is amusing, but hardly profound.

The investigation of role and individuality moves deeper in a later comedy like *As You Like It*. Here the improbability of the myth-like framing plot is deliberately heightened by the cutting of the realistic political motivation found in the source and the substitution of the unexpected conversions of both Orlando's elder and Duke Senior's younger brother. Inside this outer framework, the entire center of the play takes place within the fantastic Forest of Arden. Here the courtiers play at being outlaws and denizens of the Golden Age, but retain Renaissance court conventions—love and hunting being the accepted peacetime equivalents of heroic love and war—while their ceremonial is a relaxed version of the code practiced by the traveling noble and gentle households of medieval England. The most important of the characters is a new arrival in this setting, the disguised Rosalind, whose relationship with Orlando defies the social expectations of the period. In contemporary society, the wife was subject to her husband's authority, her duty being obedience, just as a commoner was subject to a monarch. Courtship was recognized as an atypical interlude in which the woman was transferred from the authority of her father to the authority of her husband. The period between the two normal states of affairs resembled the period under the Lord of Misrule after Christmas, originally a transition between the old and the new year: The ordinary ranking was reversed, and it was the suitor's duty to obey his mistress, the only indication she could have that after marriage she would indeed be "cherished" (the husband's side to the matrimonial contract). The woman was expected to be whimsical and, as befitted the less rational sex, even perverse. Rosalind is instead an educator, training Orlando in the wisdom of living. There is thus a double level of significance in the role playing between the two. The first is an inherited level of Plautian humor, in which the whole artificiality of the stage situation is thrown into relief; the fact that it is "just acting" and also the audience's superiority in knowledge to Orlando are called upon:

Orl. But will my Rosalind do so?

Ros. By my life, she will do as I do.

(4.1.158–59)

Here the audience is in a conspiracy with the disguised Rosalind to smile at Orlando. The second level of significance arises between the characters themselves. Orlando on an instinctive level recognizes Ganymede as Rosalind, but on a conscious level sees her only as Ganymede. He declares to Ganymede–Rosalind that he would not be cured of love, a cure the latter is proposing to undertake:

Orl. I would not be cured, youth.

Ros. I would cure you, if you would but call me
Rosalind and come every day to my cote and woo me.

Orl. Now, by the faith of my love, I will;
   Tell me where it is.

                                                    (3.2.446–51)

There is a natural pause before this last line in playing, as the instinctive pull
of subliminal recognition tugs the conscious mind into apparently irrational
action, the kind of situation that is so important and occurs so often in the life
we call real; in the fantastic, the denial of naturalism works through to deeper
levels of natural living. The same kind of duality is explored elsewhere in the
central Arden episodes, and a lot of the humor springs from it, as when Touchstone, against his better judgment and knowing full well that his passion will
not last, finds himself enamored of a country goatherd, who is associated all too
closely with the animals she tends:

Touch. Come apace, good Audrey. I will fetch up your goats, Audrey. And how, Audrey,
   am I the man yet? Doth my simple feature content you?
Aud. Your features! Lord warrant us! what features?
Touch. I am here with thee and thy goats, as the most capricious poet, honest Ovid, was
   among the Goths.

                                                    (3.3.1–9)

The point is highlighted by the fact that Touchstone's entrance immediately
follows the exit of Orlando and Rosalind quoted above. This exchange has in it
much truth to life—sexual relationships are, after all, supremely ridiculous, and
a sense of humor, or at least a sense of play, is necessary if we are to survive
them with our humanity relatively intact.

   In *As You Like It*, a wider perspective is provided by two other factors. The
first is the recurring references to the horns of Priapus and to cuckoldry. They
reach a climax in the hunter's song (and how often had not love been referred
to as a hunt in medieval and Renaissance tradition, often the hunting of a deer?),
in which it is the hunter's privilege to wear this ambiguous symbol and procreate
the species:

   Take thou no scorn to wear the horn;
   It was a crest ere thou wast born;
       Thy father's father wore it,
       And thy father bore it.
   The horn, the horn, the lusty horn,
   Is not a thing to laugh to scorn.

                                                    (4.2.14–19)

(Procreation was still at this time the dominant purpose of marriage.) The second
factor is the magnifying of this theme in the Masque of Hymen, which, despite
the misgivings of critics and sometimes of producers, *is* an integral part of the

play. Once again the fantastic is called upon, the Masque constituting a play within the Arden play within the improbable framing plot. Hymen appears from nowhere, an epiphany to be explained only if Rosalind is, in fact, the magician she has claimed in jest to be. Hymen, being totally unreal, is in consequence free to speak truth, which he does in no uncertain terms to the marrying couples; and beyond this individual truth lies the truth of nature, the drive to marriage, propagation, the continuation of the species, together with the shadowy passing of the generations, brought out in the marriage song:

> Wedding is great Juno's crown
> O blessed bond of board and bed!
> 'Tis Hymen peoples every town;
> High wedlock then be honoured.
> Honour, high honour, and renown,
>   To Hymen, god of every town!

(5.4.147–52)

The god of towns and of the civilization of the *civis* is thus celebrated in a make-believe forest as a natural force. The play within a play within a play is therefore also the level beyond level of life that makes up the social being of man. These multiple levels have been explored and presented to the audience, which experiences them sympathetically, but nevertheless from the outside, for despite its sympathy, the audience remains above the action, superior to it: Jaques's "All the world's a stage" is an observation on, not an experience of, life. For the plays of this period in Shakespeare's career, Anne Righter seems to be correct in holding that "reality" is the world of the audience, and the play its copy. But Shakespeare did not stop there, and this general formulation is not adequate to the later plays, a point she herself partially admits.[8] In his next stage of development, Shakespeare began to pull the audience into the play.

The taking of the audience into the play involves a shift in the language and in the balance of the fantastic in the play as a whole. In the plays of the period of the great tragedies, the language tends to become less rhetorical, more organic; the imagery subsumes contradictions and ambiguities and is not rationally explicit. "Pity, like a naked new-born babe / Striding the blast" in *Macbeth* (1.7.21–22) and the conflicting implications in the architectural images in the opening scenes of *Antony and Cleopatra*, the "triple pillar of the world" and "the wide arch / Of the rang'd empire" (1.1.12, 33–34) suggesting architecture allied to cosmic order through Pythagorean proportion and equally the transience of political power through the ruins of Rome, are both instances of this kind of development. Its dramatic importance is that ordinary language states a case, presents a formulated conclusion, whereas Shakespeare's language in this period catches the movement of the mind itself, half-formed thoughts merging and tumbling over each other, with an intuitive depth and resonance through strand upon strand of possibly contradictory meaning. Through the language alone, therefore, the audience tends to experience the play as its own thought process, and it is the irrationality, the presence of the fantastic in the language, that enables this experience to come about.

But the fantastic also tends to take over the whole play. The fantastic had always been present in Shakespeare, both in the play-within-the-play and in certain notable characters like Falstaff and Richard III who tend to burst the constricting bonds of the plays in which they occur through their very creative force. But there is a change in the plays of the middle period: So much of the action of *Hamlet*, *Macbeth*, *Antony and Cleopatra*, even *Othello* with its double time scheme, takes place in the mind, a point that becomes clear if they are compared, for instance, with *Richard II* (its mental action being projected outward in universal emblems that tend toward the static and impersonal, whereas the emblematic elements in the later plays move inward to mental process); and this inwardness is why the constant improbabilities, the jugglings with time and space and plausibility, are acceptable.

The techniques of significant improbability rise to a peak in *King Lear*. If the play were to be judged by naturalistic standards, Tolstoy would surely be right: The play would be unnatural, the characters "unreal" and unmotivated. But the play is precisely not a copy of ordinary life; in fact, it reverses Anne Righter's formulation of the nature of Renaissance plays, being more real than life, not in the manner of medieval drama with its conceptualized, systematized religious myth held to contain ordinary reality, but on a deeper level still, by its undercutting of all conceptualization, by its myth to end mythologies.

Its grip on the audience is not through ideas but through theatrical technique. The first scene is tripartite: an opening passage of commentary on Lear, the central court scene in verse, and a closing passage of prose commentary. The opening private conversation is curiosity arousing, and the opening grouping— Edmund slightly apart, behind his elders—suggestive of his relationship with the old order. The discussion turns on Lear's love of Albany and Cornwall, his earlier favoring of Albany being denied in the apportioning of the kingdom; a lead into the love trial theme that is presented pageant-wise again and again in the play, by Lear in this same scene, by Gloucester in the following scene, by Lear, Goneril, and Regan in the disquantifying of his train. As these opening characters move aside, they create the royalty of Lear's processional entrance by their reaction, and Lear then makes public his already published so-called "darker" purpose. In what immediately follows, Cordelia is clearly somewhat apart from the main court group, since she makes asides to the audience; and an emotive rhythm is built up, the flow of pompous speeches from Lear, Goneril, and Regan being syncopated by Cordelia's short and ominous lines "What shall Cordelia speak? Love and be silent" (1.1.63), etc. There is thus a physical polarity on stage, the basis of stage art, for, as Jacob Boehme said, "In Yes and No all things consist." Cordelia is then pulled into the main group and the two rhythms meet and explode in the confrontation between Lear and his youngest daughter:

Lear. What can you say to draw
   A third more opulent than your sisters? Speak.
Cor. Nothing, my Lord.
Lear. Nothing!
Cor. Nothing.
Lear. Nothing will come of nothing. Speak again.

(1.1.88–92)

"Nothing," a word that reechoes through the play, launches one of the main thematic complexes of the action: the nothing of chaos and death that comes of Cordelia's refusal to create, logos-like, the manifestation of love out of nothing; the nothing that Lear ironically believes will come of the nothing he gives his younger daughter; the nothing to which language tends in the semiarticulate howls and mumblings of Lear at the end; the irony of even attempting to order a tangible and quantified manifestation of love; a no-thing that owes its creative power to its status as no-thingness. William Elton's brilliant study of *King Lear* has already documented the eternal-matter versus creation-out-of-nothing controversy at the time.[9] Behind this issue lies the intuition of the two senses of the nothing from which creation can be drawn: the nothing of negation, absence, death, and the no-thing of boundless fullness, the repose of all things; the void of negation or the void of the absence of limitation. With the simple word "nothing," the heart of the thematic material of the play has begun to beat, though this theme is not the heart of the play itself; for the play is suspended between the thematic material and the onlooker (a point that will be clarified presently). This theme makes sense only through the play *in toto*, the characters and their viewpoints complementing one another. The action not being naturalistic, judgment as to whether a particular character is "right" or "wrong" in what he or she does takes attention away from the essential, for the play is concerned with something deeper than mere right or wrong action. The play must, however, command theatrical conviction, and while only the very opening of the first scene has been analyzed, this is enough to indicate that the theatrical skill here is consummate. The text has written into it the power to grip if it is performed innocently, that is, if it is played straight, fast, and in the obvious way suggested by the text itself, without having cleverness of intellectual interpretation foisted upon it: It is too intelligent a play to need "cleverness" in production; all that it requires of the director is that he remember his skills and forget himself.

Together with the thematic play around the word "nothing," another aspect of the nothing–no-thingness polarity has begun to be focused in the breakdown of the personality of Lear himself. The opening scene starts with comments on what had previously appeared and what now appears to be the state of Lear's affection for the Dukes; it proceeds through his reckless abandonment of the bonds of family and kingship; and it ends with comments that he had "ever but slenderly known himself'' (1.1.296–97). Elton has already pointed out that Lear's personality tends to break down during the play into the persons of his three daughters, and Gloucester disintegrates into his two sons, while Cordelia finds a reciprocal double in the character of the Fool, who appears when she disappears, and disappears when she reappears. During this process, Lear begins to ask an essential question:

> This is not Lear.
> Does Lear walk thus? speak thus? Where are his eyes?
> . . . .
> Who is it that can tell me who I am?
>
>   (1.4.246–47, 250)

The play is, however, more than a naturalistic case history: The breakdown of personality is not presented objectively; the play *is* the breakdown of personality. The theatrical technique becomes almost surrealistic. Not only does the Fool disappear without explanation, his first entrance is deliberately cloaked. The summons to fetch the Fool is issued some twenty lines before his entry; meanwhile Oswald has come on, insulted the King, and been beaten off stage by Kent, who trips him up and thrusts him out. Since the Fool can hardly enter over the struggling bodies of Oswald and Kent, and since the audience is watching the struggle and not looking elsewhere, the Fool comes on unnoticed, and is suddenly there, exclaiming:

> Let me hire him too; here's my coxcomb.
>
>   (1.4.105)

From there on, the world of the play is one of association and dissociation rather than cause and effect (that modern cultural norm). The stage technique of the mad scenes is the expression of this view of reality. The scene is nowhere—a disorienting void: The text informs us only that for miles about there is scarce a bush, and that at one point a hovel is in sight. In this almost un-setting, Lear begins the stripping down of his ego. He pulls off his clothes, the traditional outer uniform that varied according to rank and specific occupation in Elizabethan England; so that its removal would be instinctively received as the casting off of social role, while he seeks both equality with the masses—''Expose thyself to feel what wretches feel'' (3.4.34)—and the nature of his own true self. To the naked Edgar he says:

Thou art the thing itself; unaccommodated man is no more but such a poor, bare, forked animal as thou art. Off, off, you lendings!

                                        (3.4.110–13)

In this world roles shift: Edgar, disguised as Poor Tom, the naked, mad beggar, becomes a Persian and a philosopher in Lear's mind, while the Fool has already

gained the ambiguous status of the fool of wisdom, Kent's "not altogether fool,"
through such extended plays on words as those in his speech to Kent:

> When a wise man gives thee better counsel, give me mine again;
> I would have none but knaves follow it, since a Fool gives it.
> . . . .
> But I will tarry; the Fool will stay,
> And let the wise man fly.
> The knave turns fool that runs away;
> The Fool no knave, perdy.
>
> (2.4.75–78, 83–86)

The spatial limbo through which Edgar and the Fool move is a state of mind,
and its quality is reinforced by the ambiguity of the thunder, already noted by
Elton. Instead of being the voice of divine vengeance for sin, as it was in the
source play and in other plays of the period, here thunder may be the voice of
perhaps spiteful or indifferent gods, or it may be just the material elements, or
it may be the thunder of Lear's own mind; but whatever it is, its constant presence
is implied in the one recurring stage direction of the Folio in these scenes,
"*Storm still.*" The three characters of dislocated identity, Lear, Edgar, and the
Fool, merge in a common fantasy in the mock trial of Goneril in Act 3, scene
6, one picking up the common train of thought where the other leaves it off.
Edgar and the Fool are now "justicers" in Lear's mental state, and Tom throws
his head at the curs Lear imagines attacking him. In this situation, the asides of
Edgar–Tom the justicer, and above all the comments of the Fool, are vital in
establishing the necessary relationship between the audience and the action. It
is not merely that the Fool acts as lightning conductor for the laughter that might
cause the audience to reject the scene; it is also the establishment through his
intervention of a double perspective. Such passages as these give the audience
a double vision:

Lear. Has his daughters brought him to this pass?
   Couldst thou save nothing? Wouldst thou give 'em all?
Fool. Nay, he reserv'd a blanket, else we had been all sham'd.

> (3.4.65–67)

Fool. Come hither, mistress. Is your name Goneril?
Lear. She cannot deny it.
Fool. Cry you mercy, I took you for a joint-stool.

> (3.6.51–55)

The joint stool is just a joint stool, and at the same time Goneril; the audience
shares the fantasy, yet is outside it. This distant nearness of the action is most
important. As a modality of view, it broadens to affect the perception of social
reality, a point brought out in Act 4, scene 5, when the mad Lear and the blind

Gloucester try social justice on the basis of the distinction between the individuality of the justicer and his role, and find it wanting. But much more important
is its effect on the audience's reception of the play. Elton is surely right about
the nihilistic exhaustion of the play's conclusion, and yet an intense experience
of the play is positive—indeed there would be little point in seeing it if this
response were not so; it would be possible to stay at home and get depressed
for nothing. There is, however, nothing in that action as such to justify positivity.
Lear, apparently reformed if not "redeemed," has created a new role for himself
and Cordelia as "God's spies"; but identity in terms of any role, good or bad,
is false and vulnerable, and Lear's new role collapses with Cordelia's murder.
At the close, there is little left, and the spirit of the end is summed up in Edgar's
concluding lines:

> The weight of this sad time we must obey;
> Speak what we feel, not what we ought to say.
> The oldest hath borne most; we that are young
> Shall never see so much, nor live so long.
> *Exeunt, with a dead march.*
>
> (5.3.323–26)

The positivity is not in the action, or in the play as text–performance at all—
it is in the play as suspended between performance and audience, in the audience's
experience or rather mode of experiencing. Lear's question "Who is it that can
tell me who I am?" finds no answer in the play; but there is an answer in the
mind of the audience, in its "I amness" beyond personal names and identity,
and beyond personality as ordinarily understood, generated not as an idea (which
would be a falsification, for we are not ideas but the perceivers of ideas) but as
a direct experience through the process of distant nearness provoked by the
dramatic technique of the play. The illusion of the play is the generator of reality
in the mind of the audience, and this generation is made possible through the
use of the fantastic, in the play-within-the-play of Lear's mad scenes, to disrupt
our everyday sense of reality and to disrupt our everyday sense of identity as
dependent on personality and social role.
    It is this shift of the mind of the audience toward fundamental identity and
away from role and personality identity that links the working of the play with
Heidegger's thoughts on freedom. The process starts with the experience of the
object, the play, in intimate alienness, and then proceeds to a stage where neither
intimacy nor alienation has meaning, where meaning instead rises through the
object itself from the source of the perceiving mind. Similarly, Heidegger's
Gesinnliches Denken "begins with content which is given to it, the field of
awareness itself," from which point of view the knowledge of an object becomes
"history," a "return to origins in the sense in which intelligibility must have
its roots in what is prior to thought, must abide in what is the source of all
articulation."[10] Here lies the way to the only ultimate freedom there is, for all

other forms of freedom are partial, freedom from something or freedom to do something; and thus freedom is defined in terms of bondage. All that is needed to achieve this real freedom is, as Heidegger himself points out, "openness to the mystery," an openness that is "beyond the distinction between activity and passivity" to the "mystery" that lies "within" the object and is the source of mind. It is thus a form of *Edelmut*, noble-mindedness, in which purely subjective demands and pretensions are set aside, a form of self-transcendence that is diametrically the opposite of what is often taught as critical awareness in our universities. The result is the real *universum*, an approach to the multiple oneness of total experience hinted at by Heidegger when he speaks of the horizon of awareness as "but the side facing us of an openness which surrounds us; an openness which is filled with views of the appearances of what to our re-presenting [*Vorstellen*, literally a placing-beforeness] are objects."[11] It is precisely this tendency in the art object to project the audience toward freedom of perception that is its claim to greatness and, in a non-utilitarian sense, usefulness.

I have used the late philosophy of Heidegger to try to convey what seems to me the essence of the experience of *King Lear*, because Heidegger is Western, modern, and relatively accessible. It will be seen that my analysis has similarities to and some divergences from the powerfully cogent discussion of the *theatrum mundi* metaphor and the play-within-the-play conducted in Heideggerian terms by Howard Pearce.[12] We agree on the function of this species of the fantastic as a means of dislocating the ordinary and ossified sense of reality; but I have used the late rather than the early Heidegger because the great drama of Shakespeare tends to burst the bounds of the categories and transcendental schema of knowing posited by Kant, and only the late Heidegger allows for this. I have also avoided Husserl's concept of intentionality, the necessary linking of subject with object, or of consciousness with an object of consciousness, since this is inadequate: The state that W. T. Stace called "pure consciousness"—and defined as "not the consciousness *of* any empirical content [for] it has no content except itself"—is perfectly well recorded in human history, a relatively commonplace experience.[13] There are, I believe, clearer paradigms of the mind than Heidegger's in Taoist philosophy, Cha'an Buddhism, and the Indian traditions.[14] Older thought is, however, even less familiar to us than Heidegger in its terminology and conceptualizations, and is also encrusted in accretions of misunderstanding: Thus, Abhinavagupta's idea of *rasa* is, unless I am much mistaken, akin to the enjoyment in openness through freedom that Heidegger was talking about, though the term is, even by Indians, interpreted totally differently today.

Heidegger's ideas thus form the best leverage for articulating an experience of *King Lear*, and the experience is created by a dramatic technique that makes powerful use of the fantastic and of such devices as the play-within-the-play. *King Lear* was, of course, not the end of the road for Shakespeare. He went on with further innovations and development that culminated in *The Tempest*, a play whose consideration lies beyond the limit of length placed upon this essay. It is, however, in that play that Prospero steps outside the drama and the audience finds itself absorbed within the play to assume a status akin to that of Prospero's recently dissolved masque. The probing of phenomenological "reality" is taken a stage further, and if, like the *Sacre du Printemps*, I may end up on a note of interrogation rather than affirmation, I would ask the many-faceted central question posed by the play: Why is it that Prospero's island is so many different things to different men; why do some find the island a barren desert, while some find it a fruitful wilderness, and one even a prison-cum-paradise; and why can the castaways never seem to agree as to whether their clothing is fresher than when they first put it on, or sea salt-bedraggled from the wreck?

NOTES

1. William Shakespeare, *The Complete Plays and Poems of William Shakespeare*, New Cambridge Edition, ed. William Allan Neilson and Charles Jarvis Hill (Cambridge, MA: Riverside Press, 1942), Act 1, scene 1, lines 33–34. Further references to Shakespeare's plays appear in the text, as act, scene, and line.

2. Martin Heidegger, *Discourse on Thinking: A Translation of Gelassenheit*, trans. John M. Anderson and E. Hans Freund (New York: Harper Torchbooks, 1966), 58.

3. Ibid., 220.

4. Ibid., 83.

5. Ibid., 67.

6. Martin Heidegger, "The End of Philosophy and the Task of Thinking," in *On Time and Being*, trans. Joan Stambaugh (New York: Harper Torchbooks, 1972), 55.

7. Heidegger, "Memorial Address," in *Discourse on Thinking*, 50–54.

8. Anne Righter, *Shakespeare and the Idea of the Play* (London: Chatto and Windus, 1962), 201–3. She speaks of *The Tempest* as becoming "lost in a confusion of dreams and shadows."

9. William R. Elton, *King Lear and the Gods* (San Marino, CA: Huntington Library, 1966), 181.

10. Heidegger, *Discourse on Thinking*, 64.

11. Ibid.

12. Howard D. Pearce, "A Phenomenological Approach to the *Theatrum Mundi* Metaphor," *PMLA* 95 (1980): 42–57.

13. W. T. Stace, *Mysticism and Philosophy* (London: Macmillan, 1960), 86.

14. For Taoist aesthetics, see Chang Chung-yuan, *Creativity and Taoism: A Study of Chinese Philosophy, Art and Poetry* (London: Wildwood House, 1975).

Collage and Creation: Necessary Violence in *Thief*

Richard E. Hersh

Sometimes violence is the agent of a viable methodology. In Michael Mann's *Thief*, the violent destruction of a collage and what it represents enables the evolution of methodologies of living and moviemaking; for collage is "an agglomeration of memorable signs."[1] Signs say "Walk" or "Don't walk"; signs say "Exit" and "Do not enter." By word or image, signs refer and remind; signs discipline life, imposing order on otherwise free experience. And the methodology of collaging is that of selecting and ordering and affixing. The product is a work of art whose process of coming into being is an essentially rational one and whose function as a work of art is subordinated to meaning. For Frank, the main character of Mann's film and a thief, collage functions as a reminder of how to construct his life, as a referent for checking the correspondence of his life with his concept of life, and as a method of disciplining his living of his life. Until he destroys his art work, his story is bound to telling by the traditional narrative method of epic pattern and literary convention. However, this violence frees Frank to make up his life as he goes along—to live imaginatively. Simultaneously, a violent shift of the film's narrative method occurs as Mann begins to tell the tale of Frank's living imaginatively.

Frank has conceived and constructed his collage while in prison, and his work of art is both compact and portable, composed almost entirely of still photograph images torn from mass-audience magazines. The rough, torn edges of the images accentuate their disjunctures in their juxtaposed arrangement. And this arrangement is absolutely and arbitrarily fixed not merely by the glue that holds them together but by the concept demanding that this art work be reasoned and meaningful, and by the mental discipline that attempts to order that concept into actual and factual existence. Keen analysis and critical judgment are the faculties of a rational mind at work in the art's construction. Frank carries his collage with him at all times and refers to it at length on three separate occasions during the film.

In constructing his collage, Frank's method has been to select images representing his notions of what his past, present, and future life should be. With the exception of a single one, all the images in his collage are conceptual—abstractions drawn from the specific. While each image is an image of a specific object or thing, each has been chosen, nevertheless, for its ability to represent an idea of that thing and not the thing itself. Moreover, each image represents a distinct piece or part of Frank's model life. Each fits into his collage not in the way a unique piece fills a particular space in a jigsaw puzzle, but in the way an individual may exemplify a more general slot in a logical classification or fill a "higher" category in a hierarchy. Typicality and impersonality characterize all the images in his collage, save one. Each part of the collage, each ideal part, is but a piece subordinated to the grander concept of what Frank's life should be. In order to achieve his ideal, his life must consist of a home, a business, a wife, a child, and a father, for Frank wants to construct a past as well as a future.

As Mann's film opens, Frank is in the midst of procuring the items for his life according to his as-yet unrevealed collage–plan. The action in this scene precludes an explication of "what the film is about"; for, at the same time, he is in the process of practicing his craft—liberating jewels from a safe. At setting brightly colored precious stones free (exposing them to light and sight), Frank is an artisan. As is eventually revealed, his skill and success as jewel thief permit him to pursue his avocation of manufacturing a life and in particular a family in much the same way that he has assembled his collage.

The most specific of those images making up his collage is a wallet-sized portrait of Okla (played by Willie Nelson), an older convict, master-thief, mentor to and still-imprisoned close friend of Frank. Their affection for one another is obvious from a scene in which Frank visits him in prison. Okla tells Frank that he has angina and is not expected to live much longer. He asks Frank to help him get out so that he can die on the outside; for while he has not been able to live freely, he does want to die as a free man. For Frank, however, Okla is more than an individual human being for whom he genuinely cares. Okla has taught Frank his craft and shared similar experiences with him. Even more than that, Okla gives Frank sage advice—"Lie to no one." As their relationship suggests, Okla can fill a category in Frank's plan just as his image occupies a fixed part of Frank's collage. So ignoring or disbelieving the facts of Okla's existence and motivated by his desire to obtain a father figure to fit into the life he is assembling, Frank bribes a judge to release Okla. The release comes only in time to fulfill Okla's wish. Medical science cannot save Okla's life; it can barely prolong his death, and Frank is confounded and enraged by the failure of the doctors and their machines to save Okla. Despite his knowledge the doctor cannot alter the facts of life. Despite all the tools a rational mind can devise to fix and preserve it, a life cannot be separated from the hazards of living it.

While trying to get a father for his well-contrived life, Frank has also been looking for someone to fill the category of wife. The image in his collage representing this piece of his life is less specific than the portrait of Okla; for the image that means wife is the face of a model, someone whose identity and individuality are not significant. While a model may be an individual, its value is derived from its ability to represent the ideal and typical. The particular image in Frank's collage is an abstraction meant to represent the category of wife. Another picture of another model from another mass-audience publication might fit the collage as well, for the image was not selected for its uniqueness. Frank is working exclusively with types and general characteristics, with rational concerns. Yet in order to fill the category in his actual life, he must finally select an individual: He hits on Jessie (played by Tuesday Weld) to fill this slot. If nothing else, his courtship of her is unique. While driving with her in the rain, he reveals that he has been supporting his unprofitable but socially respectable business operations—a car dealership and bar—by his craft. "I'm a thief," he says, lying to no one.[2] Once she can accept this fact of his life, he proposes, "So let's cut the mini moves and bullshit and get on with this big romance."

Later, during one of several scenes given over to dialogue and speech making, in which both reveal more of the circumstances of their pasts, Frank shows Jessie his collage and her place in it, explaining the life he is constructing. "That is my life, and no one can stop me from making it happen," he says, handing her the collage. He has chosen her for the category he wants to fill; he has selected her for the role she will play in his well-wrought life—for the functions she can perform. Even her introduction, her entrance in the film, is through her role as cashier and not by her identity. Her name is not even revealed until much later. In a sense, the function she performs is more significant and more highly valued than the fact that she is a unique individual. As Frank conceives it, she can fill the role and perform the function of wife, and the general and obvious characteristics of femaleness are the most significant characteristics she possesses.

In her role as wife she can also fill another role, theoretically; but Jessie is not that comfortable and comforting abstraction of the collage. She is actual and individual, and she is unable to perform that other function of wife—mothering. She cannot fill both roles. Not that she lacks the desire or will to become a mother: she merely lacks the biological ability, the physical capacity to naturally become a mother. She is barren. Pointing to the collage, she says, "I can't have children—I don't fit in." Like Okla's death, her barrenness is an incontrovertible fact. She cannot help Frank fill in the blank in another part of his life. Accepting this fact of her existence, Frank says, "So, we'll adopt." To acquire the child that will complete the family he wants to assemble, Frank must go elsewhere.

Like the image representing the idea of wife, the image of child is an image or picture of a specific child but not a picture of Frank's own created child. The role of child in Frank's life cannot be filled by a familiar figure the way the role of the father was. No individual's image can mean "child" the way Okla's image meant "father." The individual who can incarnate this child image demands creation, and the fact of Jessie's barrenness thwarts generation. Yet throughout the film this method of generating images for his life–collage has not been Frank's method.

As the collage and his thus far assembled life show, Frank's method has been to select from the world around him pieces that will fit his concept of art or life and then to order and fix them together. His method has been to construct. Thus, his child need not be of his creation. Other ways of securing this part to complete his ideal family exist, and Frank and Jessie attempt to adopt a child through a legitimate adoption agency.

This scene demonstrates Frank's desire to secure a child, any child, just so long as he can have a child. During this scene no character actually sees or examines a single child. Instead, Frank and Jessie discuss the concept of child and the idea of family. Despite their obvious economic well-being (Frank is wearing an expensive tailored suit and Jessie is dressed well, too) and their apparent ability to care financially for the needs of a child, and despite their desire, nearly desperation, to have and rear a child ("You got an eight year old black, chink kid, we'll take him," Frank offers), the law (those concepts of reasonable men) forbids Frank from adopting. Very suburbanly, the caseworker states: "We establish criteria." As an ex-con Frank does not fulfill the state's ideal of proper or suitable or appropriate parent. As abstractions, laws cannot account for a particular case, although their broad application is to, in each instance, a particular case. The caseworker cannot imaginatively transcend the concept of laws and criteria, even when Frank attempts to bribe her with a flawless three-carat emerald ring.

Like the image of wife in Frank's collage, the image of child is an abstraction. One image would serve as well as another for the purposes of his rationally based art. And one individual would serve as well as another to fill that slot in his life, as long as he or she evinced the characteristics of "kid." Frustrated in his attempt to assemble the ideal life by legal means, Frank turns to the under- world for help and accepts a baby, sight unseen. The choice of a particular child is not important, for the child's significance resides in his general "kid" char- acteristics. Frank has little concern for the concrete and individual. Although he passionately pursues his goal, the well-constructed family, he works toward it impersonally. When the local godfather who provides him with an infant asks what "model" Frank wants, Frank answers, "I want a boy." Except for this one specification, Frank surrenders the selection of his child to another person, nearly eliminating his involvement in the process of acquiring a family. The fact that Frank accepts a child whom he cannot see and must assume to be a "boy" emphasizes the impersonal process at work. Frank's family will mirror his collage in substance, for it mirrors it in formation. Frank and Jessie pick up their child on the day that Okla dies. A peroxide blonde in the lobby of a rundown building hands what appears to be a bundle of laundry to Jessie. They then go to a Chinese restaurant to discover what they have received. "What you baby's name? You got cute baby," the Oriental waiter asks. Frank's response is to say nothing. Jessie tells the intruding waiter, "No name—not yet." The fact is that the child is obviously unrelated to Frank, and like Frank, who was orphaned and state reared, this child will never know its heritage. Frank and Jessie decide to call the baby "David," Okla's Christian name. As Frank has impersonally selected the typical images for his collage, he has selected the individuals for his life impersonally. In fact, impersonality is the feature of collage that attracted another artist to the form. "Collage," Rauchenberg says, "is a way of getting an additional piece of information that's *impersonal*. I've always tried to work impersonally" (italics mine).[3] And so does Frank, in both art and life.

Frank's methodology represents his concept of life. Life is a substantive thing, a thing that can be acquired or filled up or in. For Frank, life is something that can be put together, tested, and taken apart, something one can observe and tinker with. Life is a thing whose parts one can name—a thing one can step outside of in order to consider its conformity to an idea of it. Yet facts persist in disrupting the conformations of Frank's life. Just as the torn edges of the images in his collage emphasize the formal disjunctures among the images, so the facts of his life emphasize the disjuncture between the ideal and the actual.

As Frank has constructed his collage to represent an ideal, he has subordinated art's function to meaning. He has adopted a traditionally Western and traditionally rational attitude toward art and life. His assumptions about both are unquestioned parts of the mythos. To tell Frank's tale, Mann initially uses a traditional narrative method, borrowing techniques and devices from the ancient and familiar literary form—epic. As an utterly conventional narrative method (one that can be imitated easily and that follows a general pattern with standardized elements), the epic form Mann uses complements Frank's approach to life and art.

In the finest epic tradition, Mann begins narrating Frank's story *in medias res*—directly in the middle of things. Although the opening scene is an action scene devoid of speech except for the simple radio transmissions "Are we clear?"—"You're clear," it introduces the artist–hero as he practices his craft. Frank and his protégés are liberating jewels from a safe. Since normally stories begin well after the main character's birth (except in eighteenth-century novels wherein it takes the hero half the book to be born), such an opening might not mark the film's narrative method as characteristically epic. Later, however, it becomes apparent that the hero is in the process of a tremendous exploit, that of constructing an entire life—past, present, and future—a legendary task equal, indeed, to the toils of Hercules. He has completed his collage, has acquired legitimate business interests, and has begun selecting individuals to comprise his ideal family before his story begins.

Such information is conveyed in a way that further suggests epic origins: As epic convention has it, long scenes in which characters more or less deliver speeches are used to reveal those things that have gone before and to foreshadow those events that will transpire. In *Thief*, shooting these scenes usually entails placing the characters in sedentary positions while they deliver monologues or engage in dialogue that amounts to alternating speeches. In one such scene, Frank, while driving through Chicago in the rain, reveals his criminal past and present to his future wife. Both figures are sitting still, but the movement of the car and the background motion make the action around them appear vigorous and rapid. The act of narrating becomes an island of stillness in a maelstrom of energy. Later, while sitting before the picture window of a diner with color and motion again as background, Frank reveals his collage–plan to Jessie, and they exchange stories of their histories. Characteristically, action scenes in epics are interspersed with scenes of speechifying in which figures boast, predict, challenge, pledge, and promise. They attempt to accomplish in words what they would accomplish in deeds; and in the first part of *Thief* such scenes of action and speech alternate.

In pagan and Christian epics alike, goddesses and gods intervene in the affairs of men. Whether Apollo or his satanic majesty, the immortal's first duty in epics is to interfere in the lives of heroes. Indeed, a god of sorts becomes involved in Frank's life. After the opening jewel heist, the local godfather, Leo, arranges the murder of Joey Gags, the fence Frank uses. Joey Gags's body is found without Frank's $185,000, which of course Frank cannot retrieve. Thus, Frank's plans for creating a life are disrupted, for his art or craft was supporting his avocations—the legitimate but unprofitable businesses. Frank tries to steal the profits of the heist back from one of Leo's hoods, and then a conference between Frank and the local godfather is arranged. At the conference, the money is returned to Frank, and Leo ultimately persuades Frank to go to work for him. Frank feels pressured by time and trades his skills for Leo's protection and assistance in casing jobs and disposing of stolen goods. Leo attempts to persuade Frank to branch out—to steal other items besides jewelry—and to work permanently for the godfather. Frank refuses to steal anything but stones or cash but agrees to work temporarily with the underworld leader. "I don't believe in lifetime subscriptions," Frank says. By persuasion and coercion, Leo attempts to subordinate Frank's life, actions, and efforts to his purpose, even to the extent of later killing one of Frank's protégés in order to frighten Frank into allegiance. Ultimately, it is the godfather who provides the child Frank and his wife can neither create nor legally adopt. In epics, one subplot is the battle of gods for the loyalties of men, and Leo, in the role of god, knows how to get Frank's loyalty. "Kids are a miracle—a little hoochie-koo, a drop of energy." You state your model; he buys them.

Many epic heroes must journey into the underworld. Both Aeneas and Odysseus are guided to the underworld by shades. Frank's trip begins with a roust by two corrupt cops who stop him on the street, destroy one of the taillights on the car he is driving, and then arrest him for driving an unsafe vehicle. If not Hades, the interrogation room at the precinct is certainly purgatory. The set for this scene is entirely dark—dark walls, dark floors, and dark furnishings, with no windows. The lighting is likewise subdued. The corrupt cops who beat Frank dress in white shirts, and a cacophony of screaming voices makes the conversation in this scene nearly unintelligible except for the clear warnings Frank receives. Eventually, like all legendary and epic heroes, Frank returns to the daylight.

In order to perform a particularly heroic act—pulling the ultimate heist—Frank needs a special tool. He goes to a metal shop—a small, dark, cave-like place— in the recesses of a junkyard and, as Beowulf and Siegfried did before him, enlists the aid of a troll-like figure whose skill is in crafting tools. This smith contrives the special cutting torch Frank will need in order to break into the uncrackable safe. Of course, as in all epics, this tool is constructed of special materials to be a one-of-a-kind thing.

Frank requires this unique instrument in order to relieve a very well-protected hiding place of its treasure. This task has been turned down by some of the "best" thieves in the business, and the godfather even warns Frank about it: The vault is located in the bottom of a mountainous building protected by five varieties of alarm systems. The most difficult barrier Frank and his apprentices must overcome is a special voice alarm neutralized only by repetition of the code word "Mexico," an incantation discovered by one of Frank's assistants, who eavesdrops electronically on the shop owners. Once inside the store, Frank must don special clothing in order to wield his special weapon, and his protégés arm this warrior for battle.

Once the epic pattern begins, the conventions proliferate, and the film's narrative proceeds according to the literary model. Although Mann incorporates novelty into the story pattern, this pattern nonetheless remains bound to traditional narrative method.

The big jewelry heist should provide enough money for Frank to achieve his goal of constructing a secure life, and he tells his accomplices that this will be his last job. But the outcome is Leo's reassertion of dominance, which produces a reaction in Frank—the determination to dispose of his own carefully constructed life. Simultaneously, Mann disposes of the epic literary narrative method by which he began to tell Frank's tale. Mann's method includes drastically reducing the number of words in the sound track. Dialogue shifts from long to short sentences and ultimately to almost no words at all. The film turns from speech to action—from telling to showing.

Frank begins dismantling his life by sending Jessie and David away with Joseph. "It's not what was supposed to be," he tells her. "Do not take anything. Do not pack." Jessie demands to know why she and the baby must leave; she loves Frank and needs a reason. "We just disassemble it and put it back in the box like an erector set?" she asks. Frank refuses to discuss this action and does not explicate. He makes no commitment to see either wife or child again. "I'm throwing you out. Get out," he replies, and these are the last words Frank utters in the movie. His action is sudden and abrupt. The act is a fact that, although violent, enables life.

The violence of Frank's actions begins to increase exponentially; and each violent act is more imaginatively liberating, more life freeing. Once his family is removed from the house, Frank, too, leaves, and their home explodes in a series of blasts. At his next stop, the Green Mill lounge, the violence pursues him. Frank is hardly back behind the wheel of his car when the insides of the bar explode into the street. At the auto dealership, Frank becomes the agent of violence, dousing buildings and cars with gasoline and touching them off. As he watches the flames rise, he removes the collage from his pocket and studies the images one more time. He then crumples his work of art and tosses it out his car window onto the burning lot. This violence has been both necessary and valuable, for it has freed Frank from the ratiocination that ordered his actions, demeaned his craftsmanship, and subordinated the living of his life to an idea of life. With the violent dismantling of his family, life, and art, Frank has disposed of the rationality-based methodology for living. At one time he had told Jessie that "you've got to get to where nothing means nothing" in order to stay alive in prison. Now again nothing means nothing. This is the end of Frank's life but the beginning of Frank's living, for his violence has engendered a creative breakthrough in methodology. Life is no longer a substantive thing that will stand still for analysis, but a process—a journey rather than a destination.

As Frank disposes of the philosophical basis for his art and life—the Platonic theory that supported his attitudes toward life and art—Mann abruptly shifts his narrative method. He eliminates the conventional elements from the movie. Predictable scenes and devices that are the stock of epic disappear. Scenes in which dialogue or speech predominate give way to an almost wordless presentation of Frank's story. Visual images predominate as the camera eye's focus on color and motion takes precedence over the word's compulsion to explicate. Dialogue does not entirely disappear, but the few words spoken are muffled and insignificant, contributing little toward explaining the film. Communication between characters relies less on speech than on gesture. With a veil of words removed, the camera eye, rather than focusing on still characters enclosed in a setting, focuses on the motion and movement—on the "moving" in the picture. Freed from literary conventions, Mann needs no words to explain the actions.

The camera follows Frank's motion through Leo's home as he attempts to penetrate to the center and the godfather himself. The story Mann shows is the story of Frank making up his life as he goes along, as he moves from room to room. Frank must make split-second decisions, and each choice is a matter of life and death. He is going to kill the godfather if he can. He has come as a thief to steal a life, and he is an artist when it comes to stealing.

For Mann the manner of narrating is as imaginative as Frank's living. The camera moves agilely and skillfully, but as unpredictably and unexpectedly as Frank moves through the labyrinthine environment of the godfather—the all-knowing, the omniscient. But the order of the rational interior fails to befuddle Frank, the imaginative man. No longer a man of rational processes, he is a man of vision. He sees his way to the godfather, sees him die (Mann narrates this action in slow motion, graphically and lingeringly), and sees his way out.

By several increasingly and necessarily violent acts, Frank frees himself from the rational arrangement of his life and from the hierarchical subordination of that life to another's rational order. Without his own plans or the designs of others, Frank is free to live imaginatively; and he lives so by making up his life as he lives it. Without the literary traditions of epic device and convention, Mann is free to narrate imaginatively, and he does so by showing Frank's story, as it happens, by using the movement in the picture rather than the explicating word to tell the thief's tale. The instrument of such fantastic freedom is imaginative acts, necessarily violent acts.

NOTES

1. Robert Hughes, *Shock of the New* (New York: Alfred A. Knopf, 1981), 345.
2. I cite the film from viewing it rather than from reading a script.
3. Robert Rauchenberg, quoted in Hughes, *Shock of the New*, 345.

MONSTROUS AND MARVELOUS BEINGS

Those clichés of the fantastic, the monster and the miracle, perhaps enforce our most disturbing engagements with all that lies beyond human reason and comprehension, in both our outer and inner worlds. Writers of such spaces populate them with strange creatures that may defy or charm us but always provoke us to define to them our own humanity.

Marc Chagall's Fantastic Vision of La Fontaine's *Fables*

Raymond G. LePage

In 1921, on the occasion of the tricentennial birth of the great French classical poet Jean de La Fontaine (1621–1695), the well-known Parisian art dealer Ambroise Vollard offered to underwrite the cost of a new edition of La Fontaine's *Fables* with accompanying illustrations by a major artist. He felt that a newly illustrated edition was appropriate to commemorate the poet's birth, since the last illustrated edition by a well-known artist had appeared in 1868, when Gustave Doré had been commissioned to illustrate a special edition marking the two hundredth anniversary of the original publication of the *Fables*. There was opposition to Vollard's proposal, mainly from conservative circles. Some of the *literati* felt that because La Fontaine was such a great classical writer (French schoolchildren learned his fables by heart), this kind of project should be subsidized by the government rather than by a commercial establishment. Vollard deferred to the wishes of these people. His project, then, was postponed for a while. However, when the government subvention did not materialize as expected, Vollard proceeded with his own plans.

The most important decision he had to make was in the choice of artist to illustrate the new edition. Marc Chagall had returned to Paris after the war in 1922, and Vollard had always liked the works of this young artist. He asked Chagall to illustrate a Russian masterpiece, Gogol's *Dead Souls*, but before Chagall had had a chance to complete his illustrations, Vollard commissioned him to make the illustrations for La Fontaine's *Fables*. This was now 1925.

The history of this set of illustrations is interesting in itself. To begin with, it was decided by both men that only certain fables would have accompanying illustrations. This explains why we have the illustrations for only one hundred fables, even though La Fontaine wrote over two hundred. Furthermore, it was Vollard's custom to exhibit commissioned illustrations in art galleries before committing them to the color plate process for printing. Accordingly, Chagall

painted a series of one hundred gouaches for public display, completed in late
1929, and Vollard exhibited them at the Galérie Bernheim-Jeune in February
1930. The reception was not what either man had expected. The artistic world
was surprised at Vollard's choice of artist (it had been a closely guarded secret),
the public was perplexed, and the conservatives were outraged. A storm of
protest descended on the head of Vollard. How dare he commission a Russian
emigré, a Jew and a Romantic to boot, to illustrate one of the most classical of
all French works! Vollard's act was called unpatriotic, and he was accused of
making a mockery of the genius of La Fontaine. The subject was even debated
in the Paris Chamber of Deputies. The whole episode was blown out of proportion
in one of those cultural altercations for which the French are well known.
Nonetheless, the fracas generated by the disclosure of the commissioned artist
put the entire project in jeopardy. Vollard, who was bold as well as ambitious,
knew that he had to answer his critics and justify his choice of artist. He did so
by pointing out that many of La Fontaine's fables had Eastern, oriental sources.
They also had a universal spirit that transcended national boundaries. He then
went on to say:

In my opinion at least, no one has had the idea of bringing to the fore the at once magical
and tangible, poetical and prosaic quality of the "comedy in a hundred acts" constituted
by his fables and made us feel that an artist has clothed the inspirations of a great poet
with his magic spell. That is why I thought it desirable and feasible to give La Fontaine's
work a less literal and fragmentary, but more expressive and synthetic, interpretation. In
my opinion, one can only demand such a rendering from an artist of temperament, an
artist with a creative talent bursting with pictorial ideas. Now if you ask me: "Why
Chagall?" my answer is, "Simply because his aesthetic seems to me in a certain sense
akin to La Fontaine's, at once sound and delicate, realistic and fantastic."[1]

Undaunted, Vollard pursued his idea of a Chagall-illustrated edition of the
Fables. He had a special studio built and hired the famous engraver Maurice
Potin to prepare the many color plates for printing. Unfortunately, the complicated process did not do justice to Chagall's beautiful color tones, and Vollard
was not satisfied with the results obtained. He convinced Chagall to redo them
in black and white etchings, arguing that only the artist could properly recreate
his own work in transposing from color to black and white. Chagall concurred
and proceeded to do just that. He completed these etchings in 1931. The final
product proved to be satisfactory and presented no problem for the black and
white engraving process. Curiously enough, the edition went unpublished during
Vollard's lifetime; it was only after his death that it was finally published. This
edition—published by Tériade—first appeared in 1952. Only one hundred copies
of the Tériade edition were printed, thus ensuring its status as a rare and expensive
edition. Moreover, forty of the copies issued were etched with bright colors—
red, blue, yellow, or lavender—added by Chagall himself and autographed by
him. For those fortunate enough to possess such a copy, it was like having one
hundred separate, full-page etchings with each print personally autographed by

the artist. One can readily understand why this illustrated edition of La Fontaine's *Fables* has become a collector's item.[2]

In examining these illustrations, it becomes quickly apparent that we are looking at the work of a painter and not a professional printmaker. Chagall preserves the freedom and imagination of the painter in his etchings; he does not fall into the routine of the printmaker. This quality can be seen in certain technical processes such as the broken surfaces, lines, scratches, and dots associated with his style of painting. Other details also serve to enhance the painterly effect of these illustrations: For example, the engraved parts are covered with a special touching-up varnish. As interesting as these stylistic matters may be, it is especially Chagall's treatment of the fables that interests us. Here, we see the imagination of a great painter working at its best. Unlike many of his predecessors who seemed to have been somewhat intimidated by La Fontaine's work, Chagall is not dominated by the fables. On the contrary, he dominates them. He uses the fables as a medium for his own artistic creativity. Unlike some previous illustrators, he is not content merely to do in pictures what La Fontaine has already done in words. While remaining true to the spirit and essence of the *Fables* as a whole, he goes beyond and creates an atmosphere that at times La Fontaine could only suggest. Indeed, this is the major contribution of Chagall as illustrator of La Fontaine. The latter, like all fabulist writers and storytellers, treats animals in anthropomorphic terms: They are used simply to depict certain human foibles. Consequently, the satire to be found in his *Fables* is obvious. On the other hand, Chagall treats the animals as individuals, not as representatives of some human tendency. The result is that his satire is also much more subtle.

I believe it is possible to group Chagall's illustrations around certain ideas or motifs that they serve to highlight. All of the illustrations can be grouped into four broad categories: (1) the ones that heighten a significant detail in the poetic text; (2) those that stress particular mythical themes; (3) those that convey the primitive sense of the animal stories; and (4) those that show original artistic treatment of familiar themes. Lastly, it should be pointed out that Chagall does not seem to be interested in the moral that a fable expresses, because the moral of a given fable seldom comes to the fore in his illustrations. As has already been mentioned, he is more interested in the animals themselves. What emerges is a different animal world in which fantasy becomes the *sine qua non*, as it were, of pictorial representation.

The fable of "The Crow and the Fox" (plate 2) is a good example from the first major category of illustrations—those that heighten a significant detail in the poetic text. It is one of the oldest and best known of all fables. In La Fontaine's version, the fox manages to obtain the coveted piece of cheese from the crow by means of deception (that is, his use of flattering terms and observations). The moral of the fable is explicitly stated by the fox when he tells the crow that all flatterers live at the expense of those who flatter them. Chagall's illustration is not a comment on the pitfalls of flattery. It goes much further. Chagall has taken

Figure 3. The Crow and the Fox

the one significant detail in the fable that struck him—the duplicity of the fox—
and used this as a point of departure (see Figure 3). The cunning and guile of
the fox now come to the forefront. More importantly, we see how Chagall has
managed to emphasize the idea of duplicity and hypocrisy in the fox. He employs
a novel approach: He has inverted the fox's head so that if we turn the illustration
upside down we see the fox's cunning mask from the same direction or spot as
does the crow perched in the tree. Chagall's fantasy is obvious here. The crow's
perspective is further accentuated by the fact that the artistic setting of the crow
seems to overwhelm the illustration (that is, the size of the crow, the many
branches of the tree, the quivering leaves, etc.). Thus, Chagall's own artistic

Figure 4. The Lion in Love

creation interweaves with La Fontaine's and produces a noticeable shift in emphasis, a shift that is aesthetically pleasing.

Chagall's fantasy is not always as innocently playful as it is in "The Crow and the Fox." At times, it incorporates elements of myth and imagination that have intense psychological meanings. The print accompanying the fable "The Lion in Love" is a prime example of this type of illustration (plate 54; see Figure 4). Since this fable is not as well known as the preceding one, a brief synopsis may be helpful. A lion has fallen in love with a shepherdess. He approaches her father to ask for her hand in marriage. The father does not dare refuse outright.

Instead, he reveals to the lion that his daughter is a delicate and fearful creature who would turn away from his advances unless he had his paws declawed and his teeth filed down. The lion obliges foolishly. Upon his next visit to their house, the father sets loose a pack of hounds on the would-be suitor; they, in turn, tear to pieces the defenseless animal. The moral of the story is implicit in the tale: Love sometimes will make people do irrational things. Illustrators have usually depicted the lion in the process of being groomed for the special visit and beaming proudly as a peacock. Chagall's illustration actually goes beyond the story. He shows us the two protagonists in a meaningful pose: The lion is clutching the young shepherdess forcefully in his grasp. The sexual overtones are rather obvious. In doing so, Chagall has managed to increase the sense of terror and tragedy that comes across only feebly in the fable. Some people may feel that he has taken too much liberty with the poetic text in this instance. On the other hand, he has chosen to stress the one mythical element present in the fable—the universal theme of Beauty and the Beast. This theme is not only visually evident in the bearing and countenance of the lion, but it is intensified, stylistically, by the tight network of patches, brush lacerations, and thick rings that seem to hem in the lion and the shepherdess. Thus, in a moment of supreme artistic creation, the illustrator has managed to unite woman and animal into a single, mythical statement that was hidden somewhere beneath the surface of the text.[3]

At times, Chagall's fantastic vision combines the best elements of fabulation and realism. This fusion can be readily seen in those illustrations that convey the primitive sense of the animal stories. In this category, Chagall has managed to depict graphically those moments in the fables that express the primordial hostility and violence of the animal world. Like any true fantastic creation, these illustrations possess great evocative power in themselves. Here, the pictorial renderings of violence make many of the drawings riveting and explain why they manage to exert such an enduring fascination. The fable entitled "The Old Lion" is perhaps the best known in this group (plate 33). It purports to tell the story of an aging, noble lion whose time has come to fall victim to the inevitable law of the animal kingdom from which he cannot escape: survival of the fittest. Chagall's depiction of the aged lion captures the very moment when the pack of wild beasts is attacking him (see Figure 5), and he does justice to its violence. The fanciful look on the horse kicking the old lion, the wolf who is getting ready to sink his teeth in the flesh, the powerful bull goring his victim, the opportune donkey in the background preparing to attack the quarry, the sparse landscape— the action and the psychology are superb; we are witnessing a ritualistic killing in which the savage forces of a primordial nature have been unleashed. This illustration is one of a few in which a great deal of brutal realism is apparent.

An important aspect of the poem is the manner in which the lion awaits his fate in a stoical attitude of resignation. Chagall's illustration effectively captures the circumstance. The sphinx-like lion, seemingly paralyzed with age, barely dragging himself along the ground and incapable of putting up a fight, stoically

Figure 5. The Old Lion

awaits the inevitable end. Generally speaking, figures represented horizontally
in art are intended to be seen as weak—the wounded, sleeping, dying. Here,
the physically passive pose of the lion attracts the other animals, excited for the
kill. Moreover, just as La Fontaine does not show us the final humiliation of
the lion at the hands of the base donkey (it is merely suggested), so Chagall
represents the donkey in the background, off center stage. Although the theme
of decline has disturbing connotations, it is through the process of visualization
that it has been made more meaningful and has achieved a certain impact.

It is, however, in the last category of illustrations that Chagall shows the greatest originality as a fantasist. It has often been said that the true enchantment of fantasy is produced by a different creative perspective that forces us to open our minds to new concepts of interpretation. If this assumption is true, then Chagall certainly qualifies as a supreme fantasist, because his treatment of materials in this category can be remarkable. A visual assemblage will be treated from an original point of view that will, in turn, project a new insight or different emphasis than one would normally expect. The fable "The Lion and the Gnat" is a prime example of this illustrative art (plate 26). The story concerns an arrogant lion who encounters a gnat and hurls insults at him. The injured gnat has the temerity to retaliate by attacking the lion. The gnat's size and speed make it well-nigh impossible for the lion to vanquish him. On the contrary, in his frustration he manages to inflict terrible wounds on himself:

> Whereupon the Lion's rage is at its height
> The invisible enemy triumphs and laughs out
> To see the arrogant beast put to rout
> As teeth and claws draw his own blood.
> The miserable Lion tears his hide in pain,
> Scourges his agonizing sides with his tail,
> Swats the air in vain and, worn out with
> Violent frenzy, collapses vanquished on the plain.[4]

The gleeful gnat, now bursting with pride, darts off to proclaim his victory over the king of beasts only to fall victim, in his turn, to a spider's web.

The fable is presented in dichotomous terms: two instruments of force, each representing different forms of it (that is, the brute might of the lion as opposed to the cunning agility of the gnat). For this reason, the fable has traditionally been depicted as a kind of David and Goliath struggle by the illustrators. La Fontaine describes the many different phases of the combat, the lion's blind rage, and his subsequent defeat by the gnat. In fact, since most of the poem gives us a vivid account of the contest between the combatants, illustrators have shown us the lion and the gnat in actual combat—with the lion roaring or swatting menacingly. Chagall instead has chosen to portray the lion in the moment of his defeat (see Figure 6). We see the great brute fastened to the ground on his back, immobilized with self-inflicted wounds and seemingly exhausted. He is lifting his head through the abundance of his mane to gaze at the puny, victorious creature, with an expression that betrays his inability to comprehend how this defeat could have happened to him. Although the particular artistic treatment of this fable by Chagall is perhaps not as strikingly pictorial as the more conventional portrayal, it does provide us with a tantalizing paradox: The lion has now become a symbol of the agony of helpless strength. This paradoxical antithesis captures well the baroque spirit of the age when La Fontaine originally wrote the fable. One thinks of Pierre Puget's popular sculpture "Milo of Crotona," which adorned the gardens of Versailles in the seventeenth century and which dealt with the

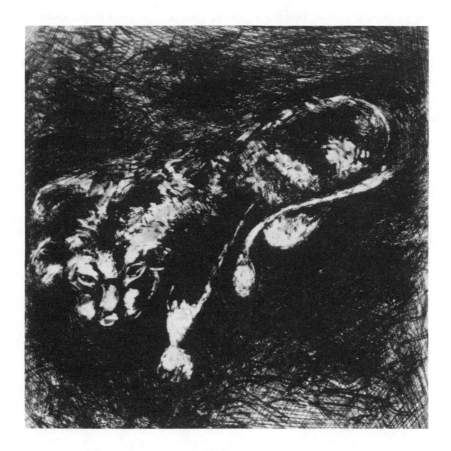

Figure 6. The Lion and the Gnat

same subject (depicting the athlete whose hand was caught in a tree and who was thus incapable of defending himself when attacked by a lion). Chagall has managed to make the fable more interesting by presenting the subject matter in a novel and significant way.

Pictorially speaking, one can study La Fontaine's *Fables* on various levels and from multiple points of view. A critical comparison of past popular editions would show that the major illustrators of these fables have mostly suppressed certain nuances while giving prominence to others. The illustrations of Marc Chagall are unique in any iconographic study of La Fontaine's *Fables*. Traditional materials are handled with shades of feelings not to be found in earlier illustrations. A fantastic world permeates these drawings. As we have seen, it is a world in which fantasy's power is enhanced by the artist's unmatched sensibility and vision. In particular, Chagall's approach to depicting animals in the *Fables* is at variance with that of practically all the previous illustrated collections that had found favor with the public. His fantastic interpretations of various animal types will probably never be surpassed. Yet, he has accomplished his interpretations while still remaining true to the author's concept of the *Fables*. Chagall, more than any other artist, has truly captured the genius of La Fontaine.

NOTES

1. Cited in Frantz Meyer, *Marc Chagall* (New York: Harry N. Abrams, 1965), 347–48.

2. The illustrations accompanying this chapter are from exemplary copy number 33, which is housed in the Lessing J. Rosenwald collection of rare books at the Library of Congress.

3. The mythical theme of Beauty and the Beast is one that Chagall is fond of portraying in La Fontaine. It is not limited solely to animals: See his treatment of the fable entitled "The Old Woman and the Two Servants."

4. Jean de La Fontaine, *Fables*, my translation.

Val Lewton and the Perspective of Horror

J. P. Telotte

The modern horror classic *Night of the Living Dead* concludes with the protagonist, Ben, survivor of a night of terror, suddenly shot down, as he is mistaken for one of the zombie flesh eaters inexplicably threatening society. Despite the sense of inevitability that clings to the scene, the conclusion is unsettling, particularly since his death occurs just as normalcy seems restored, and it is at the hands of his fellow man, trying to rid his world of those horrors. Ben is simply the victim of a certain "distanced" perspective, as he is glimpsed through the telescopic sight of a rifle; a product of the modern, technological mind, here employed rather irrationally to "kill" the already dead. I recount this scene because it effectively dramatizes a fundamental motif of the horror genre, occurring in both its modern realistic form and that older concern with monsters and an "otherness" that seems to reside threateningly outside of us, in the dark, ever ready to interrupt our normal world.

In this scene a man is confused with a monster, and in the process, that insecure self and the threatening other so clearly become one that our own sense of normalcy is radically disrupted, our view of the human realm disoriented. The means by which this identity is established—that distorted perspective, through a mechanism—insinuates a central thrust of the genre, for *Night of the Living Dead*, like the recent *Halloween*, Hitchcock's *Psycho*, and especially the films produced by Val Lewton, is implicitly concerned with a transformation that occurs when we view the world and our fellow man in an improper way, as if through a telescope. That distanced perspective, such films suggest, interprets life itself as an otherness against which we must guard; that form of vision, consequently, becomes a sort of murderous glance, which ultimately transforms the viewer into just the sort of monstrous presence he so deeply fears. In light of the recent trend in horror films to manipulate audience perspective, allying it, as the opening of *Halloween* so effectively does, with that of a killer or maniac at large, this motif seems especially worthy of exploration.

Not only the horror film, but most forms of the fantastic actually operate within the structure of this perceptual encounter with the unknown. As Tzvetan Todorov explains, fantasy narratives "essentially concern the structuring of the relation between man and the world. We are, in Freudian terms, within the *perception-consciousness* system."[1] Despite the great capital it makes from our immediate responses, then, the horror film through its disconcerting images functions in more than a merely gratuitous, anxiety-producing manner; rather, it challenges the way in which we consciously perceive—or, through repression mechanisms, fail to perceive—our world. This confrontation, as R. H. W. Dillard argues, can work "instructively," like a medieval morality play, teaching us to accept "the natural order of things and . . . to cope with and even prevail over the evil of life."[2] Or, as Robin Wood contends, such films may serve to visualize our dreams, "our collective nightmares," whose imaging on the screen empowers us to cope with subconscious fears "in more radical ways than our consciousness can countenance."[3] At the same time, of course, this perceptual emphasis invests the genre almost automatically with a metacinematic character as well, by clearly reminding us that what we see is essentially a way of seeing, a perception impressed upon us by the manipulative imagination of a narrator or filmmaker, seeking to bring our conscious and unconscious visions and fears together on the screen, as if in a kind of psychological therapy.

No single body of horror films demonstrates a greater mindfulness of this perceptual encounter than that produced by Val Lewton for RKO in the 1940s. In place of what Lewton described as those "masklike faces hardly human, with gnashing teeth and hair standing on end,"[4] the stock-in-trade of his competition at Universal, he demonstrated in films like *Cat People, I Walked with a Zombie*, and *Isle of the Dead* the great effectiveness of controlling perception. As Curtis Harrington pointed out, "Lewton had observed that the power of the camera as an instrument to generate suspense in an audience lies not in its power to reveal but its power to suggest; that what takes place just off screen in the audience's imagination, the terror of *waiting* for the final resolution, not the seeing of it, is the most powerful dramatic stimulus toward tension and fright."[5] This notion of perceptual control suggests that what we naturally perceive is essentially not dangerous, or at least not truly frightening; rather, it is the withholding of vision or its manipulation that instills dread by filling our imaginations with that that is not-life, only darkness itself, the shadows and boundaries that mark off for both the film characters and movie audience the normal world of light and life. At the same time, it implies that human beings' greatest terrors reside not necessarily within their world, contiguous with their normal environment, but possibly within the mind, which by turns represses them or projects them into that surrounding negative space of darkness and boundary, and which, prodded by its rational demand to know all, to understand and explicate the world around, too readily fills all shadows with visions of its own devising, mirror images, in fact, of that voracious instinct to grasp all things—save the self. That play of light and dark, the seen and the unseen, then, is more than simply atmospheric in Lewton's shadow-filled, low-key lit films, and by extension, more than merely a conventional trapping of horror. From those dark realms—the city streets of *Cat People* and *The Leopard Man*, the cane fields in *Zombie*, the back alleys of Edinburgh in *The Body Snatcher*—monsters truly are born; but they take shape from our own inability to dispel the darkness—physical and intellectual—within which we dwell, as Lewton reveals how that very incapacity can, after a fashion, make Frankensteins of us all, creating our own twisted versions of life, as we attempt to fill up the surrounding void with images of our compulsions, "monsters from the id," as the film *Forbidden Planet* well termed them.[6]

All of Lewton's horror films seek to sidestep our usual concern with monsters or external threats, while at the same time they clearly establish the sort of atmosphere that seems to breed and promise such menacing shapes, prompting us to look for killer cats or zombies in the shadows. In point of fact, though, their central concern is the sort of perspective we bring to that world, a perspective that, if unintentionally, lends a shaping hand to an environment that is neither malevolent nor benevolent, simply ambiguous, unknowable, yet the home of creatures who require knowledge. The greatest threats in the Lewton films, consequently, prove to be those authoritarian and supremely rationalistic figures, such as Dr. Galbraith of *The Leopard Man* and Dr. MacFarlane of *The Body Snatcher*, who, despite their great learning, ultimately turn out to be the chief horrors of their landscapes. *Isle of the Dead* probably most fully develops this horror formula, Lewton's legacy to the genre, for it establishes as a central motif that compulsion to watch over and hence control the human realm; from this impulse there naturally follow tragic consequences, including the literal transformation of man into murderous monster.

The very title of *The Leopard Man*, like the earlier *Cat People*, underscores this problem of transformation at the core of the film, although it also automatically misleads audiences accustomed to more conventional horror films. *The Leopard Man* details a series of similar grisly murders, attributable to two quite different causes: one, an escaped leopard who kills out of fear and hunger, as a product of his natural instincts; the other, one of those "men with kinks in their brains," as he is described, who murders out of some inexplicable mental aberration.[7] The latter is so clever, however, so able to divorce his conscious and unconscious selves, that he nearly succeeds in placing the blame for his own irrational, animalistic actions on that escaped cat. Through this paralleling, then, *The Leopard Man* points up the presence of a monstrous, bestial element in man that often goes cloaked or unacknowledged, but that can easily surface to render one something less than human and a threat to others.

The human transformation this film recounts begins innocently enough, although in a fashion that underscores the improper mode of vision accompanying, even precipitating the problem. The leopard is originally unleashed on society when a publicity stunt backfires. In order to create an effective spectacle, the nightclub entertainer, Kiki Walker, rents a leopard to help her make an entrance on opening night; in fact, she even plans to wear a particular black dress that she feels will make her look "just like" that dangerous cat. This implicit recognition of a kinship between the human and animal, of a certain bestial force that might be externalized and rendered symbolically, opens onto a greater complexity when Kiki finds she is unable to control the leopard because of its great strength and the fact that, as the local museum curator explains, such animals "are unpredictable; they're like frustrated human beings." Our initial introduction to Kiki, as we see her staring into a mirror, concerned with the image she will present to her audience, suggests that she is concerned largely with appearances and thus gives little thought to the potential danger she might unleash on others. It is that selfish perspective, however, that seems prevalent here and that precipitates that almost willful transformation wherein Kiki makes herself look like the leopard; the subsequent escape of that dangerous beast and the string of murders that follows symbolically denote the threat implicit in a mode of vision that detaches the self from all others.

Most fittingly, it is the person who seems most detached from these events, Dr. Galbraith, curator of the local museum and, ironically, the sheriff's expert consultant on the "cat murders," who turns out to be the killer. Perhaps not even fully conscious that he is speaking of himself, Galbraith can clinically dissect the possible murderer, explaining that he would "be a hard man to find . . . especially if he were clever. He'd go about his ordinary business calmly, except when the fit to kill was on him." In his case, the reasons for that murderous instinct go largely unexplained, are simply deferred by Galbraith's own comment on how little we know "about the forces that move us, and move the world around us." That a scientist could so easily fall prey to these violent, animal instincts, undergo such a complete transformation, and yet so effectively hide those irruptions of the unconscious, though, seems an unsettling enough comment on our normal rational pretensions. Rather than simply leave us with this iconic commentary on the darker possibilities of the self, the film depicts a similar transformation in the character of Raoul Belmonte, boyfriend of one of the murder victims. As Galbraith finally confesses to the murders, we watch Raoul's reaction, and in close-up see his eyes as they take on a frightening gleam, similar to that previously noted in close-up shots of the leopard. His sudden murder of Galbraith does, of course, represent a kind of justice, but it ultimately affords a discomfiting glimpse indeed of how easily those transformations can occur and that sense of humanity become lost.

If the metamorphosis lying at the core of *The Body Snatcher* is less radical than that of *The Leopard Man*, it is for that reason probably more disconcerting. This adaptation of a Robert Louis Stevenson story describes the problems of the medical profession in nineteenth-century Scotland, focusing especially on the many obstacles to the advance of medical knowledge in that era. The eminent Dr. MacFarlane, a surgeon and teacher of distinction, explains for his student assistant, Donald Fettes, how "ignorant men have dammed the stream of medical progress with stupid and unjust laws. If that dam will not break, the men of medicine will have to find other courses. As for me, I'll let no man stop me when I know I'm right.''[8] That rhetoric reveals much about the speaker, particularly MacFarlane's headstrong and self-righteous attitude, which allows him to place himself above the law in all questions of scientific research and application. While he voices a plea for the liberal attitude necessary for the advance of human knowledge, then, he also points up the underlying reason for such repressive laws, as a check to the possible dangers that may surface from that Faustian desire for knowledge that seems to haunt all men. MacFarlane's subsequent reminder to Fettes, that "if you're a real man and want to be a good doctor, you'll see it as I see it," suggests the dangerously autocratic nature of that point of view he maintains, as well as the will to transformation that subtly moves it, seeking to work its way upon others—as we saw after a fashion in the conclusion of *The Leopard Man*.

MacFarlane's plea for more liberal laws and a more tolerant perspective on the quest for knowledge springs from his difficulties in obtaining bodies for dissection and instruction in his medical school. To his mind, a human corpse is nothing more than a potential object of study, and a municipal council that disputes that view and regulates access to the dead he sees as demonstrating "the stupidity of the people, the idiocy of their laws." Having worked this initial transformation of the human body in his own thinking, then, he need take only a short step to transgress those "stupid" laws and contract with Mr. Gray, an old acquaintance, to rob graves and attain cadavers by any means possible— and with no questions asked. When a small girl, Georgina Marsh, needs spinal surgery so that she might walk, MacFarlane delegates to Fettes the task of obtaining a similar specimen so that he might perfect his technique before performing the delicate operation; and his student goes to Gray, as he normally does, to place an order. With no appropriate corpses available, Gray simply murders a young street singer to accommodate his customers. It is a poor bargain indeed, that one girl must die so another might walk—murder thus facilitating medical research—and it precisely points up the danger in MacFarlane's abdication from a true concern for others in his work. At the same time, of course, this episode also hints at the sort of gradual and almost imperceptible transformation the teacher has already begun to work in the consciousness of his pupil, eroding his humanistic ideals and prompting him to wink at the actions of his confederates; as Fettes later notes, MacFarlane started him on "a road that led to knowledge, not to healing." It is a knowledge that, given free reign, can eventually transform an individual, as we see when MacFarlane himself becomes a murderer, killing Gray when that henchman tries to blackmail him, and then excusing his act by noting that with him out of the way, "I'll be a new man and a better teacher." That "new man," however, is no better than a ghoul, as he presses Fettes to assist him in stealing bodies from the graveyard; "We can do our own dirty work," he informs his student with some satisfaction.

The flawed perspective that underlies this transformation is particularly underscored in the film's final scene, in which MacFarlane and Fettes return from exhuming the body of an old woman. As they ride off with their prize, the corpse repeatedly topples onto the doctor's shoulder, and he gradually begins hallucinating that the body is actually that of Gray, returned to haunt him. Confronted by this imagined sign of his crimes, a long-repressed guilt suddenly unleashed on his consciousness, MacFarlane seems to go mad and drives his carriage over a precipice. Fettes, thrown clear of the careening coach, then inspects the wreck, holding up a lamp (symbolic of his own clearer vision) to the corpse that had so frightened his tutor, and affirms that it was indeed simply the body of an old woman. The guilty vision that effectively frightened MacFarlane to death, we understand, was an image of his own distorted perspective, a projection of that internal horror he had long denied and repressed under a guise of respectability and scientific purpose.

With *Isle of the Dead*, the faulty perspective precipitating such human transformations becomes the key motif, literally framing the tale with its various formulations. It first takes shape in the character of General Pherides, known as "the watchdog" of Greece and the "guardian of his country."[9] As the film opens, the general summarily court-martials a subordinate, ordering him to take his own life, despite the fact that he is an old friend. Immediately established is the general's desire to maintain order in his army by closely overseeing every action. The other emblem of that dangerous perspective is the recurring image of Cerberus, literally the watchdog of the ancient gods, guarding the gates of Hades, which here takes the form of a statue that greets all who land on the island where the story's main action occurs. A similarity between these two figures is immediately established when the war correspondent, Oliver Davis, notes for the general, "There's another watchdog for you." Pherides disavows the likeness, though, and points up his own belief in the correctness of his perspective, reminding Oliver that Cerberus "only guards the dead; I have to worry about the living." Like the general, however, the figure of Cerberus seems ever present, watching over the action of the film, serving as a key transitional device, and providing the narrative's closing image. What those recurring shots of that mythic watchdog suggest is just how closely death lingers in this world, and how hellish human beings can make their environment by misfocusing their perspective on it and fellow human beings.

Vision for the general, we understand, is associated with warding off danger and preserving the laws of his homeland. What he sees around him is a world of chaos, of constant threats he must notice as soon as they take shape in order to counter them. One form this attitude takes is his rigid enforcement of the law, even to the point of collecting taxes from the native villagers with field artillery; he could fire on his own people, he admits, because the law dictated it, and anyone "who is against the law of Greece is not a Greek." While Pherides earnestly keeps watch, then, it is through a transforming filter, the conceptualizations afforded him by a rigid and inhuman system of laws that so clouds his true perceptions that he can deny the very nationality of his countrymen.

The advent of a truly invisible threat, the plague, as a consequence of the general's latest military victory serves both to underscore this attitude and to

illustrate effectively its danger. In fact, with the plague comes a literal transformation in the general's character, from protector to destroyer, which serves
to comment upon the perspective he brings to this world. Although of peasant
origins, Pherides sees himself as a representative of a new order, a Greece that
has abandoned the ancients and their superstitious ways; "These are new days
for Greece. We don't believe the old, foolish tales anymore," he boasts. In
place of those myths he describes as "nonsense" the general pays homage to a
rational perspective, putting his faith totally "in what I can feel, and see, and
know about." When the plague strikes, therefore, he turns to modern science,
embodied in his subordinate, Dr. Drossos, to halt its spread and keep it from
devastating his army. All that Drossos can counsel, however, is sanitary precautions and patience while the disease runs its course. Since a favorable wind
might rid them of the fleas that spread the plague, the doctor does raise a pennant,
in part to keep track of the wind's shifting direction, but more to distract the
vision of those under his quarantine; as he readily admits, it is "better to watch
the wind and hope that it changes than to watch each other and have no hope
at all." What Drossos thereby admits is the complexity and even futility of that
watching process, an activity that simply transforms human beings into potential
victims of the devastating and uncontrollable forces they unwittingly evoke.

When Drossos's precautions fail to stop the plague's progress—the disease
even taking his life—Pherides gradually returns to the long-repressed fears and
beliefs of his folk heritage. From that collective unconscious, Madame Kyra,
the old housekeeper, dredges up a superstitious explanation for the disease: the
notion that a *vorvolaka*, or evil spirit inhabiting a human form, has brought
about this affliction. Since, as he notes, "everything—every *human* remedy"
has failed, Pherides embraces this explanation and turns his attention to the
servant girl, Thea, who, in the midst of the plague, inexplicably remains healthy,
beautiful, and, as one character notes, "full of life." Pherides and Kyra, therefore, mount a constant watch over Thea, even at night while she sleeps, in hope
of catching her in some evil act; he justifies the transformation he has worked
on her character by asking her if "a *vorvolaka* in human form can remember
the evil that she did at night," and he vows that "until I know, I must watch
you." That constant surveillance and the suspicion it denotes deeply affect Thea,
undermining her view of herself, even bringing her to question whether she has,
in fact, become possessed by such an evil influence. Consequently, the general's
watching, initially prodded by his desire to save his fellow human beings, becomes less a protective activity than an injurious one, as he isolates Thea from
the others, especially Oliver who is in love with her, and forces her into a
desperate self-doubt, as she too lives in fear of those forces lingering beneath
her consciousness, threatening even those she loves. Because of the perspective
the general brings to his world, then, a human being has arrived at such a state
that the beautiful can be thought a disguise for evil, love can be denied, and the
human spirit can be suspected of the most sinister motivations.

What the narrative repeatedly underscores is just how much remains invisible, though, and thus how unavailing that watchfulness must ultimately prove to be. When the British Consul, St. Aubyn, dies, his wife asks for some proof, since, she asserts, "the breath can stop; the heart can stop. It still doesn't mean death." Visible signs, she knows from experience, can be most deceptive, for there is a history of catalepsy in her family, of trance-like states that give the illusion of death; consequently, she has always feared being buried alive. When she is apparently stricken with the plague, though, that sanitary impulse precipitates a hurried burial, and she is entombed alive, a symbolic reminder of the dangers of our limited perspective and of that mode of vision the general has brought to bear on those around him—a vision that readily sees death even in life, pestilence in the natural order, and danger in the harmless. The darkness in which all of the subsequent action takes place serves only to emphasize the difficulty of those visual judgments Pherides so precipitately makes, while allowing for the note of irony Lewton injects by repeatedly depicting Thea carrying a lamp or candle to dispel that darkness in which those around her dwell, enabling them to see circumstances all the more clearly.

In his discussion of this plague motif in literature, René Girard points out its archetypal characteristic and suggests that we should see in its narrative recurrences "a disguise for an even more terrible threat that no science has ever been able to conquer."[10] The shape of that threat appears most clearly here in the final transformation Pherides undergoes when he is himself stricken by that disease he has sought to ward off. Taunted by Madame Kyra that "you stayed your hand and now the plague punishes you," he decides to murder Thea, believing that he will thereby vanquish the *vorvolaka* she harbors within and appease the anger of the ancient gods. In effect, he becomes with this decision precisely the sort of evil and threatening spirit he seeks to remove from this human realm. Transformed into a raving maniac, he stalks Thea, only to be stopped at the last moment by the intervention of Mrs. St. Aubyn, who has escaped from her premature entombment where she has apparently undergone a similar transformation. In her own madness, then, she kills both Pherides and Kyra, visits their fears upon them, before throwing herself off a cliff. Oliver earlier warned the general of a danger far greater than the plague: "There is something here more dangerous than septicemic plague . . . and that's your own crazy thoughts." His point is simply that human beings often become their own worst enemy, harboring within the potential for their own destruction, their own monstrous shape or madness, usually repressed or lost in the unconscious, but waiting to be evoked. Fittingly, the particular form of the plague that strikes and elicits that delirious state in which the general can attempt murder is an internal disease with no visible marks, other than, as the doctor notes, a change of behavior in its final stages. Septicemic plague, it seems, eats away at the vitals, particularly the bloodstream, and etymologically suggests a rotting from within. In short, it seems carefully selected to denote the sort of internal, cancer-like danger to which we are prone, an internal violence that defies watchfulness and points up our own complicity in those threats that often seem to erupt in our world.

Lewton ends *Isle of the Dead* with a most telling juxtaposition, one that underscores the connection between that failure of vision and the terrible events that accompany it. A close-up of the dead Pherides's face, his eyes open and staring, still keeping their frightful vigil, even in death, dissolves to a long shot of Oliver and Thea leaving the island, taking their love out of this land of the dead so that it might prosper. Their departure, however, is haunted by these events, as a close-up of the statue of Cerberus is superimposed, the three snarling heads of that monstrous watchdog recalling the dangers of a vision whose only purpose is to control life.

That final image well sums up this genre's concerns with both internal and external threats, with human anxieties and those monstrous presences that often provide the objective correlatives for our vague and unformulated fears. One of Lewton's great achievements, in fact, was that he consistently managed to dramatize how interwoven these concerns ultimately are, how fully the unconscious must influence the conscious world. Like the more conventional examples of the genre, his films explore that very common fear we have of otherness, but at the same time they reveal how it may prompt us to distance ourselves from other people and to abdicate participation in that human realm we necessarily inhabit. Nietzsche's warning in *Beyond Good and Evil* that "whoever battles with monsters had better see that it does not turn him into a monster. And if you gaze long into an abyss, the abyss will gaze back into you" hints at just this sort of transformation to which we are prone when we lose an essential human perspective, the ability to look within as well as without.[11] An improper mode of vision, such as the sort that enables us to abdicate our human responsibility or see in our fellow human beings that otherness we almost instinctively fear, in the end engenders that very monstrousness from which we initially and naturally recoil.

What the horror film in its various formulations has ideally sought to do is to prod us into a more comprehensive perspective, to engender, as it were, a morality of seeing. Recent work in the genre, it has been suggested, has essentially abdicated that moral function by forcing an identification between the audience and some aberrance, through a subjective camera placing a "killer's center of consciousness in the audience."[12] Even if poorly controlled and misguided, though, that effect derives from and points back to a most important impulse in the horror genre. A major legacy of the Lewton films, more recently found in the work of Hitchcock, Brian DePalma, and John Carpenter especially, is to call attention to that frame of reference to which we normally and unconsciously cling, a framework that allows us to see marked distinctions between the self and a threatening otherness, but that may also blind us to a similar duality within the self. Our experience of the horror film clearly prompts us to perceive the world differently when we emerge from the theater, to find a new potential—both a frightening and an exhilarating one—in that world we normally inhabit. This is one transformation we sorely need, though, for the ways in which we see the world and the self are mutually dependent. Those formulas that help to foster that vision, consequently, serve a vital function, promising to make us more human, if paradoxically by forcing us to recognize a monstrous potential within.

NOTES

1. Tzvetan Todorov, *The Fantastic: A Structural Approach to a Literary Genre*, trans. Richard Howard (Ithaca, NY: Cornell University Press, 1975), 33.

2. R. H. W. Dillard, "The Pageantry of Death," in *Focus on the Horror Film*, ed. Roy Huss and T. J. Ross (Englewood Cliffs, NJ: Prentice-Hall, 1972), 37.

3. Robin Wood, "Return of the Repressed," *Film Comment* 14 (July-August 1978): 26.

4. Quoted by Joseph McBride in "Val Lewton, Director's Producer," *Action* 11 (January-February 1976): 12.

5. Curtis Harrington, "Ghoulies and Ghosties," *Quarterly of Film, Radio, and Television* 7 (1952–53): 195.

6. Dialogue transcript from the film *Forbidden Planet*, MGM, 1956.

7. This and subsequent quotations are dialogue transcripts from *The Leopard Man*, RKO, 1943.

8. This and subsequent quotations are dialogue transcripts from *The Body Snatcher*, RKO, 1946.

9. This and subsequent quotations are dialogue transcripts from *Isle of the Dead*, RKO, 1945.

10. René Girard, "The Plague in Literature and Myth," *Texas Studies in Literature and Language* 15 (1974): 845. Girard believes that we should see in this insistent and universal motif of the plague "a generic label for a variety of ills that affect the community as a whole and threaten or seem to threaten the very existence of social life" (p. 834).

11. Friedrich Nietzsche, *Beyond Good and Evil*, trans. Walter Kaufmann (New York: Random House, 1966), 89.

12. For a discussion of the possible implications of this unsettling visual identification, see Roger Ebert's "Why Movie Audiences Aren't Safe Any More," *American Film* 6 (March 1981): 56.

The Dragon Is Not Dead: Le Guin's *Earthsea Trilogy*

Margaret M. Dunn

"When we feared the dragons," asks Carl Sagan in *The Dragons of Eden*, "were we fearing a part of ourselves?"[1] Sagan's question may in one sense encapsulate the history of Western man, a history that is, in effect, a gradual process of internalization. For unlike his legendary progenitors who did battle with real, fire-breathing colossi, contemporary man has internalized his dragons and thus fights not the enemy without, but the enemy within. In her *Earthsea Trilogy*, however, Ursula Le Guin reasserts the necessity for fantasy, objectifies in the figure of the dragon the age-old powers of darkness, and clearly shows that such darkness is a necessary and inevitable part of life.

In the earliest known creation myths, in the Anglo–Saxon *Beowulf*, and in the medieval romances, the dragon was the ultimate embodiment of evil—a real, physical presence to be met and defeated if man was to master his world. In the nineteenth and twentieth centuries, however, those dragons that had once been so terrifyingly real fell prey to the rational onslaught of science; they had been "internalized" so that man had now to do battle not with a concrete, flesh-and-blood monster, but with his own elusive psyche. By this time, the dragons of yore had become mere symbols, picturesque but relatively unimportant artifacts of ages less rational and less learned. Some authors were still writing about them, of course, but intelligent people knew that dragons were no more numerous than pterodactyls, and those who took their literature seriously knew that one encountered such beasts only in that escapist subgenre in which science fiction and fantasy were so ingloriously lumped together.

Then, in 1936, Professor J. R. R. Tolkien ushered in what one critic has called "a distinctly striking moment in the history of the modern imagination, the resurgence of a critical grasp of the mythological perception of radical evil."[2] In two now-famous lectures given in 1936 and 1938, Tolkien first defended the monsters and dragon of *Beowulf* against charges that they were "irrelevant," and then expounded upon his own developing theory regarding the place of fantasy and myth in modern literature. He had pondered long and hard, said Tolkien, upon the profoundly revelatory way in which myth and fantasy can deal with moral and spiritual issues, and he had found that the dragon—as a symbol of embodied radical evil—holds a special significance for modern readers; for this dragon inhabits an other world, a "perilous land" that may at times be the mind's only recourse when forced to flee from the ironies and injustices of life. After glimpsing this other world, and after considering the importance of its fabled denizen, said Tolkien, he became convinced of the terrible necessity for dragons, and he knew that he himself "desired" them with a "profound desire."[3]

While Tolkien was working out his theory of fantasy, he was at the same time writing and publishing *The Hobbit* and *The Lord of the Rings*, and it is these works that greatly influenced Ursula Le Guin as she was herself beginning to write and publish. For Le Guin, too, recognized the need for dragons, and she echoed the professor in a talk she delivered in the early 1970s. Modern, rational people, she said, are afraid of fantasy because "they know that its truth challenges, even threatens, all that is false, all that is phony, unnecessary, and trivial in the lives they have let themselves be forced into living. They are afraid of dragons because they are afraid of freedom."[4] Le Guin was talking, of course, as was Tolkien, about the inward journey that fantasy forces one to take, and about the self-revelation that may result from such a journey. To be free is to face and come to terms with the dragons within us, the dragons that we may otherwise bury in the superficial details of our busy, busy lives.

Le Guin, then, knew instinctively about dragons, and it is in her *Earthsea Trilogy* that she once and for all establishes the necessity for them. Thus, in Book 1 *(A Wizard of Earthsea)*, her protagonist defeats the Dragons of Pendor in a contest that parallels the time-honored struggle of man versus beast. But in Book 3 *(The Farthest Shore)*, these traditional adversaries actually join forces in order to combat a common enemy who threatens to subvert the natural order of life—an order in which man and dragon, good and evil, joy and pain, the known and the unknowable are necessary counterparts. Consider, then, Le Guin's account of the adventures of a wizard named Ged.

In her trilogy, Le Guin spins a magical tale of adventure set in the kingdom of Earthsea, a watery archipelago inhabited by warriors noble and barbaric, by magicians humble and powerful, and by enchantresses beneficent and fey. Many are the characters whom Le Guin feeds into the fabric of her tapestry, but it is the life story of the wizard named Ged that ties the three volumes together. In Book 1 we follow him in his youth and growth to manhood; in Book 2 we read of a quest undertaken by him in the prime of his life; in Book 3 we follow his final, magnificent triumph and the incipient waning of his powers. Although dragons make a significant appearance only in the first and third volumes, it is the dragons around which the underlying theme of the trilogy revolves; for the dragons of Earthsea are not interlopers in a kingdom of men, but are rather creatures accepted as part of the natural order of life.

Le Guin's Dragon of Pendor in Book 1, in fact, might well have been spawned with the *Beowulf* dragon or with Tolkien's "Smaug." Generations ago, the creature had come out of the West upon the Lord of Pendor while the Lord and his men sat feasting in the tower of the great island castle. Smothering them with the flames of his mouth and driving the townsfolk into the sea, the dragon then laid claim to the island and all its treasure. The townspeople of the neighboring islands knew, as did the unnamed thief in *Beowulf* and Bilbo Baggins in *The Hobbit*, that the removal of even one small cup from a dragonhoard would enrage its owner. Through countless years, therefore, the Dragon of Pendor and his ill-gotten treasure remained unmolested. Some few years ago, however, a she-dragon had come to the castle on Pendor and left her eggs for the old dragon to lair. These young dragons were now growing in the ruined marble hallways of a tower long despoiled, and soon the eight young ones would feel hunger for the food their dead island–home could not afford them. "Slow to wake, but hard to sate,"[5] their all-devouring appetites would ravage the farms and the towns. Ged, still a young wizard, decided at this point to go in pursuit of the family of fire-drakes rather than wait for the carnage that was sure to come.

Upon reaching the island of Pendor but staying in his boat a short distance away, Ged issued a challenge to the old he-dragon. Six young ones answered his call, and six young ones he dispatched. Then, "black with the scalding wormblood, and . . . scorched about the head with fire," Ged stared in awe at the sight for which even the old songs and tales had not prepared him:

The highest tower slowly changed its shape, bulging out on one side as if it grew an arm. . . . What [Ged] had taken for a part of the tower was the shoulder of the dragon of Pendor as he uncurled his bulk and lifted himself slowly up.

When he was all afoot his scaled head, spike-crowned and triple-tongued, rose higher than the broken tower's height, and his taloned forefeet rested on the rubble of the town below. . . . Lean as a hound he was and huge as a hill. (pp. 88–89)

As puny before this menacing immensity as a leaf before a hurricane, the young wizard faltered not and bought the safety of his countrymen with the only weapon that could hold the monster in check. Ged had discovered what no other man knew—the dragon's true name; and in Earthsea, it is such knowledge that gives one mastery over him whose true name is known. In boundless rage at his defeat, the old dragon rose up, "breaking the tower with the writhing of his body, and beating his wings that spanned the whole width of the ruined town" (p. 93). But Ged was already sailing away, secure in the knowledge that the oath of the dragon named Yevaud, who had sworn by this his true name, would hold.

In Book 1, then, Ged engages in a contest that has been sung since the beginning of time. He becomes both Dragonslayer and Dragonlord as he meets and defeats a foe that Le Guin tells us explicitly is of "an older race than man" (p. 90). Like Beowulf and Bilbo before him, Ged is a participant in a contest between the forces of good and the incarnation of evil, and in each case it is the dragon that is the heart, the center of the work. "A dragon," said Tolkien, "is no idle fancy."[6] Indeed, this is no buffoonish creature from Disney World, no pale, anemic symbol. Clearly the spawn of an ageless darkness beyond the ken of man, the dragon is rather a monumental embodiment of all that lies beyond the purview of human reason and comprehension. To die in combat with him, as did Beowulf, is to embrace the knowledge that man's magnificence lies in his willingness to accept a challenge that must ultimately end in defeat; to elude him, as did Bilbo, is to realize with humility the terrible strength of the foe; to reach a standoff with him, as did Ged, is to accept the inevitability of an evil force that, since it cannot be eliminated, must be acknowledged. Thus, we must all struggle with evil, and Ursula Le Guin, in this first volume of her trilogy, recognizes the necessity of the struggle as she restores the dragon to his rightful place as the focal point—as the embodiment of all that is unknown and unknowable in life.

After receiving only passing mention in Book 2, Le Guin's dragons once more appear in Book 3 of the trilogy. By now Ged has become the most powerful wizard in Earthsea. With a companion of princely birth named Arren, he sets out on a quest upon whose outcome rests the fate of the kingdom. A deadly but invisible menace threatens the natural order of life in the lovely archipelago. No beast of awesome power and ferocity, no concatenation of destructive natural elements, this menace is a man, a mage—but one who has achieved immortality, one who through the mastery of death itself threatens the ultimate subversion of the natural order of life. A wise man turned evil through his burning desire for power, he has gained control over the gateway between life and death and thus has broken the balance of nature in Earthsea. As they journey by land and sea, Ged and Arren observe a kingdom that is debased and sickened. A debilitating lassitude, a baffling lethargy has taken hold of its people. Villagers tend neither to their children nor to their fields; townspeople sit in drug-induced stupors while flies cluster in their mouths and ears; even the trees and shrubs stand mute, unable to blossom. It is as if a creeping, deadly miasma exudes from the very rocks, hills, and streams. Now it is that Le Guin brings man and dragon together, not as adversaries, but as allies. For in a world in which death itself is threatened, a world in which the natural order may thus be destroyed, all the powers that make up that natural order must unite in its defense. Man, whose experience of joy and hope and life is meaningless if he knows not the existence of evil and pain and death, and the dragon who embodies these nemeses of mankind—these traditional foes must thus join forces to protect the balanced system of which they are both a part.

Summoned by Orm Embar, one of the greatest of the ageless beasts, Ged and Arren arrive at the island of Selidor where the foe whom they have been seeking awaits them. There, they and the mighty dragon face the emissary of death-in-life. And there it is that Orm Embar, the creature spawned in darkness aeons before the advent of man, the creature who suffers the very existence of man with contemptuous amusement—there it is that this creature gives its life so that

Ged and Arren may live to defeat their common enemy. As the man and boy stand in the grip of a spell that holds them powerless to move, and as the enemy reaches with his sword toward Ged, suddenly

over Ged and Arren, over their heads, vast and fiery, the great body of the dragon came in one writhing leap and plunged down full-force upon the [enemy], so that the charmed steel blade entered into the dragon's mailed breast to its full length: but the man was borne down under his weight and crushed and burnt.

Rising up again from the sand, arching his back and beating his vaned wings, Orm Embar vomited out gouts of fire and screamed. He tried to fly, but he could not fly. Malign and cold, the metal lay in his heart. He crouched, and the blood ran black and poisonous, steaming, from his mouth, and the fire died in his nostrils till they became like pits of ash. He laid down his great head on the sand.

So died Orm Embar where his forefather Orm died, on the bones of Orm buried in the sand.[7]

Ged and Arren must now continue to pursue their enemy as he crawls, burned and shriveled, into a darkness visible; they must still heal the rent between the world of the living and the world of the dead. But they will be able to do so because of the sacrifice of the magnificent beast. Much later, when they are both spent beyond the point of exhaustion, it is Kalessin the Wise, the eldest and most feared of all the dragons of Earthsea, who will find them, permit them to mount behind his fearsome head, and soar with them away from the vale of death and back to the land of the living.

Le Guin, then, not only restores the dragon to his rightful place as the embodiment of the incomprehensible forces of darkness, but in Book 3 of the trilogy she also allies him with man to assert the importance and inevitability of such forces within the natural order. As Le Guin knows, and as Tolkien knew, and as those long-ago ancestors who sang the exploits of Beowulf knew, there is that in life that will forever be unknowable except in terms of myth and imagination. The world is "improbable and unmanageable," says Le Guin, and we must realize that "realism is perhaps the least adequate means of understanding or portraying the incredible realities of our existence."[8] Shall we not, then, return to the dragon? Shall we not, then, acknowledge his importance? His significance? "The dragons are not all dead!" cry the villagers of Earthsea when Kalessin arrives in the west with his human passengers. Indeed, the dragon is not dead. Whether he lives in each of us in the frightening labyrinth of the subconscious, or whether he lives apart somewhere, beyond the abyss of time, space, and human comprehension, he and all that he embodies are as relevant and important to us today as when the scops sang at the campfires and in the great halls.

Before they reach Selidor but as they approach the neighboring islands, Arren has his first sight of dragons in flight. Le Guin describes his reaction thusly:

Arren saw the dragons soaring and circling on the morning wind, and his heart leapt up with them with a joy, a joy of fulfillment, that was like pain. All the glory of mortality was in that flight. Their beauty was made up of terrible strength, utter wildness, and the grace of reason. . . .

Arren did not speak, but he thought: I do not care what comes after; I have seen the dragons on the wind of morning. (p. 147)

To see the dragons on the wind of morning is to enter into that ageless kinship of seers, scops, and poets—all those who, in the words of C. S. Lewis, "brood much on the remote past or future, or stare long at the night sky."[9] To see the dragons on the wind of morning is to comprehend the power of human imagination, to realize the depths to which humans can fall and the boundless heights to which they can aspire.

To see the dragons on the wind of morning is to know the glorious pain, and the painful glory, of being human.

NOTES

1. Carl Sagan, *The Dragons of Eden: Speculations on the Development of Human Intelligence* (New York: Ballantine, 1977), 150.

2. Randel Helms, *Tolkien's World* (Boston: Houghton Mifflin, 1974), 3.

3. J. R. R. Tolkien, *Tree and Leaf* (Boston: Houghton Mifflin, 1965). This volume is the reissue of Tolkien's 1938 Andrew Lang Lecture, "On Fairy Stories."

4. Ursula Le Guin, "Why Are Americans Afraid of Dragons?" in *The Language of the Night: Essays on Fantasy and Science Fiction by Ursula Le Guin*, ed. Susan Wood (New York: Putnam, 1979), 44.

5. Ursula Le Guin, *A Wizard of Earthsea* (1968; reprint, New York: Bantam, 1975), 77. Further references appear in the text.

6. J. R. R. Tolkien, "*Beowulf*: The Monsters and the Critics," in *An Anthology of Beowulf Criticism*, ed. Lewis E. Nicholson (South Bend, IN: University of Notre Dame Press, 1963), 64. This essay is a reprint of Tolkien's 1936 Israel Gollancz Memorial Lecture.

7. Ursula Le Guin, *The Farthest Shore* (1972; reprint, New York: Bantam, 1975), 169–70. Further references appear in the text.

8. Ursula Le Guin, "National Book Award Acceptance Speech," in Wood, *Language of the Night*, 57–58.

9. C. S. Lewis, "On Science Fiction," in *Of Other Worlds: Essays and Stories by C. S. Lewis*, ed. Walter Hooper (New York: Harcourt, Brace and World, 1967), 73; reprinted in *Science Fiction: A Collection of Critical Essays*, ed. Mark Rose (Englewood Cliffs, NJ: Prentice-Hall, 1976), 103–15.

Werewolves and Unicorns: Fabulous Beasts in Peter Beagle's Fiction

Jean Tobin

"Would you call this age a good one for unicorns?" asks the elder of two hunters riding through the first pages of Peter Beagle's *Last Unicorn*; "Times change," the other mutters. By the end of a brief conversation, the elder has made a judgment. Breaking out of the lilac wood, he shouts back over his shoulder as if he knows the listening unicorn can overhear: "Stay where you are, poor beast. This is no world for you."[1] Elders in fairy tales are wise, and the hunter may be right. This world—our world—*is* no world for unicorns. Indubitably, people believed in the existence of unicorns for a thousand years and more, but they do no longer. Belief in unicorns, in werewolves—indeed in a whole menagerie of mythical and legendary beasts—vanished over two hundred years ago with the coming of the Enlightenment. People on the streets of San Francisco and New York, Indianapolis, and Miami know about but do not believe in either werewolves or unicorns. How, then, in such an age, for such an audience, does any contemporary writer create a compelling novel or short story based on a myth? A good number of writers have done it, of course, but among them Peter Beagle is one of the very best. In *The Last Unicorn* (1968) and *Lila the Werewolf* (1974), Beagle manages to give his readers fresh, contemporary versions of both the unicorn myth and the werewolf legend while retaining all the traditional and satisfying familiar elements of each.

In *The Last Unicorn*, Beagle's fabulous beast both looks and acts like unicorns in the classical and Christian accounts. Marvelously, she meets physical criteria from both versions of the myth. As she first appears, looking nothing "like a horned horse, as unicorns are often pictured, being smaller and cloven-hoofed" (p. 1), she is one of the caprine unicorns reported in the *Physiologus*, or "The Bestiary," a collection of moralistic animal tales gathered in third-century Alexandria and popularized throughout Europe during the next thousand years. When perceived by unsuspecting villagers merely as a "white mare with strange eyes" (p. 97), however, Beagle's lovely last unicorn is equally one of the equine unicorns of earlier, classical accounts. The physician Ctesias first wrote of such creatures, on his return home to Greece in 398 B.C. after seventeen years in the Persian court, that "their bodies are white . . . and their eyes dark blue. . . . The animal is exceedingly swift and powerful."[2] The last unicorn has the mane given to her by Aelian, who wrote in the *Historia Animalium* that "this animal is as large as a full-grown horse, and it has a mane, tawny hair, feet like those of the elephant, and the tail of a goat."[3] Hunters in *The Last Unicorn* even repeat the elder Pliny's somewhat later description of the unicorn as having characteristics of horse, deer, elephant, and bear, with "a deep bellowing voice, and a single black horn" (p. 4). Only when she is frightened, however, does the last unicorn's seashell horn turn black, and then "even Molly Grue" is unable to prevent herself from recognizing the unicorn's absurdity "when the shining has gone out of her" (p. 118).

The last unicorn meets other traditional criteria as well. Her single horn has the curative powers first given it by Ctesias; she has memories of the unicorn hunts described in "The Bestiary." In this European and Christian account, the unicorn, symbolic of Christ, is vulnerable to capture only by chaste young maidens, symbolic of the Virgin Mary. In the past, Beagle's unicorn recalls, "I went to them all and laid my head in their laps" (p. 89), but now she allows herself to be touched only by Molly Grue, who though bedraggled is pure in heart, and whose name is the common form of Mary. There are other traces of the medieval unicorn hunt in *The Last Unicorn*, for one of the hunters retells a family story of how a unicorn came to his grandmother, who was generally afraid of large animals; and later in the fairy tale, recalling the virginity test long associated with the unicorn myth, an anxious princess intent on marriage and her indifferent prince are seen flourishing a golden bridle and calling unicorns. However, even though most unicorns, as symbols of Christ, are male and even symbols of male potency, the last unicorn is female. From the moment the unicorn appeared to him, according to Beagle, "she was female."[4]

Beagle's werewolf is similarly female, but female werewolves are more common.[5] In both novels considered here, Beagle shows the fabulous beast being transformed into a young girl, for in *The Last Unicorn* the unicorn becomes the Lady Amalthea, the beautiful, gentle, chaste maiden required by the legend. In *Lila the Werewolf*, however, the werewolf becomes Lila. As sexuality is often part of the werewolf legend, Beagle emphasizes this element by merging it with the Talmudic tradition of Lilith, a vampire-like nocturnal female demon.[6] In addition, in Beagle's long story, all the standard elements of the Central European werewolf legend are present, or at least mentioned: stakes in the heart, wolf bane, bags of garlic, "cold iron, silver, oak, running water," the drinking of blood and howling at the full moon.[7] In using all this ancient and traditional material, however, Beagle recreates his werewolf—and his unicorn—in narratives that are new and compelling for contemporary audiences.

In both *The Last Unicorn* and *Lila the Werewolf*, Beagle places his fabulous beasts in a recognizably modern landscape, and this in a world almost without wonder, where unicorns and werewolves are generally acknowledged not to exist. This paradox is most obvious in *Lila the Werewolf*, in which Beagle's werewolf, Lila, is a girl from the Bronx who began turning into a wolf monthly, under the full moon, with the onset of puberty, and who now lives in an apartment on Ninety-Eighth Street with an accommodating young man called Farrell. When Farrell first sees that Lila is a werewolf, three weeks after they have begun living together, he breathes in "the wild smell of the wolf" and finds it difficult to simultaneously accept the two realities: "That smell and the Miro prints on the walls" (p. 11). Even when Farrell later that morning goes up on the roof and discovers that the Russian wolfhound he has been dog-sitting is dead, bloodless, its throat torn out of its body, he has difficulty finding a place for real werewolves in his modern consciousness: "The coffeepot was still chuckling when he came back into the apartment, which struck him as very odd. You could have either werewolves or Pyrex nine-cup percolators in the world, but not both, surely" (p. 12). A major part of the reader's delight in *Lila the Werewolf* comes from precisely this juxtaposition of two realities, from seeing the entire, totally familiar Central European legend—even to the use of a silver bullet to kill a werewolf— newly worked out in the context of an equally familiar, and very realistic, modern American city. Throughout the story, Beagle insists upon juxtaposing the marvelous with mundane details and ordinary places: His characters converse sensibly about werewolves in the Automat; his werewolf is hunted down Columbus Avenue and Riverside Drive, through Central Park and near Lincoln Center; the Lithuanian—or Latvian—building superintendent who shoots at Lila with the silver bullet is fined by the New York police for possessing an unlicensed handgun. Werewolves, as we all know, do not exist in New York or in other large American cities; but in Beagle's *Lila the Werewolf*, at least one werewolf, Lila, most improbably but realistically does.

In *The Last Unicorn*, Beagle places his fabulous beast in a less realistic but no less modern setting. When Beagle sends his last unicorn off in quest for all the lost unicorns, he has her leave her lilac wood, where time has passed her by, and traverse the landscape of the modern world. The unicorn may travel through fairy-tale villages and towns, be detained a short while at Mommy Fortuna's Midnight Carnival, and wander through the Greenwood; but these realms of the imagination are now sadly diminished, and always her destination is Haggard's kingdom. When she—and companions Molly Grue and magician Schmendrick—reach Haggard's realm, they find a parched, barren, wintry land, where nothing grows and children are neither desired nor born. We as twentieth-century readers recognize the place, for we have been here often before. More than any other in the twentieth century, the landscape that has lingered in our minds is T. S. Eliot's image of spiritual sterility and physical desolation—the Waste Land. Later in the fairy tale, as if in confirmation of this thought, Haggard's successor is justly informed that his kingship is over a wasteland that has always had only one king: "fear" (p. 233). Indeed, the kingdom has been "wasteland in Haggard's time" (p. 239).

As the years of the twentieth century have worn on, and the mud and trenches of World War I have been supplanted by the cratered battlefields of World War II and eventually by the defoliated jungles of Vietnam, Eliot's image of a barren, unproductive land has lost none of its power. Countless writers have used the image since the publication of *The Waste Land* in 1922: The most memorable early use is probably F. Scott Fitzgerald's creation of the Valley of Ashes in *The Great Gatsby* (1925), but among later works dominated by the image—so argues Raymond Olderman in *Beyond the Wasteland* (1973)—are novels by writers as various as Ken Kesey, Stanley Elkin, John Barth, Joseph Heller, Thomas Pynchon, John Hawkes, and Kurt Vonnegut.[8] Indisputably, the Waste Land is a twentieth-century landscape. It is strange to see a unicorn in the Waste Land.

In publishing his long poem, it will be remembered, Eliot acknowledged his debt to James G. Frazer's *Golden Bough* (1890) and Jessie L. Weston's *From Ritual to Romance* (1920).[9] Both works have to do with myth. Frazer investigated vegetation myths and rituals celebrating the death and resurrection of primitive gods intimately related to the seasons. Weston applied Frazer's insights to trace the legend of the Holy Grail back to its source in those mystery religions originating in vegetation myths, and examined the medieval versions portraying an ailing and sexually impotent fisher king ruling over a cursed, barren land to be saved only by a questing knight. The Waste Land of the twentieth century, Eliot suggests, is similarly much in need of renewal, in part because myth and ritual have lost their power to lend wonder to our daily lives. Almost by definition, then, the presence of the Waste Land in Beagle's book suggests that in *The Last Unicorn* is a world where myth has lost its potency—where unicorns, for instance, are not generally acknowledged to exist. The narrative supports this surmise. As the younger hunter insists in the opening pages, "Unicorns are long gone . . . if, indeed, they ever were" (p. 3). The villagers and townspeople in Beagle's book are recognizably like ourselves. They see no unicorns in their world; they experience little wonder.

Thus, in *The Last Unicorn*, as in *Lila the Werewolf*, Beagle places his fabulous animals not only within recognizably modern landscapes, but also among characters to whom he has given modern consciousness. One expects contemporary attitudes from the realistic New Yorkers in *Lila the Werewolf*. When Farrell shouts his story of werewolves to his friend, Ben, above the clatter of the Automat, no one expects the New Yorkers to look up, because nothing can surprise New Yorkers; and besides, as Beagle accurately points out, "New Yorkers never eavesdrop. . . . [They] hear only what they simply cannot help hearing" (pp. 13–14). But it is startling while reading a fairy tale like *The Last Unicorn* to hear one character tell another in blunt disbelief that neither of them knows anything about unicorns: "for I've read the same books and heard the same stories, and I've never seen one either" (p. 3). Beagle's fairy-tale characters share our modern knowledge of the origins of myths and legends as well as our lack of wonder regarding their content—such as werewolves and unicorns.

Schmendrick talks to the unicorn herself about how "the whole silly myth got started" with the rhinoceros (p. 126). Captain Cully, who lives in the Greenwood with his band of unmerry men, lets Molly know that Robin Hood, as mere myth, demonstrates how "heroic folk-figures [are] synthesized out of need." In a brief lecture he explains that, since our need for heroes cannot be filled by men of ordinary size, "a legend grows around a grain of truth, like a pearl." (p. 76).

Like other characters in and readers of twentieth-century literature, the characters of *The Last Unicorn* find that their knowledge of myths, legends, and fairy tales forces them to acknowledge the present lack of heroes. As a nameless townsman grumbles about the loss of "old standards" and "values" (p. 97). Some may carry an honorable title—Magician, Prince, Witch—but they are self-consciously aware they do not fill the roles. Schmendrick tells the unicorn, describing how he entertains carnival-goers with "miniature magic, sleight of hand . . . accompanied by persuasive patter" (p. 24). Schmendrick humbly admits that he welcomes the appearance of Prince Lír because he has "been waiting for this tale to turn up a leading man" (p. 109). But Prince Lír is merely the fat fiancé who idly flipped through a magazine while his princess unsuccessfully sang for unicorns. Prince Lír may be tall, but being also flabby and lazy he is no hero. Molly Grue, who lives in the Greenwood with Captain Cully, greets Schmendrick in a caustic, curiously modern, self-deprecating way: "Dress and dirty hair tattered alike, bare feet bleeding and beslimed, she gave him a bat's grin. 'Surprise', she said. 'It's Maid Marian' " (p. 82). Even the witch, Mommy Fortuna, is disillusioned that her youthful dreams of evil have ended in "meager magic, sprung of stupidity" (p. 32).

Some of Beagle's characters are still blindly self-promoting, of course. Mistaking Schmendrick for the wandering Child collecting songs for his *English and Scottish Popular Ballads*, Cully reveals his hopes "to be collected, to be verified, annotated, to have variant versions, even to have one's authenticity doubted" (p. 71). Mistrusting the folk, Cully has written thirty-one ballads himself; he now urges his minstrel to practice for the day when he will be "field-recorded." Those characters in Beagle's *Last Unicorn* who have looked at themselves with clear eyes, however, are shamefaced at their unheroic stature. Only ordinary, they know they do not measure up to their dreams.

All of the characters need the last unicorn, and a very few recognize her. Schmendrick the magician and the witch, Mommy Fortuna, accustomed to enchantment, know her for what she is: "a rare creature," "myth," "memory" (p. 57). King Haggard knows, and in his greed would pen her up in an attempt to keep her elusive beauty forever. Molly, too, recognizes the unicorn, first scolding, then weeping that the unicorn has come "now, when I am *this*" (p. 83). Molly serves the unicorn, becoming her handmaiden. Almost no one else, however, truly sees the unicorn, who is bewildered that unicorns are not merely forgotten but not seen at all or seen as "something else" (p. 9). The last unicorn knows then that human beings and the world have changed "because the unicorns are gone."

In *Lila the Werewolf*, Beagle's New Yorkers, equally ordinary sorts, react variously to the mythical creature in their midst. Only one, the Lithuanian—or Latvian—building superintendent, recognizes her for a werewolf while she is in the guise of Lila. He drops the chair he is carrying, cowers, and makes the sign of the cross. Telling his friend, Ben, about the superintendent's terror, Farrell remarks, "I guess if you believe in werewolves and vampires, you probably recognize them right away. I don't believe in them at all, and I live with one" (p. 23). Apparently having little belief in myth, most of the dog owners who witness the werewolf slashing at their Pomeranians and Chihuahuas on West End Avenue just before dawn are less able to admit to themselves what they have seen. Adjusting a mythical experience to their modern expectations, most call Lila a "killer dog," although some insist she is a wolf. Beagle comments further: "As for the people who had actually seen the wolf turn into a young girl when the sunlight touched her, most of them managed not to have seen it, though they never really forgot. There were a few who knew quite well what they had seen, and never forgot it either, but they never said anything" (p. 43).

The people who know Lila well—Farrell; her mother, Bernice; her psychiatrist, Schechtman; and, at second hand, Ben—accept the fact that Lila is a werewolf as easily and with as much certainty as characters in any Lithuanian forest, but for their own contemporary reasons. Farrell, whose "gift was for acceptance," tells Ben he hates confrontations: "If I break up with her now, she'll think I'm doing it because she's a werewolf. It's awkward, it feels nasty and middle-class." Ben scolds Farrell—"You see why nobody has any respect for liberals anymore?"—but takes more than werewolves on faith for friendship's sake: "If there's such a thing as werewolves, the other stuff must be real too" (pp. 14–15). The psychiatrist, as variously reported, explains it in his own terms: "Lila's shrink says she has a rejection thing, very deep-seated," says Farrell (p. 15); "Dr. Schechtman says it's a sex thing," says Lila (p. 21); "[It is] Dad's fault" (p. 19), according to Lila's stereotypical Jewish mother, who worries about how and when her daughter will get married. Lila herself sees being a werewolf in terms of the monthly inconvenience: "I missed a lot of things. Like I never could go to the riding camp, and I still want to. And the senior play, when I was in high school . . . they changed the evening, and I had to say I was sick" (p. 20). Eventually, as Bernice spitefully reports to Farrell, Lila marries a Stanford research psychologist. In response to Farrell's hesitant question, Bernice crows: "Does he know? . . . He's proud of it—he thinks it's wonderful! It's his field!" (p. 44).

The effect of these modern New Yorkers' bland tolerance for werewolves is to neutralize the power of myth in their lives. They ignore, or accept, or explain, or investigate the phenomenon, but are unchanged by it. This is not to say that Beagle—or his narrator—is unaware of myth's power. Beagle even intensifies it, by adroitly combining the werewolf myth with elements of Talmudic traditions. As mentioned, his werewolf Lila is also Lilith, that nocturnal female vampire long associated with lustful sexuality in Jewish folklore. The smell of

Lila's lovemaking joins with the smell of the wolf as "wild, heavy zoo smells, warm and raw and fearful, the sweeter for being savage" (p. 16). Sexual disgust is strong in *Lila the Werewolf*, particularly when as a werewolf Lila goes into heat and runs in the streets of New York with a mangy pack of dogs. "The hell with it," even Farrell says then; "She wants to mess around, let her mess around" (p. 34). As werewolf and as Lilith, Beagle's Lila eventually turns on her dog lovers, for the blood.

Beagle allows his narrative to gain power from other myths. His building superintendent, for example, pursuing Lila through the city by underground passageways, "using the keys that only superintendents have to take elevators down to black sub-sub-basements" (p. 33), becomes momentarily a modern equivalent to Pluto, pursuing his Persephone. At that moment, the spirit of Demeter is briefly revealed in Lila's mother, for as Beagle describes her, with "her plum colored hair all loose, one arm lifted, and her orange mouth pursed in a bellow, she was no longer Bernice but a wronged fertility goddess getting set to blast the harvest" (p. 32).

But it is Beagle and his narrator who perceive such power. The usual reaction of the New Yorkers is to make the mythical and marvelous reassuringly mundane. Farrell's early response is characteristic:

The thing is, it's still only Lila, not Lon Chaney or somebody. Look, she goes to her psychiatrist three afternoons a week, and she's got her guitar lesson one night a week, and her pottery class one night, and she cooks eggplant maybe twice a week. She calls her mother every Friday night, and one night a month she turns into a wolf. You see what I'm getting at? It's still Lila, whatever she does, and I just can't get terribly shook about it. (p. 14)

In the end, Farrell is largely unchanged by living with a werewolf. She fit into a pattern in his life, after all: "It's the same good old mistake," he thought at the time, "except this time the girl's hangup is different" (p. 22). Four years later, he feels wistful about Lila, for he is living with a girl with a "really strange hangup" (p. 45). Thus, the characters of *Lila the Werewolf* attest to the continued presence of myth in our lives, but not to its power.

In contrast, by the end of *The Last Unicorn*, not only Beagle but also his major characters triumphantly assert the power of myth. However diminished that power may seem in our present age, it is real, as is the power of the imagination and love and beauty. One of Beagle's best images for the *seemingly* diminished power of myth occurs in Mommy Fortuna's Midnight Carnival. The witch—now akin to mere superstition rather than powerful good or bad fortune— has caged the epic creatures of Greek myths and Norse sagas. Gesturing toward the cages, Schmendrick tells the unicorn, "Look at your fellow legends and tell me what you see." She stares disbelievingly at a dog, an old ape with a twisted foot, a crocodile, and a lion beneath signs marked Cerberus, Satyr, Dragon, and Manticore. Then she sees in each cage a "second figure" produced by magic.

The lion was "tiny and absurd" compared to the manticore. "Yet they were the same creature." (p. 21). Fittingly, before the unicorn continues on her quest, the caged creatures of the imagination are freed.

Later in the journey, while the diminished and very ordinary characters of Beagle's Greenwood—Cully, Willie Gentle, shrill Molly Grue, and the unmerry men—look on, Schmendrick calls up the heroes of medieval ballad and legend in his first act of real magic; and Robin Hood, Alan-a-Dale, Maid Marian, Will Scarlet, and the others stride silently across the clearing at more than human size. Even as Cully denies that Robin Hood exists, Molly rebukes him, saying that the reverse is true; they themselves do not exist. "Robin and Marian are real, and we are the legend" (p. 76). Much later, it is Schmendrick who informs Molly that they are controlled by the plot of the fairy tale they are in, that it is the unicorn who is "real" (p. 109).

The power of the unicorn is such that even those who cannot see her truly are altered by her presence: "there were women who woke weeping from dreams of her" (p. 55). The mayor's men, sent to capture her, do not know why, later, "they laughed with wonder in the middle of very serious events, and so came to be considered frivolous sorts" (p. 62). As for the three who accompany the unicorn on her quest—inept Schmendrick, unlovely Molly, and flabby Lír—they believe and work, lose weight, and eventually grow in stature, until they become characters fit for a fairy tale: powerful Magician, fair Beloved, heroic Prince. The power of the unicorn, of beauty, when accompanied by the imagination and aided by love and by self-sacrifice, is great. Together, the four do battle with greed in the guise of King Haggard—who is real—and with fear—which is not, but seems so—in the guise of the terrifying Red Bull. Beagle allows them to triumph and, more affirmative than Eliot and more certain of the power of myth in our lives, lets all the found and freed unicorns sweep in a wave across the parched Waste Land, bringing green leaves and spring flowers to that scene of twentieth-century desolation.

The Last Unicorn is a young man's book. Even six years later, Beagle had something very different to say about myth in *Lila the Werewolf*. But in both book and long story, he succeeds in presenting ancient and fabulous beasts in fresh and significant ways for a twentieth-century audience.

NOTES

1. Peter S. Beagle, *The Last Unicorn* (New York: Ballantine, 1968), 4–5. Further references appear in the text.

2. In Odell Shepard, *The Lore of the Unicorn* (New York: Barnes and Noble, 1967), 27–28.

3. In Shepard, *Lore of the Unicorn*, 36.

4. Telephone conversation with Peter Beagle, 16 March 1978.

5. Brian Frost's collection of werewolf stories in *Book of the Werewolf* (London: Sphere, 1973), for example, includes stories of female werewolves by Sir Gilbert Campbell, Elliott O'Donnell, Manly Banister, Beverly Haaf, and Dale Donaldson.

6. See Louis Ginzberg, *The Legends of the Jews* (Philadelphia: Jewish Publication Society of America, 1925), vol. 1, pp. 65–66; vol. 5, pp. 87–88, 143–48.

7. Peter S. Beagle, *Lila the Werewolf* (Santa Barbara, CA: Capra Press, 1974), 15. Further references appear in the text.

8. Raymond Olderman, *Beyond the Waste Land: The American Novel in the Nineteen-Sixties* (New Haven: Yale University Press, 1973). Chapter 8 is about Beagle.

9. T. S. Eliot, *The Complete Poems and Plays 1909–1950* (New York: Harcourt, Brace, and World, 1952), 50.

THE FANTASTIC AND SEXUALITY

The fantastic enables startling reversals of sex roles, including basic functions of feeling, reproduction, and mortality. As sex "play" becomes serious social and political action, horrific or comic, the fantastic releases complex structures of desire.

Symbolic Sex-Role Reversals in the Grimms' Fairy Tales

D. L. Ashliman

Once upon a time there was a proud and haughty princess who refused to accept any of the suitors selected for her by her father. She was especially emphatic in her rejection of one of his choices, a king with a misshapen chin, whom she mockingly christened "King Thrushbeard." As fitting punishment for her obstinacy, her father gave her in marriage to a man in rags, whom he supposed to be a beggar, but who was actually King Thrushbeard in disguise. Her new husband heaped one indignity after another on the princess, until finally her self-will and independent spirit were broken. Only then did he reveal himself as King Thrushbeard, the suitor whom she previously had rejected with scorn, but whom she now only too happily accepted.

I lied. This story did not happen "once upon a time." Read it for yourself in the Grimm brothers' fairy tales. In spite of its inclusion in this collection, "King Thrushbeard" is not a magic story; it even lacks the traditional formula opening of fairy tales, "once upon a time." The narrator gives us no signals that this story happens in a fantasy world, a realm of a different time and place than ours. Nothing sets the tale apart from the everyday world of 1812 when it appeared in the Grimms' collection. Even then, fathers were giving their daughters in marriage to unattractive "King Thrushbeards," who in turn were transforming them into the household Kates they wanted. This was the norm.

However, there is a large group of fantasy tales, well represented in the Grimms' collection as well as other folklore sources, in which this norm is reversed; tales in which it is not the man who reforms his self-willed bride, but rather the woman who transforms her bridegroom—normally one selected for her by her father—into a person to her liking. I am referring to the long-lived and widespread cycle of animal bridegroom tales. These stories, contrary to the real-life context of "King Thrushbeard," are set in a remote world of fantasy and magic, a world whose logic is covered by a curtain of symbolic language.

Easily the most famous German fairy tale in which the transformation from beast to man takes place is "The Frog King," number one in the Grimms' collection, and a perennial favorite for folklore interpreters. But very few, in my opinion, have elucidated the most significant symbolic moment in the tale:

The princess was afraid of the cold frog; she did not dare to touch him, and yet he was supposed to lie next to her in her bed; she began to cry and did not want to at all. Then the king became angry and commanded her to do what she had promised. There was no helping it, she had to do what her father wanted, but in her heart she was bitterly angry. She picked up the frog with two fingers and carried him upstairs to her room, and climbed into bed, but instead of laying him next to herself, she threw him bam! against the wall. "Now you will leave me in peace, you ugly frog!" But the frog did not fall down dead, but rather when it came down onto the bed, it was a handsome young prince. And he was her dear companion, and she held him in high esteem as she had promised, and they fell asleep together with pleasure.[1]

Most interpretations of this passage appropriately dwell on the evolution of the young woman's attitude toward sex from one of repulsion to one of pleasure, but the significance of the timing of this important change is seldom mentioned. The frog's metamorphosis (and with it the princess's reward) comes at exactly the moment when she throws the frog against the wall, thus breaking the promise that she had made and openly refusing to obey her father. It is not her acceptance of traditional values, but rather her violent assertion of sexual independence, that brings her satisfaction. Unlike the bride of King Thrushbeard, this princess does not allow herself to be remade by her husband; the sex roles are reversed in this tale. She remakes him, transforming him literally from a repugnant creature into a handsome prince.

The Grimms' collection includes more than a dozen tales that belong to the animal bridegroom group, a significant number of which illustrate the effectiveness of a bride's rejection of her husband's beastly nature, often in a violent manner. Symbolically throwing one's animal bridegroom against the wall, or—as happens in other folktales—burning his beastly hide, whipping him to a bloody pulp, and cutting off his head, are fairly clear-cut expressions of the female storytellers' desire for a measure of power, authority, and independence in the marriage partnership. These advantages may have been denied them in real life, but in the fantastic world of the magic tale, nothing is impossible.

And I mean absolutely nothing. Of all the sex roles assigned to the female members of the human race, none are more pervasive than those directly related to the conception, bearing, and nursing of children. But in the fantastic world of the fairy tale, even here the roles can be reversed. A marvelous example of this particular symbolic sex-role reversal is offered by the Grimms' version of "Little Red Cap," better known in English as "Little Red Riding Hood" (no. 26).

In addition to its entertainment value, this famous tale also contains a fairly obvious warning to young women about the dangers inherent in encounters with members of the opposite sex. Every element in the story, as recorded by the brothers Grimm, contributes to this sex-education interpretation. Even the open-ing motif, the girl's gift of a red cap, easily can be seen as a symbol of her sexual maturation with its accompanying onset of menstruation. We are told that from the day she received the red cap she would wear no other, and that she looked so good in it that every one called her "Little Red Cap." Like many adolescents of both sexes, she revels in her newly achieved sexual maturity, even to the extent of flaunting it. Perhaps for this reason her mother gives her explicit instructions not to leave the established path en route to her grandmother's house, for if she does, she is warned, she may fall down and break the bottle that she is carrying—a symbol that scarcely needs elucidation. And the wolf's opening remark to her, when he meets her on the forest path, is even less dependent on interpretation. He straightforwardly asks what she has under her apron. Nor are the events that follow overly ambiguous. He starts the seduction by tempting her with flowers and music (wildflowers and bird song). And he ends the process in bed, with naive little Red Cap growing uneasy only as she discovers the unexpected size of his various body parts. But Red Cap discovers her danger too late, and the wolf devours her. Then, having satisfied his appetite, the wolf falls asleep.

If this were nothing more than a didactic story, it might well have ended on this tragic note as a warning to young women everywhere to be aware of wolves in bedclothing. But the Grimms' version does not mirror the real world with its injustice and undeserved suffering; instead, this fairy tale creates a fantasy world with its own miraculous system of justice. Red Cap is restored to life and health when a hunter happens on the scene and cuts the wolf open. The first stage of justice—restoring to the victim what she has lost—is thus quickly achieved; and the second stage—appropriate punishment—follows immediately. In real life, the consequence of premarital sex is often unwanted pregnancy—a consequence that almost always is more devastating to the female than to her male partner, and a consequence that often is borne by her alone. In Red Cap's world, however, there is a reversal of the accustomed order. There is no unwanted pregnancy for her; in fact, she fills the wolf's open belly with stones and then sews him shut. She impregnates him. The wolf, upon awakening and finding himself burdened with an unexpected and thoroughly unwanted "pregnancy," goes into convul-sions and dies. The fairy tale thus creates an order of justice that one can only dream about in the everyday world.

It is appropriate that the earliest recorded historical document concerning the Germans, an account written by Cornelius Tacitus some nineteen hundred years ago, contains clear statements about their moral values, especially those expected of their womenfolk. The Roman historian writes that for German women, "the loss of chastity meets with no indulgence: neither beauty, youth, nor wealth will procure the culprit a husband. No one in Germany laughs at vice."[2] Certainly the women did not laugh at it, for, as we learn from other sources, the punishment was swift, sure, and often cruel for a married woman who brought shame to her husband or for a single woman who disgraced her father's house by yielding to the forbidden pleasures of the flesh. Nor has this preoccupation with female chastity been limited to the pre-Christian Germanic tribes, as countless legal, historical, and literary documents from the succeeding centuries will testify. Nineteen hundred years of history and tradition have borne out Tacitus's observation about the Germans' concern for women's virtue.

This, of course, is not to suggest that Germany is unique among its European neighbors in this regard. Two obvious linguistic examples of our traditional concern for our women's sexual purity illustrate the point: My Duden dictionary of the German language unhesitatingly defines "ein gefallenes Mädchen" as an unmarried young woman who has engaged in sexual intercourse. There is no hint that the adjective "gefallen" could also be used to define a male who has had similar experience. English offers an extension of this example: According to my Webster's unabridged dictionary, the adjective "fallen" carries implications of femaleness, lost chastity, and degradation. As is the case with the German language, the English dictionary gives no indication that a man who has similarly "lost chastity" also would be labeled "fallen" by society.

Whatever reasons a society might have for granting its males freedoms that are forbidden to its females, these prohibitions and taboos are certainly a source of frustration and anxiety—actually to the whole of the society, but most specifically to those directly concerned, its women. Here, as in other areas, the household fairy tale—told primarily by women—provides a vehicle for the expression of forbidden desires. This vehicle, created and steered by female storytellers, carries teller and listener alike into a realm where women enjoy the same sexual freedoms that men have in the everyday world.

Of the several tales in the Grimms' collection that can be read as symbolic expressions of women's desire for more sexual freedom, none is more obvious than the tale of "The Worn-Out Dancing Shoes" (no. 133). This fantasy story tells of a king who had twelve daughters, each one more beautiful than the other. But their beauty was not complemented with good behavior. In spite of the fact that the king himself bolted their bedroom door each night, every morning, upon unlocking their chamber, he discovered that they had danced their shoes into holes. This nocturnal activity so alarmed the good king that he proclaimed that whoever should discover where and how the princesses were dancing their shoes to pieces would receive one of them in marriage and would become the next king.

To appreciate why the good king was so upset about the violation of his daughters' shoes, it is necessary to understand a symbolic convention in European folklore so deeply rooted and so widespread that most tellers and hearers of this story must have perceived, at one level of consciousness or another, that this was a story about an activity much more severely prohibited than dancing in the night. This convention is the very frequent use of the shoe in European folk customs and literature to symbolically represent the female genitalia. For many centuries the folklore of Europe has used the symbol of the shoe in an amazingly consistent manner.

If the shoe represents the vagina, then it is suddenly quite understandable why it is that the little old woman who lived in her shoe had so many children she did not know what to do. Another Mother Goose rhyme that takes on new meaning is the old favorite:

> Cock a doodle doo,
> My Dame has lost her Shoe;
> My Master's lost his Fiddle Stick
> And knows not what to do.
> . . . .
> Cock a doodle doo,
> My dame has found her shoe,
> And master's found his fiddling stick,
> Sing doodle doodle doo.[3]

The Germany of the Grimm brothers also offers numerous examples of the shoe symbolizing the vagina. A popular superstition still prevalent at the time of the Grimms dictated that after having given birth to a child, a mother was to be given a new pair of shoes. Local marriage customs in many areas called for the male friends of the groom to steal one of the bride's shoes during the wedding festivities, which had to be ransomed back by the bridegroom before he and his bride could retire for the night.[4] And the legal statutes of the city of Ulm formerly compelled a man who had had intercourse with an unmarried virgin to recompense her with a new pair of shoes.[5] German folk songs and tales also frequently use the shoe as a vaginal symbol. Perhaps the best example in this regard is the famous shoe test in the Cinderella tales, with the prince recognizing his true lover by the fit of her shoe.

In the tale of twelve daughters who danced their shoes into holes every night, in spite of the bolt on their bedroom door, a soldier, with the help of a magic cape, follows the sisters into a subterranean realm, where they have been spending their nights dancing with twelve enchanted princes. He makes his report to the king, who takes measures to halt his daughters' nocturnal excursions, and who honors his agreement. The soldier is named successor to the throne, and is given his choice of the king's daughters for a wife.

In the present context, it is important to note that the soldier chooses the oldest daughter, although it is perfectly clear that she had been the principal instigator of the prohibited nightly adventures. In real life she would have been labeled a "fallen woman," and would have been shunned by respectable suitors. But in the fantasy world of this fairy tale, no aspersions are cast on the woman who led her sisters to an underground realm of forbidden pleasures. She loses nothing. Unlike the fallen women of ancient Germany described by Tacitus, she is not denied a husband; on the contrary, she marries the man who will replace her father as king, and she herself will be the queen. There is a punishment to be paid for the violation of prohibitions, but in this fairy tale, as opposed to everyday life, the men involved—and not their female partners—are punished for the transgression. The princes with whom the twelve sisters had nightly danced were enchanted for as many additional days as the number of nights they had spent with the princesses. Males have long had the right to "sow their wild oats" without being stigmatized as having lost their honor. The traditional sex roles are reversed in the fantasy tale "The Worn-Out Dancing Shoes." Here the women are symbolically allowed premarital sexual adventures, and they pay nothing, whereas their male partners receive the entire punishment.

The longevity and widespread appeal of fairy tales such as those contained in the Grimm brothers' collection suggest that these deceptively simple stories address a number of basic human concerns. One of these concerns derived from the inequities surrounding traditional sex roles. If the tellers of these stories felt powerless to correct the sex discrimination in their own lives, then at least they could create a make-believe world where all such problems would find a fantastic solution.

NOTES

1. *Kinder- und Hausmärchen der Brüder Grimm: Vollständige Ausgabe in der Urfassung*, ed. Friedrich Panzer (Wiesbaden: Vollmer, n.d.), 65. All translations from German tales used in this essay are mine. Fairy tales from the Grimms' collection are referred to by the numbers that have been standard since the seventh edition of the *Kinder- und Hausmärchen* (1857).

2. "Germany and Its Tribes," paragraph 19, in *Complete Works of Tacitus*, trans. Alfred John Church and William Jackson Brodribb, ed. Moses Hadas (New York: Modern Library, 1942), 718.

3. William S. Baring-Gould and Ceil Baring-Gould, *The Annotated Mother Goose* (New York: New American Library, 1967), 56–57.

4. For documentation on the numerous folk customs involving shoes, see the listing for "Schuh," in *Handwörterbuch des Aberglaubens*, eds. Eduard Hoffmann-Krayer and Hanns Bächthold-Stäubli (Berlin: de Gruyter, 1927–1942), vol. 7, cols. 1292–1363.

5. Franz Carl Müller-Lyer, *The Family*, trans. F. W. Stella Browne (New York: Alfred A. Knopf, 1931), 235.

The Function of Eroticism and Fantasy in the Fiction of André Pieyre de Mandiargues

David J. Bond

André Pieyre de Mandiargues is a poet, novelist, essayist, and writer of short stories whose works have always received high praise from the critics. Although these works have never been widely read, especially outside France, professional critics and reviewers show great esteem for them. Their comments usually single out as the two most striking aspects of his writing his use of fantasy and his evident taste for the erotic. "In André Pieyre de Mandiargues's work, the fantastic never loses its power," says one critic. He has been called "Prince of the imaginary," the "great poet of oneiric prose," and "diviner of the unusual," and his work has been described as "a kingdom where the unusual reigns supreme." Others, focusing on the erotic content, claim that his writing is full of "a delicate and cruel eroticism" that it is "subtly erotic in its passion for troubling fragrances and baroque shapes," and that "love and eroticism give warmth to M. de Mandiargues's world."[1] My intention here is to show that these two apparently different strands of Mandiargues's work, the fantastic and the erotic, are interwoven in his fiction and that they have the same function.

It should be noted from the outset that Mandiargues readily admits to a fascination with the erotic. He has said, "I do not hide the fact that I am an *érotomane*,"[2] and, "In truth, I believe myself to be a sado-masochist."[3] Among the works on which he has written are Marquis de Sade's *Justine*, Pauline Réage's *Histoire d'O*, Pierre Louÿs's *Trois filles de leur mère*, and Guillaume Apollinaire's *Les onze mille verges*. He has translated Mishima's *Madame de Sade* into French and has himself written a sado-erotic novel called *L'Anglais décrit dans le château fermé* (originally published under a pseudonym). Nearly all his other fiction also has a strong erotic content.

One may attribute some of this interest in the erotic to a desire to shock, for Mandiargues argues that art should "create disorder and disturb the senses" (*Le Belvédère*, p. 207). He certainly tries to achieve this in his own work, and the preface to one volume of his short stories warns the reader: "The essence of these adventures is to shock the observer or the listener. He is shocked in his most honorable feelings, in his beloved culture, in his modesty and in his tastes" (*Porte dévergondée*, p. 13). These remarks should not be taken, however, as an apology for art that titillates through mere smuttiness. Mandiargues has said, "Everything that has been called 'dirty jokes' or (wrongly in all likelihood) 'Gallic humor' is as irksome in eroticism as the midday sun to an owl" (*Le Cadran lunaire*, p. 204).

Mandiargues approaches the erotic seriously and with sincerity of purpose. He wants to shock his readers into *thinking*, into considering carefully the role of sexuality in our lives. Mandiargues's interest in human sexuality is part of a wider interest in human nature and human emotions in general. He is, in other words, in a long and time-honored French tradition that goes back at least as far as the seventeenth century: the tradition of the *moralistes* who studied the workings of the human heart and mind. He views much of the erotic writing of others as being a study of human nature, and he quotes with approval those critics who describe Sade as a *moraliste*. He adds, "I believe that I am both an erotic writer and a *moraliste*."[4]

The particular aspect of human psychology that Mandiargues most frequently links to the erotic is humankind's eternal desire to escape the limits of the self, to loosen the bonds imposed on the individual by personal identity. He believes that all human beings have felt the need, at some time during their lives, to escape the bounds of their being and to become other than they have always been. This desire is expressed by one of his characters who, gazing up at the night sky, is filled with "that old pagan sadness that wrings a groan from those whose destiny it is to be unique among all the species in the world" (*Le Musée noir*, p. 128). Elsewhere, he writes eloquently of this age-old longing: "There are hours in our life . . . when there can be felt the imperious need to break out of ourselves, when we are finally ashamed of the personality in which birth has deposited us and habit imprisoned us, of the species to which we belong . . . moments when we are assailed by the tedium of a sexual identity that is always despairingly the same, of the unchanging drama and comedy that it has got us into since our adolescence" (*Les Masques de Léonor Fini*, preface).

Sexual activity seems to provide this longed-for release from the self in several ways. First of all, it affects the individual's perception of time. One of the most obvious restraints on the freedom of the self is temporal flow, but eroticism seems to loosen the grip of time on us by halting it. Lovers, for example, seek to make pleasure last, to string together a "multitude of splendid, exquisite moments, without past or future" (*Le Belvédère*, p. 84). For lovers, the present alone exists, and the writer who would convey the pleasure of lovers must depict a series of present moments. As one of Mandiargues's characters observes, sexual pleasure is "the illusion of the continuity of the present" (*Mascarets*, p. 60). This sense of continuity is why, Mandiargues writes in *Le Belvédère*, Pierre Louÿs's *Trois filles de leur mère* and many of Sade's works consist of a sequence of similar erotic scenes all set in the present, all repeating the pleasure of the moment. Although he does not mention it, his own work *L'Anglais décrit dans le château fermé* is another excellent example of such repeated scenes of erotic abandon that seem to exist in a timeless present.

Even in his less openly erotic works, Mandiargues still depicts eroticism as a force that suspends time. The hero of the novel *La Marge*, while on a business trip to Barcelona, learns that his wife and child have died. He pushes this knowledge from his mind and spends three days in the prostitutes' quarter. The erotic dreams with which he fills his mind, and the prostitute whom he hires, help to create a period set "en marge," removed from the normal flow of time. In other stories, certain scenes take place in timeless moments. "La Marée" tells how a young man has oral sex with a girl on an isolated part of a beach. First, however, he removes his watch and ensures that the incoming tide has cut them off from the outside world. The moment of sexual climax comes at the precise time of high tide, that is to say at a moment suspended between two essential movements of time, balanced between two parts of the day. In *La Motocyclette*, Rébecca's lover removes his watch before making love to her, telling her that "when coming to meet him . . . she had placed herself outside of the time of her usual life" (p. 198). Vanina, the heroine of *Le Lis de mer*, leaves her watch behind when she goes to meet her lover because "it was not permissible to keep the free use of time and the power to measure it on a dial fixed to her wrist" (p. 126). In the short story "La Grotte," the main character tells the prostitute whom he has hired, when she asks him the time, "there is no time where we are" (*Porte dévergondée*, p. 77).

Other means have also been used by man in an attempt to escape his identity. Mandiargues writes that drugs, masks, and games have all been made to serve this purpose, and they prove that "men have no sooner taken on bodily form than they have felt the need to escape from it" (*Le Cadran lunaire*, p. 137). But eroticism has always had a privileged role to play in this attempt. "The amazing attraction of eroticism," he writes, "is that it finally leads to loss of the personality" (p. 201). He argues that it "makes you slip, to your delight, through the narrow gap into another world where you are no longer yourself" (p. 202). One might mention, as an example of this loss of self through eroticism in Mandiargues's own work, the scene in "Le Pain rouge" where several men with bees swarming all over them are experiencing such a keen erotic pleasure that it "could be compared only to a saint's in the midst of the most convulsive ecstasy" (*Soleil des loups*, p. 130). Another character, in the act of sex, achieves "a kind of nothingness or emptiness" that makes him lose all sense of his individual being (*Porte dévergondée*, p. 87). Jean de Juni in "L'Enfantillage" uses a prostitute to reach a state in which "his spirit tended towards a kind of zero" (*Feu de braise*, p. 199).

Frequently Mandiargues's characters use sex to escape not so much into nothingness as into the world around them. They become part of the natural world, losing their personal identity in it. When Vanina is possessed by her lover in a forest, her consciousness seems to expand to encompass all around her, and she communes with the night sky, the moon, and the flowers growing nearby. Her hair mingles with the soil, and her breasts seem to draw force from the moonlight, until she feels "a sort of essential analogy or relationship between them and these heady flowers and the moon" (*Le Lis de mer*, p. 140). At this point, "she felt, at last, as she had so often desired, that she was 'communicating with the whole of nature' " (p. 142). Rébecca in *La Motocyclette* has similar experiences. When her lover first came to her, "she committed her body and her consciousness to violence and to the night, as, in other seasons, she had committed them to the sun and the clear water" (p. 98). On another occasion, as she made love in a woods, the surrounding world seemed to absorb her, and she was "so scattered in it all that she was no longer at all certain of existing as a distinct person" (p. 151).

In "Le Sang de l'agneau," it is with the animal world that the heroine achieves contact. Marceline Caïn is abducted by a Negro butcher and taken to his hut, where she is so overcome by the odor of the sheep in it that she is "transformed into an animal among all the other snorting, bleating, munching animals . . . all around her" (*Le Musée noir*, p. 66). When the butcher rapes her, she has become so much a part of the animal world that the only sound she can produce is a kind of bleating. One more particularly striking instance of this kind of communion with nature may be found in "La Marée." As the male character forces the girl to have oral sex with him on the seashore, the incoming tide becomes a symbol of the life forces in the world, and it is with them that the man achieves contact. He says "Never had I succeeded in finding myself in such firm and intimate communication with nature; I felt flowing within me the great vital current that streams among the planets and which goes perhaps as far as the most distant stars; I was participating in some way in the breathing of the universe" (*Mascarets*, p. 25). He seems, at this point, to escape from his bodily form to become part of creation itself.

Mandiargues refers to moments such as these as instances of "panic" communion, since they convey communication with some force deep in nature, and, in classical mythology, the god Pan was associated with these natural forces. It is as though, at such times, the life forces in his characters, which manifest themselves in sexual urges, are linked directly to the "panic" in nature. Mandiargues writes in several places of "panic" inspiration in literature, which he defines as "the use of the dark forces of nature and the deep energy of the unconscious, awareness of animality, complicity with the growth of vegetable matter, and even with the nervous energy of the mineral world" (*Bona l'amour et la peinture*, p. 38).

There are, in this escape through the erotic, obvious overtones of mysticism, for the mystic too seeks to escape himself.[5] The similarity between mystical union with the deity and sexual ecstasy has been pointed out too frequently to need dwelling on here. As for Mandiargues himself, although he denies being a "man of faith" (*Le Désordre de la mémoire*, p. 141), he shows a certain taste for art with a mystico-religious dimension. He praises the work of the Mexican artist Toledo as "a mystic endeavour" (*Troisième Belvédère*, p. 93), the Dada movement as "the last mystic current to which the Western world was able to give birth" (p. 97), and the Surrealists for saying that the artist must turn "toward the teaching of the occultists, the alchemists, and certain mystics and illuminati" (*Le Belvédère*, p. 65). One should not, however, overemphasize his "mystic" tastes. What he depicts in his fiction is not the usual Christian mystic's attempt to escape this world and achieve union with a transcendent deity. Mandiargues's characters seek release from themselves in order to be at one with the world.

The final escape from the self comes, of course, with death. Because it seems to halt the flow of time, and because it is an affirmation of the life forces, Mandiargues often depicts the erotic as an antidote to death. He says it is "the exaltation of the sexes through antagonism to death and in association with the life instinct" (*Troisième Belvédère*, p. 202), and he cites Bataille's opinion that it is "the approval of life unto death" (p. 321). His novel *La Marge* illustrates this point admirably, for the hero's awareness of his wife's death is kept at bay for several days as he engages in erotic activities and daydreams in the prostitutes' quarter. At one point, he buys a bottle of liqueur shaped like the Columbus Monument in Barcelona. This obviously phallic object is placed beside his bed, on top of the letter containing news of his wife's death, thus acting as a kind of seal. Only when he removes the bottle and reads the letter does he fully accept his wife's death and the inevitability of his own suicide.

But Mandiargues is also aware that eroticism and death are inextricably bound together in the human consciousness, that they have obvious similarities. He says that this is "a notion buried in the darkest unconscious, and it is one of the most generous sources of inspiration to which poets, narrators, and artists can have recourse" (*Le Désordre de la mémoire*, p. 181). In his own fiction, the link between eroticism and death is established by a variety of allusions and comparisons. Sigismond compares women's sexual organs to "an open tomb" (*La Marge*, p. 97); the hotel where another character takes a prostitute is called "Sarcophage Hotel" (*Porte dévergondée*, p. 73); Rébecca, when she sees the spilled blood of her virginity on the bed sheet, thinks of it as being "as black as on a hundreds-of-years-old shroud" (*La Motocyclette*, p. 102). Certain incidents in other works continue the analogy. In "Armoire de lune," a couple make love on a tomb that opens and swallows them; in "Le Nu parmi les cercueils," a man has a vision of a voluptuous naked woman surrounded by coffins, who tells him that undertakers' premises are often found in the prostitutes' quarter because "it is well known that nothing inspires man with the desire for prostitutes as much as imagining his death or that of his acquaintants" (*Feu de braise*, p. 122). The hero of *Marbre* witnesses a strange ceremony in which a dying woman is exposed to the eyes of the male population of the town. Her body is shaken by spasms resembling sexual ecstasy, and she seems to be embracing an invisible partner, while all the men watch with bated breath. When she finally dies, they experience a "curious release of tension" (p. 181). In *La Motocyclette*, Rébecca dies in a traffic accident, and her mind is full of thoughts of her lover as "thousands of blades plunge into her and it seems that they make one single wound through which her lover spreads inside her" (p. 212).

This consistent linking of eroticism and death underlines the idea that the erotic is escape from the restraints of life, a means of dying to oneself and breaking the bounds within which one is normally confined. When Rébecca experiences sexual ecstasy, she is given a foretaste of the freedom that she will eventually encounter in death. In this case, as in nearly all the others in Mandiargues's work, the erotic is witness to a longing to escape the limits that are part of life.

Mandiargues makes many statements about the erotic. Although he admits the importance of fantasy in his work, and has said "my taste tends towards the sudden appearance of the fantastic" (*Troisième Belvédère*, p. 106), he says little about why he uses fantasy. However, certain comments on the role of fantasy in literature, made by the critic Marcel Schneider, are useful for filling these gaps left by Mandiargues. For Schneider, fantasy is a search for something beyond this life, for a dimension where we are liberated from the constraints of society, of official doctrines, of ideologies, and of life itself. "The fantastic," he writes, "is a continuous, irrepressible protest against what is, against the created world and the life one leads in it. . . . Thanks to it, we may give free rein to our most avid desires, our most tenacious hopes, and give shape to our hope."[6] This is, of course, precisely how Mandiargues sees the erotic. An examination of certain elements of his fantasy reveals that it is also how he sees and uses the fantastic.

Erotic incidents in Mandiargues's work are attempts to escape time, but his fantasy fiction as a whole represents a denial of time. *La Motocyclette* recounts a journey extending over a definite period of hours, but within this framework the heroine's mind ranges over the present, the immediate past, the distant past, and anticipation of the future. As in a *nouveau roman*, the reader is placed inside the character's mind and shares her perception of time, living her memories and her imagined future with her. While this activity goes on, the reader has only the vaguest notion of time in the outside world, for Rébecca has left her watch behind when embarking on the journey. "Le passage Pommeraye" is a short story set in a mysterious covered side street that constitutes a world set apart from the rest of the city. The silence and stillness of the place, the dusty and deserted shops, the strange glaucous light all suggest a world outside of time, and the reader shares the narrator's feelings when he says, "I no longer had any notion of the time elapsed since I had entered the passage Pommeraye" (*Le Musée noir*, p. 101). In "Le Diamant," the heroine takes off her watch before examining a diamond. She seems to fall inside the precious stone, and finds herself in a timeless world where she can gauge the passing hours only approximately by the approaching rays of the sun.

Certain other stories attempt to destroy the very idea of time. "Le Marronnier" consists of a discussion of whether it is possible to disappear completely from time. The characters have removed their watches, and the discussion takes place at an indeterminate time of day, somewhere between the end of daylight and nightfall. The hero of "Le Triangle ambigu" meets a woman whom he persuades to come home with him. At the last moment, she changes her mind, realizing that she has seen him in a recurring dream. In her dream she kills him, and she is afraid that this act may come true. A dream experienced in the past thus intrudes into the present and destroys an anticipated future. Marie Mors, the heroine of "L'Etudiante," is able to see future events taking place in the window of a nearby building. Since she herself figures in these scenes, she is able to live in the future in the present merely by watching them.

In some of the most fanciful tales, it is not even clear whether events have taken place, whether they even have a place in time. "Les Formes charnelles" is the story of a man who seems to be watching a striptease show while his mind dwells on a murder that he has just committed. Or perhaps he is being questioned by the police about the murder, and he is imagining the striptease in order to evade the questions. In any case, we cannot be sure what has happened, or when. At the end of *Marbre*, a similar state of doubt is created when Mandiargues invites the reader to invent his own conclusion to the novel. The hero's future, in other words, varies with the individual reader.

Many of Mandiargues's stories are based on dreams or contain dream sequences. The strange street in "Le passage Pommeraye," the scenes that Marie Mors witnesses in the window, and Sigismond's wanderings in Barcelona all have a dreamlike quality. Other works depict dream affecting reality: The heroine of "Le Songe et le métro" goes to a métro station that she sees in a dream, hoping to make the dream come true. Clearly, dream is a basic element of Mandiargues's fantasy, and, like eroticism, it too denies time. As we all realize, the normal flow of time as we know it in the waking world has no place in dreams, where time follows a different logic. Indeed, dreams are a manifestation of the unconscious, which, in the words of Thomas Mann, "knows no time, no temporal flow, nor any effect of time upon its psychic process."[7]

Mandiargues himself acknowledges the importance of dream in his work: "But I believe that my work in its entirety is a kind of great dream or vast rêverie" (*Le Désordre de la mémoire*, p. 187). He also recognizes that dreams may have the same liberating effect as the erotic, and he has written that "Eros is probably the only guide capable of . . . giving us a little of that absurd happiness that we have sometimes felt in dreams" (*Le Cadran lunaire*, p. 202). In other words, this basic element of his fantasy is yet another means of escape from limits on the self. Mandiargues has even admitted that he has always tried to view life as a dream because that seems "the best way of making it bearable" (*Le Désordre de la mémoire*, p. 188).

Another technique of his fantasy, closely allied to the use of dreams, is a sudden change of environment. Characters sometimes find themselves plunged into a world of strange and new experiences. Sarah Mose in "Le Diamant" finds herself inside a diamond; Conrad Mur in "L'Archéologue" is transported to the sea bed; the main character in "Le Pain rouge" enters a crust of bread;

the hero of *Marbre* goes inside a hollow statue. In all these instances, individuals elude the confines of reality as it normally encompasses them, break out, as it were, from their usual state of being.

Sometimes the characters themselves change shape or size. Sarah Mose shrinks in size before entering the diamond, as does the hero of "Le Pain rouge" before he enters the bread. In "L'Homme du parc Monceau," there is a man who can assume any shape at will, who can roll his body into a hoop or flatten it to pass under a gate. That these changes are manifestations of a deep-seated human longing is conveyed in a tale called "Clorinde." Here a man discovers a tiny, perfectly formed woman, and is at once seized with a desire to shrink to her size in order to possess her sexually. His longing, described as "a powerless rage" and a "frenzy" (*Soleil des loups*, p. 104), is explicitly linked to eroticism, for, like eroticism, his desire to change size is a sign of a basic human wish to be different.

Mandiargues's fantasy is also tied to death, and many of his works end in death: Sigismond kills himself when he fully realizes that his wife and child are dead; Rébecca dies in a traffic accident; the lovers in "Armoire de lune" are swallowed by a tomb; Captain Idalium in "L'Opéra des Falaises" meets death after following a girl in the expectation of sexual adventure. Like moments of erotic "panic" communion with nature, these deaths, too, represent escape from the self and absorption in the world. Rébecca's motorcycle crashes into the back of a truck bearing a grinning face of Bacchus—the trademark of the beer it is carrying. But Bacchus, or Dionysus, also represents the secret forces of nature, the "panic" element in the world. When Rébecca is swallowed, as it were, by this face, her last thoughts are, "The universe is dionysiac" (*La Motocyclette*, p. 212). She is absorbed at this point by the forces of nature itself, becoming at one with the world. Captain Idalium's death is somewhat similar, since it occurs in a cave deep in the earth. Conrad Mur's body falls into a stream, where he, too, is absorbed by nature.

In all these instances of Mandiargues's fantasy, we witness the same will to escape the prison of selfhood as in his erotic scenes. The fantastic and the erotic are interwoven in his fiction precisely because they serve this same purpose. By filling his fiction with fantasy and eroticism, he tells us something about human nature, about a longing that possesses all men at some time, and he demonstrates that both may be used in literature to convey a serious message and a subtle psychological truth.

NOTES

1. Quotations taken respectively from André Gascht, "André Pieyre de Mandiargues: un réaliste de l'imaginaire," *Biblio* 34 (November 1966): 8; Gascht, "André Pieyre de Mandiargues," 1; Marc Alyn, "André Pieyre de Mandiargues: *L'Age de craie*," *La Table Ronde* 172 (May 1962): 119; Alain Clerval, "André Pieyre de Mandiargues: Un érotique baroque," *NRF* 224 (August 1971): 77; Robert Kanters, "Mandiargues et la

mort en suspens," *Le Figaro Littéraire* (June 5–11, 1967): 19; Marcel Schneider, *La Littérature fantastique en France* (Paris: Fayard, 1964), 369; Mark J. Temmer, "André Pieyre de Mandiargues," *Yale French Studies* 31 (1966): 102; Robert Kanters, "Parmi les livres: André Pieyre de Mandiargues," *La Revue de Paris* (January 1968): 116. Translations of these and all subsequent quotations from the French are mine.

2. Isaure de Saint-Pierre, "Les Mandiargues," *Elle* 1729 (August 6, 1978): 51.

3. André Pieyre de Mandiargues, *Le Désordre de la mémoire* (Paris: Gallimard, 1975), 249. I have also quoted from the following works by Mandiargues, and page references are inserted after quotations in the text: *Le Musée noir* (Paris: Laffont, 1946); *Soleil des loups* (Paris: Laffont, 1951); *Marbre* (Paris: Laffont, 1953); *Le Lis de mer* (Paris: Laffont, 1956); *Le Belvédère* (Paris: Grasset, 1958); *Le Cadran lunaire* (Paris: Laffont, 1958); *Feu de braise* (Paris: Grasset, 1959); *La Motocyclette* (Paris: Gallimard, 1973); *Porte dévergondée* (Paris: Gallimard, 1965); *La Marge* (Paris: Gallimard, 1967); *Bona l'amour et la peinture* (Geneva: Skira, 1971); *Troisième Belvédère* (Paris: Gallimard, 1971); *Mascarets* (Paris: Gallimard, 1971); *Les Masques de Léonor Fini* (Paris: La Parade, 1951).

4. Saint-Pierre, "Les Mandiargues," 53.

5. For an examination of Mandiargues's work as a mystic endeavor, see my article "Mystic and Erotic Experience in the Fiction of André Pieyre de Mandiargues," *Kentucky Romance Quarterly* 27 (1980): 205–13.

6. Schneider, *La Littérature fantastique*, 30–31.

7. Thomas Mann, "Freud and the Future," *Essays of Three Decades*, trans. H. T. Lowe-Porter (New York: Alfred A. Knopf, 1947), 416.

"Death-Cunt-and-Prick Songs," Robert Coover, Prop.

Ann R. Morris

To judge by Robert Coover's two best books, it is not baseball but sexual fantasy that is the great American game. In *The Universal Baseball Association, Inc., J. Henry Waugh, Prop.* and *Pricksongs and Descants*, Coover shows the sexual fantasizing of his characters, young and old, rich and poor, male and female. Almost always juxtaposed with this sexual fantasizing is an awareness of human mortality, the possibility of death behind any door we enter. An examination of these themes in the two books will reveal some reasons for their juxtaposition in Coover's work.

Robert Scholes in *Fabulation and Metafiction* has spoken of Coover as one of the writers he calls "fabulators," a group that "tends away from direct representation of the surface of reality but returns toward actual human life by way of ethically controlled fantasy."[1] Certainly *The Universal Baseball Association* moves away from reality. In that novel Coover creates a middle-aged bachelor accountant named J. Henry Waugh who devises a game modeled on baseball and played with dice and charts. As the novel progresses, the game becomes for Henry such an obsession that although he as fabulator has disappeared by the end of the book, the game goes on with players he has created in his fantasy now having made the game into a religious ritual. Along the way Henry has imagined his players' sexual fantasies, even making up a song about a well-endowed pitcher named Long Lew and his first time with the coy Fanny.[2] Henry himself has a celebratory romp after the perfect game. In this romp he imagines that he is the young pitching star–Christ figure, Damon Rutherford, and that his partner, the aging, baggy B-girl, Hettie, is player Sycamore Flynn's beautiful virgin daughter. Henry and Hettie kid about "scoring" and "getting a hit," as she holds his "bat" and play begins:

"Damon," she greeted, grabbing—and that girl, with one swing, he knew then, could bang a pitch clean out of the park. "Play ball!" cried the umpire. . . . And Damon whipped the uniform off the first lady ball-player in Association history, and then, helping and hindering all at once, pushing and pulling, they ran the bases, pounded into the first, slid into second heels high, somersaulted over third, shot home standing up, then into the box once more, swing away, and run them all again, and "Damon!" she cried, and "Damon!" (p. 29)

Hettie enjoys Henry's game so much, in fact, that she later invents "her own magic version, stretching out as the field, left hand as first base" (p. 206).

Coover's tone in such sexual fantasies is playful, but he keeps reminding us that death and chaos lurk in the dugout. Both Damon Rutherford and Jock Casey, the two most promising young players, die in accidents, and the other players know that age eventually "got them all" (p. 167). Coover shows us, however, that sex is one way to combat death. When Henry tells Hettie about the players' deaths, she squeezes his bat harder "as though afraid now to let go" (p. 28). After Damon's funeral his brother Brock raced for home, "dragging his missus behind him, and there, pressed by an inexplicable urgency, had heisted her black skirts, and without even taking time to drop his pants, had shot her full of seed: yes, caught it! she said, and even he felt that germ hit home" (p. 93). After the funeral Henry and Hettie also find consolation in sex: "Earthy. Crude, in fact . . . . In and out, high and low, just rear back and burn it in" (p. 170). Again and again, as in these examples, sex is described in ballpark lingo, reminding us that baseball itself has been traced to ancient fertility rites in which a ball was used in springtime ceremonies to represent either the sun or the head of Osiris, both symbols of growth and fertility.[3] Thus, Coover shows that sex, linked through baseball with religion, is part of existential man's answer to meaninglessness and death.

In the twenty short fictions in *Pricksongs and Descants*, Coover again shows us the relationship between sexual fantasy and death and the pervasiveness of both in man's life. In his prologue for this book, Coover dedicates himself to "the use of the fabulous to probe beyond the phenomenological, beyond appearances . . . beyond mere history."[4] Because he sees sexual fantasy and death as universal ways of probing, he has suggestively called the tales "pricksongs" and "descants" or, as Granny calls them in the opening story, "death-cunt-and-prick songs." Coover himself has explained the musical terms used in his title: " 'Pricksong' derives from the physical manner in which the song was printed— the notes were literally pricked out; 'descant' refers to the form of music in which there is a *cantus firmus*, a basic line, and variations that the other voices play against it."[5] The musical terms thus suggested to him the pattern of his stories, variations on a basic narrative line or on some story already so familiar to his readers that it is in effect dead. Still discussing the title, he adds, "Of course, there is also the obvious sexual suggestion. In this connection, I thought of the descants as feminine decoration around the pricking of the basic line. Thus, the masculine thrust of narrative and the lyrical play around it" (p. 151). The sexual connotations of the title are then supported by the epigraph from

Fanny Hill: "He thrusts, she heaves." Thus, in a number of ways, Coover forewarns the reader that his tales are variations on the themes of sex and death. The variations range from retellings of fairy tales ("The Magic Poker," "The Door," "The Gingerbread House") to the television-oriented masterpiece "The Babysitter." The protagonists include modern man, as in "The Elevator" and "A Pedestrian Accident," and biblical characters as in "The Brother" (a retelling of Noah and the Ark from the viewpoint of Noah's drowning brother).

The first story, "The Door: A Prologue of Sorts," serves as an introduction or door to the entire collection. This tale is an amalgamative interpretation of three familiar stories—"Jack and the Beanstalk," "Beauty and the Beast," and "Little Red Riding Hood." In Coover's story, Little Red Riding Hood is, in traditional fashion, on her way to Granny's house, but there the conformity to tradition ends. The tale is told first from the viewpoint of Little Red's father, Jack, who long ago climbed the beanstalk, and her granny, formerly the Beauty who married the Beast. Both Jack and Granny have been disillusioned by life and they are worried now about Little Red who, they realize, is approaching the door to sexual awareness. As she waits for Red Riding Hood to come with her basket of goodies (pun obviously intended), Granny imagines the child wandering through the woods and guesses why she is late:

I know who's got her giddy ear with his old death-cunt-and-prick songs . . . composing his polyphonies outa dread and appetite . . . a new fuzz on her pubes and juice in the little bubbies . . . her skirts up around her ears well let her . . . trip on her dropped drawers a few times and see if she don't come running back to old Granny. (p. 17)

Granny reminds us that she knows all about the Beast, for she was the Beauty who married him. However, her Beast never became a Prince; although she was "split with the pain of his thick quick cock" and then watched her beauty slowly decline as the end of her life approached, she still had "no Prince."

Little Red's arrival at the door is seen through her own eyes and is redolent with Freudian imagery. As she pauses before the open door, the sun "jerk[s] westward," and Little Red realizes that once she enters the door to this comedy she will never return. Assailed by fantasies of "fierce sinuous images" that will "devour her childhood," she nevertheless smiles faintly at the "big production" that awaits her. Knowing that the experience will offer "towers and closets . . . and more doors," she drops her red cloak and firmly puts the latch (p. 19). The westward-moving sun suggests that Little Red Riding Hood will end like Granny, old and disillusioned, but that while life lasts she can enjoy what Coover calls "the elaborate game, embellished with masks and poetry" (p. 18).

Closely aligned to "The Door," "The Gingerbread House" is a retelling of the story of Hansel and Gretel who, like Little Red, are being initiated into the world of sexual knowledge. The gingerbread house is described in obviously erotic terms. Hansel breaks off the peppermint stick chimney, then tumbles into a rainbarrel of pudding. Gretel, trying to help him, also slips and falls. Then, with obviously erotic pleasure, they "lick each other clean," and she admires "the red-and-white striped chimney" the boy holds up for her (p. 75). As they had followed their father through the forest on the way to the house, the children had found a dove that Gretel nestled suggestively between her legs. The little bird was dead because the witch had extracted its heart, which she uses as a sexual lure to seduce first the father and then the boy Hansel. The dove's red, burnished heart continues to pulse "gently, evenly, excitingly." Similarly, the door of the gingerbread house is shaped like a heart and is red as a cherry, "always half-open, sweeter than a sugarplum, more enchanting than a peppermint stick" (p. 72). A good fairy with "ruby-tipped breasts," "dimpled knees," and "glowing buttocks" hovers nearby, but also hovering near is the old witch, who in her black rags seems to symbolize death (p. 74). The children see the door "pulsing softly, radiantly," but beyond it they hear "black rags flapping" (p. 75). Obviously, the initiation into sex is also an initiation into the terror of death.

Thus, these reworkings of fairy tales probe into the human concerns behind them. Robert Scholes has remarked that Coover

senses an order beyond fiction and beyond phenomena, which may be discovered. . . . The "flux and tedium" of phenomenal existence is not reality but the thing which hides it. For Coover, reality is mythical, and the myths are doors of perception. . . . Magic is real. The fairy tales are true. Beast and princess are not phony symbols but fictional ideas of human essences.[6]

In short, Coover shows us that behind the fairy tales we learned as children lurk the realities of sex and death. Thus, while he is flaunting traditional narrative conventions and insisting on the multiple possibilities of fiction, he is also demonstrating the unchanging human fascination with our sexual being and our eventual demise.

This insistence on multiple narrative possibilities and fascination with sex and death is as evident in the other stories in *Pricksongs and Descants* as it is in the fairy tales. Consider, for example, "The Elevator," a story that plays variations on a number of fantasies associated with the elevator as a box with doors that open and close, and with riding up and down a shaft. This story is about Martin, an unexceptional man who works in an office building that has fourteen floors and a basement. That is all the reader knows for sure. The fifteen fragments (corresponding to the fifteen floors) develop several possible story lines, some or all of which may occur in Martin's imagination. He may, for example, instead of going to the fourteenth floor as he has for seven years, punch the "B" button that will take him to the basement or to hell. He may meet the excited stare of the beautiful elevator operator and realize that she loves him. He may ride to the fourteenth floor with seven other employees whose blank faces depress him. He may walk to the fourteenth floor and hear the elevator crash below. He and the beautiful girl may get to the thirteenth floor where the cable snaps; as the elevator falls he will throw himself under her to absorb the impact. Several of the fragments develop this story line with various alternatives: "Her soft belly presses like a sponge into his groin" (p. 133). Weeping in terror, she "presses her hot wet mouth against his" while he strokes her soft buttocks soothingly and notices that she has taken off her skirt. Then, a few fragments later, as the elevator plummets downward, "their naked bellies slap together, her vaginal mouth closes sponge-like on his rigid organ. Their lips lock" (p. 134). In another fragment, he rides to the fourteenth floor with fellow workers who, led by the bully, Carruther, taunt him unjustly as the stench of intestinal gas offends their nostrils. Again, he may board the elevator and, declaring himself omnipotent, doom them all to death. In one particularly bawdy fragment, an observer tells a story of this guy, Mart, or Mert, or Mort, who has a "doodang" so long that he has to carry it over his shoulder (it was so long, in fact, that the Italians after the war thought he was a God). Anyway, as the storyteller continues, when Mort boards the elevator, the other guys are teasing "the little piece who operates that deathtrap." Carruther lifts the girl's skirt and discovers that "the little quiff ain't wearing no skivvies! It's something *beautiful* man I mean a sweet cleft peach right outa some foreign orchard." When Mort quite naturally becomes excited, his remarkable penis "rears up," knocking Carruther to the floor. "And that poor little cunt she takes one glim of that impossible rod," finishes the storyteller, "and she faints dead away and tumbles right on that elevator lever and man! I thought for a minute we was *all* dead" (p. 136). In these various fragments in "The Elevator," we see, as we did in "The Door" and "The Gingerbread House," the emphasis on sex and death. Here, fantasizing that his sexual powers have inspired legends gives the impotent worker Martin a sense of importance.

This interweaving of fantasy, sex, and death is apparent in a number of the other stories in *Pricksongs and Descants*. In "The Marker," for example, a young man named Jason puts a marker in his book, turns out the light, and crosses the room to the bed where his beautiful nude wife waits. He has just begun to make love to her when five policemen burst into the room and throw on the lights. Jason discovers to his horror that his wife is not only dead but rotten and that, most terrifying of all, he is stuck in the disgusting corpse. In this allegorical tale, Coover is apparently suggesting that modern man has been making love to something long dead—perhaps the traditions and conventions he accepts unthinkingly. In "A Pedestrian Accident," another nightmarish tale with a similar message, a young man named Paul steps off a curb and is hit by a truck. As he lies dying in the street, a crowd gathers to watch the ineffectual policeman and doctor bumble about officiously. Charity Grundy, a fat, old woman whom Paul has never seen before, entertains the onlookers by fantasizing that the dying man is her lover, though he "humps terrible." Nevertheless, she bemoans his loss in a speech rife with bawdy sexual puns: "Done in! A noble man lies stark and stiff! *Sic transit glans mundi!* . . . And at the height of his potency!" (p. 189). Like Jason in "The Marker," Paul in this story seems to represent conventional, unthinking man; having lost both his ability to speak and his creative powers, he is left to die unattended except by a beggar who wants his clothes and a dog who wants his flesh.

Fortunately, not all of Coover's stories are so gruesome. "Quenby and Ola, Swede and Carl" deals primarily with the sexual fantasies of a man named Carl who is vacationing on a lake where he fishes with big, brutal Swede and, possibly, makes love to Swede's wife and daughter, Quenby and Ola. The fascination of the story is that, like the incidents of "The Elevator," any or all may be only fantasies. The situation seems to be this: Carl is sitting stranded with Swede in a small motorboat in the middle of the lake. Carl is worried not about getting the motor going but about whether Swede might have seen him making love to Quenby or skinny-dipping with the fourteen-year-old Ola. Carl remembers hearing that the violent Swede killed Ola's cat just for stepping in his pie. Intermingled with fears that Swede might kill him just as casually as he did the cat, Carl thinks of the passionate Quenby, "hot, wet, rich, softly spread" (p. 151), and of the lovely naked Ola and their "wet bodies sliding together" (p. 154). In typical fashion, Coover leaves the reader wondering how much of this really happened and how the story ends.

Even more bewildering than Carl's story, "The Babysitter" is the longest of the twenty stories and generally acknowledged to be the best. The themes of sex and death we have been examining are apparent in the summary by William Gass:

She [the babysitter] arrives at seven-forty, but how will her evening be? ordinary? The Tucker children bathed and put away like dishes, a bit of TV, then a snooze? Or will she take a tub herself, as she seems to have done the last time? Will she, rattled, throttle the baby to silence its screaming, allow it to smother in sudsy water? Or maybe a mysterious stranger will forcibly enter and enter her? No—she will seduce the children; no—they will seduce her; no—Mr. Tucker, with the ease and suddenness of a daydream, will return from the party and (a) surprise her in carnal conjunction with her boyfriend, (b) embrace her slippery body in the bath, (c) be discovered himself by (i) his wife, (ii) his friends, (iii) the police . . . or . . . All the while the TV has its own tale to tell, and eventually, perhaps, on the news, an account will be given of . . . While the baby chokes on its diaper pin? While the sitter, still warm out of water, is taken by Mr. Tucker? While both she and the children are murdered by Boyfriend and Friend? No. . . . But our author says yes to everything. We've been reading a remarkable fugue—the stock fears and wishes, desires and dangers of our time.[7]

By the end of the 107 fragments that compose this story, the reader has seen enough lust, seduction, rape, murder, accidental death, and incidental violence to be thoroughly convinced of modern man's emptiness and confusion.

And yet Harry Tucker, the bored and lecherous husband in "The Babysitter," is not so different from Jack-become-the-giant, and Dolly Tucker is not so far from Granny who married the Beast-who-was-still-no-Prince. Little Red Riding Hood, Hansel, Gretel—are they so unlike the babysitter, the boyfriend, Jack, his friend, Mark? Children still grope toward maturity through sexual doors, and adults still try to forget death and disillusion through erotic fantasies.

Ronald Wallace has said of *The Universal Baseball Association*, "Death is a felt presence throughout the novel. . . . And yet sex, as a symbol of union and continuity, seems a possible counter to extinction."[8] The same might be said of these death-cunt-and-prick songs. Here, too, the contradictory impulses of sex and death are held tenuously in balance as Robert Coover, Proprietor, simultaneously ridicules and celebrates the continuity of life.

NOTES

1. Robert Scholes, *Fabulation and Metafiction* (Urbana: University of Illinois Press, 1979), 3.

2. Robert Coover, *The Universal Baseball Game, Inc., J. Henry Waugh, Prop.* (New York: Random House, 1968), 112–13. Further references appear in the text.

3. Ronald Wallace, *The Last Laugh: Form and Affirmation in the Contemporary American Comic Novel* (Columbia: University of Missouri Press, 1979), 126.

4. Robert Coover, *Pricksongs and Descants* (New York: Dutton, 1969), 78. Further references appear in the text.

5. Frank Gado, *First Person: Conversations on Writers and Writing* (New York: Union College Press, 1973), 150–51.

6. Scholes, *Fabulation and Metafiction*, 120–23.

7. William Gass, *Fiction and the Figures of Life* (New York: Alfred A. Knopf, 1970), 105–06.

8. Wallace, *The Last Laugh*, 127–28.

GENRE AND FANTASTIC GAME PLAY

Texts in the mode of the fantastic may exult at the boundlessness of the imagination or despair at the limits of rational control, reflexively gaming with the limit of the text itself. Genre, fictionality, and metaphor become points of fissure opening to the fragmentation of experience, the inconclusiveness of the world and of writing.

The Mystery of Hesse's *Das Glasperlenspiel*

Kurt J. Fickert

The fantasy underlying Hermann Hesse's futuristic novel *Das Glasperlenspiel* is rather limited in scope. The world in the twenty-third century, as Hesse envisions it, has not changed in essence from what it is in the twentieth. As a matter of fact, means of transportation seem to have retrogressed: Locomotion on foot prevails, and travel by air is not even mentioned. Only in respect to the book's two central symbols has Hesse essayed an imaginative approach to the future. He has invented a country, Castalia, where an intellectual elite harbor and preserve the cultural achievements of mankind and where these chosen few engage in an activity known as the glass bead game. These two endeavors on the part of the Castalians are supported by their less-gifted kindred throughout the world in the belief (it must be assumed) that the activities of the Castalians will give meaning to their own insignificant lives. Castalia and the game are intimately related: The country exists for the sake of promoting the practice of the game and for an annual public demonstration of its subtleties. The game itself is therefore the unifying factor in the novel, the focal point in the life of its protagonist, and the touchstone by which he judges his associates. As a symbol of such monumental import, the game has unfortunately, but perhaps necessarily, rather vague contours.

An account of the genesis of *Das Glasperlenspiel* must begin with a notation Hesse made on the back of a letter he had received. He outlined there a novel that would concern itself with the successive reincarnations of a protagonist that were to take place in various historical epochs, beginning with the primeval and ending with the yet-to-be. "Even less actuality, even more fantasy" is Hesse's admonition to himself in regard to this future state of affairs.[1] In extended comments on this last phase in the unidentified protagonist's series of rebirths, Hesse elaborates on the symbol of the glass bead game he has already named. He reminds himself that the game will not be easy for the reader to visualize, "since it is very complicated, and has furthermore not yet been invented."[2] In

these tentative notes, the game, so Hesse suggests, represents "the world symphony," consisting of many categories—music, history, space, mathematics
(underlined). "X," the novel's featureless hero, is depicted by Hesse as playing
the game as though it were an instrument, varying its pseudo-music according
to the styles of Bach and Mozart, but also in the manner of Plato. The players
of the esoteric game, so Hesse proposes, devote themselves to it to the exclusion
of all else, specifically all purposeful activities. Hesse soon began to flesh out
this hastily drawn skeleton of a novel, and he subsequently published in various
magazines brief sections, principally the *Lebensläufe*, the protagonist's "biographies," as he finished them, together with some of *Das Glasperlenspiel*'s
poetry. In the meantime, he described his progress on the work to his friends.
He confided to Thomas Mann that he was writing a book concerning a mental
musical–mathematical game.[3] Another reference in his correspondence has led
George Wallis Field to conclude that the concept of the game was derived from
the card game of *Dichterquartett* and that "the beads were first used as a kind
of abacus to record points won—blue for the poets, red for the musicians, etc."[4]
Except for these passing remarks on the game while the novel was being written,
Hesse left it in essence unexplicated, a play of fancy in the work itself. Following
the publication of *Das Glasperlenspiel*, he commented only on his unwillingness
to expound on its features other than as they appear in the book.

The historian–biographer who introduces the story of Josef Knecht also gives
an account of the origin of the glass bead game. It came into being, he reports,
in a bourgeois age as an activity that provided a refuge for those overwhelmed
by the sham culture of a money-oriented society. The game had a crude system
of notation subsequently supplanted by an abacus-like arrangement of glass
beads, which Bastian Perrot of Calw had proposed. The next improvement in
the game involved the elimination of the beads themselves; the ideas they represented became independent of any physical presence. Hesse here implies that
the game has dispensed with writing, the use of words, and that therefore it is
not a patent symbol for the literary arts. At this point, so the story goes in *Das
Glasperlenspiel*, Joculator Basiliensis developed what had been the private pursuit of intellectuals into a game of universal scope; Castalia came into existence,
together with the Castalians, their hierarchy, and their educational system. Now,
in the biographer's purview, Josef Knecht enters upon the scene, educated in
the schools of Castalia and chosen to continue his studies in exclusive institutes
of higher learning in order to be trained to become one of the expert players of
the glass bead game. Eventually he is made *magister ludi*, the master of the
game, and achieves the rank of a legendary figure in the history of this country
harboring all of culture and an arcane activity.

The autobiographical element predominates in this account of the career of
the most famous of the *Glasperlenspieler*. In the person of the biographer who
draws upon reminiscences, official papers, juvenilia, unpublished poetry—that
is, all available sources—Hesse is again the compiler of documents that the

editor of Harry Haller's, the Steppenwolf's, papers was; he is the historian of the League of Travelers: H. H. He tells his own story: The anonymous chronicler Hermann Hesse explores the life and work of Josef Knecht; the name is the new pseudonym for Hermann Hesse. Knecht—also Dasa and Famulus in the "Biographies"—depicts the author as servant and conveys Hesse's belief that the artist has a mission: He lives his life and recreates it in service to mankind. "Art," he has said, "is as indispensable as bread; for that reason I have devoted my life, often at the cost of personal sacrifice, to being an artist. . . . Art belongs to the functions of humanity that serve to ensure that humanity and truth continue to exist."[5] Therefore, the name Josef is also appropriate, since it designates the artist figure; at the time of *Das Glasperlenspiel*'s composition, Mann, with whom Hesse felt he had a special affinity, was publishing his series of Joseph novels concerning an outsider–intellectual who becomes a "provider," the protector of his people. The relationship of Castalia to the world that supports its existence duplicates that that exists between the artist and the public. The Castalians are not allowed to be productive in the sense that they might manufacture a product or plant a crop. They engage only in a play of fancy, represented as the glass bead game. Like the artist, they live for the sake of exercising their imaginations. In his analysis of the meaningfulness of artistic endeavor, Hesse proposes that the promulgation or publication of the results of the artist's playfulness is important only insofar as a few more people will thereafter also be inspired to become artists.

In the novel the glass bead game is further developed through the efforts of such incipient Castalians. One of them, Bastian Perrot of Calw, had first introduced the use of glass beads: He is Hermann Hesse once more, since "Perrot" refers to the clockworks factory in which Hesse once worked as a young man, and "Bastian" is probably a passing reference to Johann Sebastian Bach. I find it less likely but not improbable that Bastian is a shortened form of Saint Sebastian, who generally represents the suffering outsider–artist. Hesse's invention of names for the novel's characters and places has the complexity and playfulness of the game itself. The final phase in its development, as the chronicler in *Das Glasperlenspiel* reveals, came about through the efforts of Joculator Basiliensis, who dispensed with the glass beads so that the abstractions they symbolized could function by themselves. "Joculator" suggests the clown; in his article "Hagiography and Humor in Hesse's Glasperlenspiel," Erhard Friedrichsmeyer proposes that "Perrot" in its similarity to the French "Pierrot" is a prior form of "Joculator."[6] Once again, in associating this contributor to the game with the city of Basel, where he lived for a number of years, Hesse identifies himself as the game's creator; and once again he makes the point that its essential nature is its fancifulness. Since Basel is indeed the home of Jacob Burckhardt, perhaps Hesse is foreshadowing the appearance of Pater Jakobus; in this event playfulness would be rampant. As Friedrichsmeyer has also emphasized, the situation is expressly paradoxical, since Hesse takes his fancies seriously: His glass bead game is humanity's greatest achievement, defined as "the *unio mystica* of the separate branches of the *universitas litterarum*,"[7] that is, the sum total and intrinsic worth of all the arts.

The high point in the life of Josef Knecht is his seven-year tenure as *magister ludi*, master of the game; his contributions to it constitute the basis for his having become the legend the novel sets out to tell many years after his death. He has been responsible for both the perpetuation and the refinement of the glass bead game. The novel's events and characters—such as they are—reflect Josef Knecht's confrontations with the *Glasperlenspiel*. His decision to devote himself to a career in Castalia comes about because of his adulation of the Old Music Master. This saintly man—his death is a kind of transcendence—exemplifies tranquility for Hesse–Knecht, the artist who does not have to struggle with words to express what exists in the world of the imagination. But Knecht lacks the capacity to emulate the serenity of the Old Music Master. Furthermore, as a musician rather than a composer, he, unlike Knecht, has no desire to become *magister ludi*; indeed, he even expresses some reservations about the significance of the game. Under these circumstances, it becomes difficult to accept the theory, put forth by I. Halpert, that the Music Master is a literary portrait of Goethe, drawn by Hesse in blind devotion. Field has helped to clarify the relationship between music and the game by indicating that they manifest a parent–child kinship: Music is a reproduction of the concept that originally came into being in the imagination. The composer, in creating music, has been involved in the playing of the glass bead game; the musician, in playing the music, is a once-removed participant. In this way, Knecht's achievement is ultimately greater than his mentor's, and Hesse finds consolation in being a writer.

The *magister ludi*'s most devoted disciple among the Castalians, Fritz Tegularius, is another portrait of a player of the game, but one who lacks Knecht's brilliance. Critics generally agree that the character is related symbolically to Friedrich (that is, Fritz) Nietzsche. As a *Dichter* (writer and poet), Nietzsche represents an artist whose role is closer to Hesse's than that of the composers whom he envies. Because of the flawed performance of Tegularius, the Nietzsche surrogate, and Knecht's acknowledgment of it, the reader of *Das Glasperlenspiel* is enabled to distinguish between the game as a symbol for the literary arts and the game as a symbol for the more nebulous but more significant art of creative thinking, the interplay of ideas, an act of creative imagination. Tegularius's fault seems to be arrogance, the inability to differentiate between the importance of the game and the brilliance of the player. Apparently, Hesse felt that Nietzsche considered the artist to be greater than his art. For Knecht the lot of the individual Castalian is insignificant in the face of the necessity of ensuring that the game survive. Although the hierarchy insists that his superior performance as *magister ludi* precludes his abandoning his post, Knecht perseveres in carrying out his decision to leave Castalia. Knecht's actions at the end of the novel are not those of the master of the game, but those of an individual writer, namely Hesse, who is still a player of the glass bead game, even though he must put the world of Castalia behind him. To an extent, Mark Boulby has considered the book to be for Hesse the equivalent of playing the game: "And the game which Knecht plays," he suggests, "is similar to that game played by the author of the novel, 'to make Castalia visible', to evoke for the reader an ideal dream."[8]

The symbol of the game, nevertheless, has a wider significance than that of representing the writing of a novel. Castalia's game does contain some parallels to Hesse's literary career, as critics have pointed out. Joseph Mileck, for example, compares Knecht's seven games as *magister ludi* to Hesse's seven major tales.[9] Concurrently, he finds that "the game becomes the passion for Knecht that writing had become for Hesse."[10] In a more general way, Mark Boulby equates the game with literature: "It is evident," he proposes, "that the periodic stylistic mutations of the Game are a metaphor for literature."[11] The fact that Thomas von der Trave, whom Knecht follows as *magister ludi*, is patently a literary portrait of Thomas Mann of Lübeck on the Trave River likewise leads to the too-pat conclusion that literature and the game are synonymous. But Hesse's word-picture of Mann does not lack an element of gentle satire. As a master of the game, Thomas von der Trave is too much the novelist whom critics have labeled the ironic German. Hesse respects the sharpness of Mann's intellect, the sophistication of his humor, but he seems to find lacking in Mann's work *das Märchenhafte*, the touch of the poet, that is present both in the inventions of Hermann Hesse and in the games of Josef Knecht, the legendary glass bead game player.

An episode in Knecht's career that causes him to take an objective look at Castalia and its game, his visit to Pater Jakobus, should—it would seem—provide occasion for the reader to gain further insight into the nature of the game. Jakobus, head of a Benedictine-like order, has a real-life counterpart, someone like Mann whom Hesse admired, the Swiss historian Jacob Burckhardt. In the novel he conveys a skeptical point of view in regard to Castalia's contributions to mankind. Jakobus is less a representative of the Church hierarchy than a historian, as Hesse portrays him; therefore, his suspicion of intellectuals and writers is difficult to account for, if not perhaps his suspicion of artists. In essence he is a realist who is convinced that playfulness and idealism, which created Castalia and the game, are transient phenomena, like all phenomena. These reservations on the Pater's (and Hesse's) part about the durability of art and the concept of immortality are set aside by Knecht's good nature and his deftness as an ambassador. Reality acknowledges the importance of the fanciful; Pater Jakobus is won over. At the same time, Knecht has discovered that the artist has a counterpart in the world outside of Castalia, the intellectual whose ruminations lead to action instead of works of art. Knecht also finds some part of this worldliness in himself. He takes this self-recognition back to Castalia with him; and while he is most successfully involved in creating with the imagination, he holds in abeyance his newly recognized desire to take action. At the end of the novel, he chooses Pater

Jakobus's world of participation over Castalia's world of contemplation, know-ing, however, that Castalia and the glass bead game will persevere and that his devotion to it has not been in vain.

The game Hesse's fancy produced has the boundlessness of the imagination itself. To an extent, the history of its coming into being in Hesse's mind can be traced, for it is clearly related to Plato's concept of ideals and somewhat less clearly to Kant's speculations about *das Ding an sich*. It must also be assumed that Hesse had read in one of his favorite authors, the German Romanticist Novalis, about a game of ideas played on a chessboard. Of more immediate import, one of Hesse's cherished memories must have been an instance in which his father's fondness for games played a part. In his memoir about his father, he recalls their last meeting. His father lay on his deathbed. They spent their last hours together reciting Latin maxims, alternately and in alphabetical order. In Hesse's work, an inkling of what is to be the glass bead game first comes into play in "Klein und Wagner," where the concept of the Magic Theater is evolved. This realm of the free exercise of the imagination is fully elaborated in *Der Steppenwolf*. In the same book, the individual's free play of fancy is complemented by the depiction of the sphere inhabited by the Immortals, Hesse's symbol for the indestructible world of art. This magic realm Hesse transposed in *Die Morgenlandfahrt* into the League of Travelers. But the concept of the imagination in all its grandeur and ambiguity found its most apt expression in *Das Glasperlenspiel*. According to Joseph Mileck, "only simile and metaphor can shed light [on it]"[12]—and, I would hope, to some extent this wide-ranging analysis.

NOTES

1. Autograph in the Hesse *Nachlass*, Marbach a. N., reproduced (in translation) in Joseph Mileck, *Hermann Hesse: Life and Art* (Berkeley: University of California Press, 1978), 256.

2. Ibid.

3. Hermann Hesse, *Briefe* (Berlin: Suhrkamp, 1951), 125.

4. George Wallis Field, *Hermann Hesse* (New York: Twayne, 1970), 151.

5. Hesse, *Briefe*, 176: "Dass Kunst so notwendig sei wie Brot, ist auch mein Stand-punkt, eben darum habe ich mein Leben, und oft unter Opfern, darauf verwendet, Künstler zu sein. . . . Die Kunst gehört zu den Funktionen der Menschheit, die dafür sorgen, dass Menschlichkeit und Wahrheit fortbestehen." My translation.

6. Erhard Friedrichsmeyer, "Hagiography and Humor in Hesse's Glasperlenspiel," in *Hermann Hesse Heute*, ed. Adrian Hsia (Bonn: Bouvier Verlag Herbert Grundmann, 1980), 259–60.

7. Hermann Hesse, *Die Romane und die grossen Erzählungen* (Frankfurt: Suhrkamp, 1971), 7, 37: "Unio Mystica aller getrennten Glieder der Universitas Litterarum." My translation.

8. Mark Boulby, *Hermann Hesse: His Mind and Art* (Ithaca, NY: Cornell University Press, 1967), 302.

  9. Mileck, *Hermann Hesse*, 275.
 10. Ibid., 271.
 11. Boulby, *Hermann Hesse*, 273.
 12. Mileck, *Hermann Hesse*, 333.

Horror Shows, Inside and Outside My Skull: Theater and Life in Tennessee Williams's *Two-Character Play*

Francis Gillen

In his *Two-Character Play*, Tennessee Williams uses the traditions of the play-within-the-play to question the nature of reality and the creative act itself. In this work the theater itself becomes an image of Williams's convictions both that we are all trapped within our own skins and that we desperately need to make connections. As he presents two players, the actor, Felice, and his sister, Clare, trying to present a play, the couple become alternately themselves, the characters they play in the drama, and the authors and improvisors of the play. We, the observers, are the audience before whom the actors perform, the towns-folk in the play itself, and the human persons toward whom the human outcry of an anguished playwright is directed. The set on which the play and the play-within-the-play are enacted suggests the limited range of rational control both over ourselves and over the works through which we attempt to reach others. On the interior stage are just two flats, the incomplete interior of a Southern room. Beyond the flats and occupying most of the stage are "scattered unassembled pieces of scenery for other plays than the play-within-the-play which will be 'performed'."[1] Clearly, the small, lighted area is that over which we hope to extend control; the scattered scenery suggests for the author "the disordered images of a mind approaching collapse," and for the audience "the phantasmagoria of the nightmarish world that all of us live in at present" (p. 308). A traditional play, with its convention of beginning, rising action, and resolution, is itself a device for imposing order on that nightmarish world. But, as Williams will illustrate, a play, like life, can present only an illusion of order, an appearance of meaning. Though the characters or we the audience may choose to be "in the play," that is, in some imaginary or temporarily comforting order we have created, the final reality is not our construct but the chaos.

The play opens on this note of disorder. The theatrical tour, like life, has taken brother and sister on a "tour which has been far more extensive than was expected" (p. 309). All the other members of the company have deserted, and the two must perform as best they can with no support. Felice, the actor, is dominated by a fear that has no limits, and longs to cry out, "Take care of me, I'm frightened, don't know the next step!" (p. 310). But to do this would be to panic Clare and keep her from giving a good performance. So he must act not only in the play but outside the play and put on a performance to bolster Clare's failing courage.

To warm up to begin the play-within-the-play, Felice starts a tape recording of a guitar and faces downstage:

Felice: Fear is a monster vast as night—

Clare: And shadow-casting as the sun.

Felice: It is quicksilver, quick as light—

Clare: It slides beneath the down-pressed thumb.

(p. 311)

The obvious use of rhyme and the rhythm of the music both suggest the attempt to assert control through art. Fear itself, spoken about and presented on stage, is fear already begun to be brought under control. But such control breaks down quickly in the face of the chaos of their situation. Felice and Clare do not even remember how they got there, only that they must perform for "restoration of— order!" (p. 313). There is no going back: "With no place to return to, we have to go on, you know" (p. 316).

And so Felice and Clare get ready to perform *The Two-Character Play* even though parts of the set and many of the props are missing. They will have to improvise, but improvisations will not be bad if they can get caught up in the play itself: that is, lose themselves in the work of art.

The play-within-the-play begins with an outcry, Clare on the telephone trying to reach someone outside. The phone is disconnected. In the performance a brother and sister, Clare and Felice (played by Clare and Felice), have returned home from mental institutions where they have supposedly been recovering from the shock of the murder–suicide of their father and mother, the father taking his own life after shooting the mother. Both are afraid of the reaction of the town, see monstrous mutations outside, and hear the smashing of projectiles against the house. The townspeople know the scandal, and the deaths cause both Felice and Clare to feel absolutely isolated from them. Yet they want to reach someone: "I want to go out! Out, out, human outcry, I want to go out!" (p. 334). If they did leave the house, however, they would have to "act" before the town: "I'd have on my face the grimace of a doll and my hair would stick to the sweat of my forehead" (p. 336).

Meanwhile, on stage, the play itself constantly breaks down before the outside-the-play fears of the "actors" Clare and Felice. Felice, for example, uses the word "confined," and the word terrorizes Clare, who insists the word is not in the script. When Felice asks Clare if nature shows any kindness to mutations, monsters, freaks, Clare simply responds that she has no recollection of lines in the play that could provide an answer to such a question. Moreover, as both look out front, they see not just an audience but an interpreter through whom their words and lines must pass. Whether this be the critics who may misinterpret the play, or in a broader sense the mind-sets, the whole array of personal experiences and concerns we the audience bring to the play, the point is clear. The unique, fantastic message of the play, the heart's unpremeditated outcry, never reaches anyone in its full impact. As Felice and Clare are trapped within the theater, the characters they play within a house, so the playwright, too, is trapped within himself, never knowing if the reality that he perceives is ever understood by anyone, and hence doubting its reality and perhaps his own. Williams wrote *Out Cry*, which later became *The Two-Character Play*, at a time that he describes vividly in his *Memoirs* as "going to pieces in 'the sixties,' my stoned age."[2] It was a seven-year depression following the death from cancer of Williams's companion, Frank Marlow, and culminating with Williams's own confinement in the violent ward of the Friggins Division of Barnacle Hospital. He describes his experience there in theatrical terms as "a continual performance of horror shows, inside and outside my skull" (*Memoirs*, p. 280). "Confinement," he writes later in the *Memoirs*, "has always been the greatest dread of my life: that can be seen in my play *Out Cry*" (p. 294). Like Felice and Clare, Williams was, during this period, "aware of death's attraction" and certain that the ability to communicate was his sole lifeline. "As long as you can communicate with someone who is inclined to sympathy, you retain a chance to be rescued" (p. 258). Yet it was also a time when the popular success and critical acceptance Williams had enjoyed from *The Glass Menagerie* up through *The Night of the Iguana* had almost vanished. *The Milk Train Doesn't Stop Here Anymore, Kingdom of Earth, Small Craft Warnings,* and *In the Bar of a Tokyo Hotel* had all been considered inferior Williams, with the last-mentioned play, for example, lasting only twenty-five performances off-Broadway. So at one level, as critic Thomas P. Adler perceptively notes, the play "is a parable about the artist whose very existence and self-identity depend upon being heard by others, and yet because of fear of continued rejection by those who do not hear is afraid to expose his work—and therefore himself—to an audience."[3] "Confined," then, suggests not only being retained within an institution, but an author whose anguished meaning is no longer being heard.

As Felice, the character in the play, uses that word "confined" that Williams so dreaded, he reopens the unlimited fears in the actress, Clare. She must say the word, he claims, because "when it's prohibited its silence increases in size" (p. 338). Yet when she does speak the forbidden word, it touches fears inside of him and he silences her by thrusting a pillow over her mouth. Momentarily he has lost control of the play. Neither can remember what had been planned to come next. The play breaks down, and all they can do is call for an interval.

What Williams has presented in the first act of the play, then, is the image of a play as our effort, and to some extent his own attempt, to gain control over the irrational in life. The illusion of rational control, like the illusion of dramatic plot with its beginning, middle, and end, is a convention, a stage device. It is no more real than a play. We, like Felice and Clare, find it more comforting to be ''in the play,'' for there is support in its supposed order, its apparent communication. But as Clare and Felice, as so many of Williams's characters at the end of their rope, and as Williams himself as playwright, we find it more and more difficult to keep the illusion going. We find ourselves more and more obsessed by the irrational demons inside us, the haunting memories of personal, familial, and professional failure that defy light and expression. And though as artists we would like to believe that the attempt to put in words our greatest fears, like being confined, alleviates them, our own fears staged before us are just as likely to drive us more deeply toward them and to make the demons only larger for having been seen. Silence and speech alike increase the pain.

Act 2 opens with Felice and Clare still trapped in the house. They consider reverting to childhood, blowing bubbles, but because there is an audience present, they cannot act as children. Nor can they simply remain where they are, for supplies from the local store are no longer brought to the house since the insurance company has refused payment ''in the event of a man killing his wife, then himself, and . . . unkindly forgetting his children'' (p. 343). Yet each is afraid to leave the other to go out, for there is death in the house and the one who remains may act as the father did. Since his own confinement in an asylum after he had allowed himself ''to lose contact with all reality'' (p. 346), Felice has been obsessed with locked doors. The alternative to remaining in the house and living with death is to act out for the town the appearance of customary habits. Clare would go upstairs to give Felice the socially acceptable jacket and tie that would suggest such an appearance, but the set is incomplete and there are no stairs. So Felice is handed an invisible tie and jacket to ''look like a gentleman with excellent credit''(p. 349). They go through the door of the interior set and face the audience. In their full view, Clare is shaking too badly to sustain the illusion of calm security and, despite her brother's efforts to prevent her, retreats back into the house. Felice then speaks directly to the audience, telling them that he is defeated by the call that seems to come from within the house. ''You can't go away. Give up. Come in and stay'' (p. 353). And so he returns, avoiding the eyes of his sister, to the confinement he dreads.

There is, however, a logical, dramatic end to *The Two-Character Play*. Felice touches Clare's hand, ''which is a signal that I am about to speak a new line in *The Two-Character Play*'' (p. 355). He asks Clare if she remembers coming across the box of cartridges for the revolver; when she replies ''No!'' he reminds her that her answer in the script is ''yes.'' Feeling now securely ''in the play,'' he defies the audience by blowing bubbles serenely at it and looks assuringly at the gun on the table. Together they imagine the soap bubble ''rising through gold light, above the gold sunflower heads'' (p. 356) and take comfort that they at least can sometimes see the same things at the same time. There is still some communication, and they have traveled too long now for separation. In any conventional play, the curtain would now fall on their union in death, the idea finished, the form complete.

But in Williams's play, Clare simply notes that at some undistinguishable moment the audience had left and the house is completely empty. For a moment Felice had been lost in the play; now neither knows what to do or where to go. As they accuse one another of changing the lines and perhaps spoiling the play, Clare notes that their dialogue still sounds like *The Two-Character Play*: "Is it possible that *The Two-Character Play* doesn't have an ending?" (p. 360). Unlike drama, it does not reach a conclusion; like life, it "seems to stop just short of something important" (p. 360). Felice tries to go outdoors to ensure their reservations in the local hotel, but finds the doors of the theater locked from the outside. As the characters were trapped in the house, so the actors are now trapped within the theater. Clare's repeated plea, "Out, out, out! Human outcry," receives no response, and Felice quietly speaks the words from the Song of Solomon, "A garden enclosed is my sister." The actors now are closed within the irrational word spoken in the play, "confined." And Clare now talks to Felice as one might talk to Williams, the author of the play, saying that if she might escape from the play, she would see for herself "if these mysteries you've reported to me are exactly as you've reported." "Do you think that I've imagined them, dreamed them?" Felice responds (p. 365).

As the empty theater grows colder and colder, only one alternative seems open: to go back into the play, to find there the ending wherever it is hidden. The play commences again, this time with no audience. The opening lines are repeated until Felice breaks the illusion again to ask Clare to go straight to the sunflowers, keep her eyes on them. While they look at the sunflowers, Clare retrieves the revolver. Neither can use it, and admitting defeat they cling together as the curtain falls.

Is it a play now, *The Two-Character Play* that Felice has written? Or have Felice and Clare stepped once more out of their parts, desperate actor and actress looking for a resolution? Or is it Tennessee Williams the playwright, himself reflecting on his own confinement and that of his sister, Rose, considering his recent critical failures and wondering if anyone cares or listens anymore? It is, of course, all of these, and by constantly obscuring the boundaries between acting and living, control and the irrational, writing and being, reality and play, Williams reminds us how narrow those boundaries are and how imperceptibly we, too, step across them.

NOTES

1. Tennessee Williams, *The Theatre of Tennessee Williams* (New York: New Directions, 1976), vol. 5, p. 308. Further references appear in the text.

2. Tennessee Williams, *Memoirs* (New York: Bantam, 1976), 256. Further references appear in the text.

3. Thomas P. Adler, "The Dialogue of Incompleteness: Language in Tennessee Williams' Later Plays," *Quarterly Journal of Speech* 61 (1975): 55.

Fantasy in Structure: Layered Metaphor in Stoppard

Joseph J. Feeney, S.J.

Tom Stoppard has an imagination that feeds on analogies. "Things are so interrelated," he once commented in an interview; and in writing his plays Stoppard frequently finds himself discovering (often to his own surprise) various "convergences of different threads," "structural pivots," and points of "cross reference."[1] In these plays, the themes, characters, plots, language, and setting somehow become curiously linked and, through multiple metaphors, end up standing parallel to each other. In *Jumpers*, for example, philosophy resembles gymnastics, which is like casual sex, which resembles academic politics, which . . . And so the metaphor-making sparkles along in the Stoppard imagination. These metaphors, furthermore—often bizarre and fantastic ones—then get built into the very structure of a Stoppard play.

For the casual theatergoer, the Stoppard imagination seems only a near-bottomless source of fantastic puns, incongruities, plot twists, and verbal surprises. Critics, too, often concentrate on Stoppard's absurdity and celebration of irrationality.[2] But underneath the surface of Stoppard's plays—and of his imagination—is an intelligence and a dramatic craft that are carefully ordering those diverse elements that only *seem* to be so spontaneous, arbitrary, and chaotic. The real Stoppard, however, is a supreme organizer, a craftsman who knows that his plays "hinge around incredibly carefully thought-out structural pivots which I arrive at as thankfully and as unexpectedly as an explorer parting the pampas grass which is head-high and seeing a valley full of sunlight and maidens."[3]

This "structural pivot" is very frequently a set of parallel metaphors whose points of similarity Stoppard works out as carefully as a seventeenth-century metaphysical poet. Through metaphor after metaphor Stoppard links together bizarrely diverse elements, and this metaphor—or, more accurately, series of metaphors or layers of metaphor—provides structure, form, and shape for the play. These layers of metaphor continue for the full length of the play, and each layer of the comparison illuminates and is illuminated by the others. Thus,

Stoppard's dreamiest flights of fantasy are reined in, through metaphor, by his mind and his imagination. He sees similarities, works out continuing points of comparison, and builds these metaphors into his plays in such a way that the parallels are fantastic yet consistently coherent. Fantasy becomes structured through metaphor. And this rare combination of wild fantasy and clear structure becomes a Stoppard trademark that forms a potentially centrifugal play into a coherent unit. A number of his plays demonstrate this characteristic of Stoppard's imagination; here I consider three of them: *Jumpers, Every Good Boy Deserves Favor*, and *Professional Foul*.

A preliminary clarification may help on the question of structure. Each of these plays, to be sure, has a traditional plot structure; the traditional urge of suspense drives each play forward: Who murdered the gymnast, and what will happen to George Moore? What will be Alexander's fate for speaking the truth about Russia's political freedom? Will Hollar's philosophical essay be successfully smuggled out of Czechoslovakia? These questions, and the plots they spawn, propel each play forward and provide its basic structure. But Stoppard adds his layers of metaphor as an alternate structure. This layered metaphor, with its multiple levels of similarities, adds its own form, unity, and structure to each play. These fantastic metaphors also provide much of each play's brilliance, its *tour-de-force* quality; the metaphors—together with Stoppard's verbal pyrotechnics—also give the play its sense of fun.

Jumpers (1972) is a play whose major conflict is a dispute between philosophies, and all the other conflicts in the play—about sex, gymnastics, academic appointments, murder, even the astronauts on the moon—are merely metaphoric parallels for the central philosophical dispute.[4] On one side is George Moore, a philosopher, who generally follows the philosophical positions of the English philosopher G. E. Moore (1873–1958) (whose name, of course, is also George Moore). The philosophical hero (like Stoppard I will call him "George") is, at the beginning of the play, preparing a lecture for a university symposium that very evening. Opposing recent developments in English philosophy and ethics, he comments that he "hoped [that evening] to set British moral philosophy back forty years, which is roughly when it went off the rails."[5] Following what he, and historians of philosophy, call the "intuitionist philosopher" G. E. Moore,[6] George holds that there is an absolute metaphysical base for affirming what is *good* and what is *bad*; goodness, he maintains, is a *fact* that, by intuition, is recognized when it is seen (pp. 40, 48, 67). Moreover (and unlike G. E. Moore), George, arguing as a philosopher, actually affirms that there is a God (pp. 26, 67, 71–72). Standing in the long tradition of Aristotle, Aquinas, and the Judeo–Christian philosophical heritage, he affirms a God of Creation and a God of Goodness "to account for existence and . . . to account for moral values" (pp. 26, 28, 29).

On the other side of the philosophical dispute stand the more recent English philosophers—the current "orthodox mainstream" according to George—who are represented in the play by Sir Archibald Jumper ("Archie," says Stoppard) and his followers, including the recently murdered Professor McFee (p. 49). These contemporary philosophers are, at one point, catalogued and lumped together as "logical positivists, mainly, with a linguistic analyst or two, a couple of Benthamite Utilitarians . . . lapsed Kantians and empiricists generally . . . and of course the usual Behaviourists" (pp. 50–51). This group holds, according to George, that "things and actions . . . can have any number of real and verifiable properties. But good and bad, better and worse . . . are not real properties of things . . . just expressions of our feelings about them" (p. 41). The play's question, then, becomes this: Can goodness and badness be objectively grounded (at least by intuition), or are they only subjective feelings without any objective philosophical foundation? This is the play's philosophical conflict and the crux of its plot.

In *Jumpers*, however, this cerebral dramatic conflict, itself enfleshed in George and Archie, is further expressed in a series of bizarre metaphors; Stoppard finds parallels of this philosophical disagreement in the realms of gymnastics, sex, academic power, national politics, murder, astronauts on the moon, and human feeling. And while these metaphors at first seem fantastic and strange, on examination they make full sense and provide a complex structural network for the play. Archie (Sir Archibald Jumper, the philosopher without metaphysical foundation) is himself a gymnast—physically and philosophically—and also the manager of a group of gymnasts whom he hires out to perform at parties; these jumpers are young and "relevant," physically skilled, technically brilliant at somersaults, but have no solid foundation. In contrast, George is physically dull, boringly stable, but grounded on the firm, solid earth. Furthermore, Archie— the jumper—also leaps from bed to bed and has seduced George's own wife; George, his marriage shaky, is troubled—both morally and sexually—by Archie's actions, but is himself moral enough to refrain from such sexual acrobatics. Archie, further, is a man of academic power, vice-chancellor of George's university and the professor in charge of academic appointments; George, seeker of truth and man of moral integrity, is totally powerless and holds the lowly reputed chair of moral philosophy. In politics (to go to the next metaphor), the jumpers are Radical–Liberals; George holds a more traditional position. In life, the jumpers, since they hold no moral position as absolute, are willing to resort even to murder; George, recognizing moral limits, could not imagine himself murdering anyone. The characters' habits, too, differ: During the play the jumpers are enjoying a free-flying party in George's living room and bedroom while George is in his study preparing his lecture in isolation from others.[7] Even the lunar astronauts take part in *Jumpers'* multilayered metaphor. On television the American astronauts are seen walking on and violating the moon, and when they take off for the return to earth, one astronaut chooses self-preservation at the cost of the other's life; George and even his wife prefer altruistic courage and also mourn the loss of the old romantic, stable view of a distant and lovely moon. The jumpers, finally, see their bodies as only brilliant machines, are always coolly in control of a situation, but care little about love; George, though he cannot express his love to his wife, still cares about her, and even about his tortoise, Thumper, and his hare, Pat. Yet George, isolated but still holding to objective morality, even at play's end, remains a victim of slapstick and a philosopher in a pratfall.

On this set of incongruous metaphors, then, is the play built: philosophy = gymnastics = sex = academic chairs = national politics = murder = parties = astronauts = love = slapstick = George and Archie. Stoppard has chosen such fantastic linkings to dramatize his worries about order, reason, morality, and responsibility in the modern world. The play *Jumpers*, then, while funny and sparkling, is also very serious and—most to the point—very carefully structured.

Every Good Boy Deserves Favor (1977) and *Professional Foul* (1977) are equally funny and equally serious; they are both also structured with great care. Dealing with political repression and with freedom of expression, *Every Good Boy Deserves Favor* shows a political prisoner kept in a Russian mental hospital, and *Professional Foul* is a television play about free expression in Czechoslovakia.[8] Both plays, like *Jumpers*, are built on parallel layers of metaphor carefully linked together.

The title of *Every Good Boy Deserves Favor* puns on the musical notation E, G, B, D, F (the play's title is the British version of our "Every Good Boy Does Fine"), and the work is described as "a piece for actors and orchestra."[9] André Previn wrote the music, and both actors and orchestra share the stage. On the stage two men are confined in a Russian mental hospital; Alexander, a political prisoner because he criticized the repression of dissent, and Ivanov, a certified madman who believes he has an orchestra in his head (he thinks the cellos are rubbish!). At issue in the play is the difference between clinical madness and the human sanity–political madness of dissent in a repressive society. The play, as it progresses, jokes about Ivanov's imaginary orchestra, shows Alexander's determination to be honest and to speak the truth frankly, and dramatizes his young son's desire to free him. The plot—such as it is—is resolved crazily when a colonel enters and unwittingly confuses the two men; he asks Alexander whether he hears an orchestra in his head ("No," he says) and Ivanov whether the Soviet government puts sane men in lunatic asylums ("I shouldn't think so," he says) (p. 38). Both men are sent home and the play ends happily.

Despite the ghastly political and human situation, the play is funny. Many of the lines and situations are zanily comic; Ivanov is a humorous character; even the musical score is a parody of modern Russian music. Stoppard adds to the humor and incongruity with layers of incongruous metaphors. In Russia any statement about government repression—statements that are morally right and as obvious as geometry and logic ("To thine own self be true. / One and one is always two.")—somehow means political dissent (p. 37). Such dissent is treated as madness and as a refusal to play one's part in the orchestra of the State (here, ironically, existing only in the mind of a madman). These political themes and conflicts appear in the lines of the characters, in the logic or illogic of their utterances, in the mental-hospital setting, and in the orchestra's music.

On one side stands the sane, dissenting Alexander: frank in politics, morally truthful, logically and mathemetically accurate (one and one *do* make two), quite sane, possessing no imaginary orchestra, forthright in word, honest to his opinions; on the other side, the madman and good Communist Ivanov: amoral in his madness, inventing an unreal world of relations and even a new orchestra in his mind, crazy in word, with opinions unconnected with reality. Like Russian Communism he lives within a crazy, closed system. And even the State-as-orchestra is not very competent and plays music that is a parody. Thus, Stoppard builds up the incongruous but clear metaphors on which the play's structure stands: Alexander and Ivanov = politics = morality = logical mathematics = sanity = madness = music = verbal style = character = society. The play's richness as well as its humor and irony are all based on these layers of metaphor.

Even a play as seemingly—and actually—realistic as *Professional Foul* is based on similar fantastic parallels structured through metaphor. The play, one of Stoppard's rare pieces for television, dramatizes a lesson in applied ethics as learned by Professor Anderson, a Cambridge ethicist and rabid soccer fan. This ninety-minute drama begins as several British philosophers are flying to Prague to deliver papers at an international philosophical congress. Anderson, who has always carefully kept his philosophy separate from his life and politics, has prepared a lecture on "Ethical Fictions as Ethical Foundations" (p. 48). (The treatment of ethics as a fiction, incidentally, recapitulates Archie Jumper's position.) But if truth were to be told, Professor Anderson is *really* going to Prague to catch the World Cup qualifier soccer match between England and Czechoslovakia, which will be played in the Czech capital at the time of the congress. But when Anderson reaches his Prague hotel, he is unexpectedly visited by his former Czech student, Pavel Hollar, who asks Anderson to carry his thesis—on human rights—to England for publication. Anderson, unwilling to offend his Czech hosts by such smuggling and "bad manners," refuses (pp. 60, 63). But the next day, on his way to the soccer match, Anderson finds that Hollar has been arrested; angered, he then presents to the international congress not his own paper on "ethical fictions" but Hollar's strong views on human rights and on their real, objective foundation. Anderson, then, chooses to speak out in place of the imprisoned Hollar and even decides to smuggle Hollar's thesis to the English printers. The play ends as Anderson smuggles the thesis out of Czechoslovakia in the briefcase of an unsuspecting British philosopher—a relativist in moral theory—who unreasonably complains that a "principle" has been violated. Anderson counters that since for the relativist philosophy is merely a "game" anyway, how could an alleged non-real "principle" be violated? (p. 124). (Hollar, a traditional objectivist in moral theory, with philosophical consistency was willing to be imprisoned for his opinions and principles.) In any case, says Anderson, the smuggling was merely a "professional foul" or "necessary foul"—an action similar to England's tackle in the soccer game as the Czech player was driving to the goal.[10] And why should an English relativist complain in such a case?

In *Professional Foul*, then, Stoppard once again creates a very odd, layered metaphor: in this case soccer = politics = philosophy = academic life = Anderson and the other characters. The soccer foul is necessary for England to prevent a Czech goal; similarly, it is necessary to hide the thesis to protect (from the Czech police) Hollar's statement on political freedom and individual rights. Hiding the thesis in a relativist's briefcase (unknown to the relativist) is furthermore just part of the philosophical game for a man who holds to no objective principles. Whether such a concealment is "foul," then—much less immoral—is seen to depend on one's ethical theories and principles. Thus, at the drama's end, the relativist's complaint—"It's not quite playing the game is it?" (p. 124)—sets Anderson up for the play's brilliant final lines: "Ethics is a very complicated business. That's why they have these congresses." All five levels of the play— soccer/politics/philosophy/academics/characters—come together beautifully and ironically in the play's closing words. The comparisons generated in Stoppard's imagination have been organized and controlled through the play's structure of metaphor. Through the ironies of the metaphor, the reader comes to see that philosophy, politics, and the commitment involved in both cannot be called games in any sense at all.

Tom Stoppard has frequently shown himself willing to discuss the creative process behind his plays, and in many interviews he offers glimpses of how his imagination works. A few of his comments, when read together, clarify the metaphor-making typical of his imagination. In 1979 he said, for example, that he "enjoys writing dialogue but has a terrible time writing plays."[11] It is at this "terrible time," one might speculate, that Stoppard surprises himself by dis- covering the "convergences of different threads," the "cross references," and "structural pivots" that characterize his plays.[12] At such moments, it seems, Stoppard sees new similarities and proceeds to construct the complex interlink- ings that constitute his plays. He characteristically catches those interrelations he talked of through a series of metaphors.

Stoppard himself once described the joining of these interrelations in a play as "carpet-making" with its "different threads."[13] But this particular metaphor of crosshatching, though offered by the playwright himself, does not fully catch the great clarity and parallelism of Stoppard's metaphor-making. Rather, Stop- pard seems to express his clearly perceived parallels by clearly designed meta- phors that overlie and enrich each other like the layers of a French petit-four, a Viennese torte, or even, perhaps, an English trifle. Or again, in less gustatory terms, Stoppard's imagination is as rich, as analytically clear, and as enticing as the imagination of a Donne, of a Herbert, or of some medieval exegete or allegorist.

NOTES

1. Interview with Ronald Hayman, 12 June 1974, in Ronald Hayman, *Tom Stoppard*, Contemporary Playwrights Series, 3rd ed. (London: Heinemann, 1979), 2–4, 13.

2. For Stoppard criticism and bibliography, see C. W. E. Bigsby, *Tom Stoppard*, Writers and Their Work Series (London: British Council/Longman Group, 1976); Kenneth Tynan, "Profiles: Withdrawing with Style from the Chaos," *New Yorker* 53 (19 December 1977): 41–111; Hayman, *Tom Stoppard*; Victor L. Cahn, *Beyond Absurdity: The Plays of Tom Stoppard* (Rutherford, NJ: Fairleigh Dickinson University Press, 1979); Joan FitzPatrick Dean, *Tom Stoppard: Comedy as a Moral Matrix*, Literary Frontiers Edition (Columbia: University of Missouri Press, 1981); Lucina Paquet Gabbard, *The Stoppard Plays* (Troy, NY: Whitston, 1982); and Jim Hunter, *Tom Stoppard's Plays* (London: Faber and Faber, 1982).

3. Interview, in Hayman, *Tom Stoppard*, 2.

4. A. J. Ayer, in an essay on *Jumpers*, also maintains that the play fundamentally deals with a conflict between philosophies (quoted in Cahn, *Beyond Absurdity*, 118). Another philosopher's analysis is Jonathan Bennett's "Philosophy and Mr. Stoppard," *Philosophy* 50 (1975): 5–18.

5. Tom Stoppard, *Jumpers* (New York: Grove Press, 1972), 46. Further references appear in the text.

6. On G. E. Moore's positions and on those of his opponents in *Jumpers*, see Mary Warnock, *Ethics Since 1900*, 2nd ed. (London: Oxford University Press, 1966), 1–114, 140–47; G. J. Warnock, *English Philosophy Since 1900*, 2nd ed. (London: Oxford University Press, 1969); and W. D. Hudson, *Modern Moral Philosophy* (Garden City, NY: Anchor/Doubleday, 1970).

7. Bobbi Rothstein analyzes the isolation of the characters in *Jumpers* in "The Reappearance of Public Man: Stoppard's *Jumpers* and *Professional Foul*," *Kansas Quarterly* 12 (Fall 1980): 39–40. Cahn (*Beyond Absurdity*, 117) is wrong in seeing *Jumpers* as a largely unorganized play.

8. On the political events behind these plays, see, for example, Milton Shulman, "The Politicizing of Tom Stoppard," *New York Times* (23 April 1978): 3, 27; and Hayman, *Tom Stoppard*, 135–36.

9. Tom Stoppard, *Every Good Boy Deserves Favor* and *Professional Foul* (New York: Grove Press, 1978), 7. Further references appear in the text.

10. Rothstein ("Reappearance of Public Man," 42) offers a good definition of a professional foul in soccer: "a foul intentionally committed in order to keep the other team from gaining a sure point."

11. Mel Gussow, "Stoppard's Intellectual Cartwheels Now with Music," *New York Times* (29 July 1979): 22.

12. Interview, in Hayman, *Tom Stoppard*, 2–4.

13. Ibid., 4.

Leapfrog and Ambush in Stoppard

Gabrielle Robinson

"Leapfrog" and "ambush," two terms that recur persistently in Stoppard's plays as well as in his writings about them, are helpful in explaining his work and its direction from *Lord Malquist and Mr. Moon* to *Dogg's Hamlet, Cahoot's Macbeth*. Leapfrog and ambush create a parody that shows both the fragmentation of experience and the quest for a leap of faith that would put an end to leapfrog and ambush. But since such a leap proves impossible, Stoppard is committed to, or trapped into, "a sort of infinite leapfrog," which, however, in its coherent and farcical way helps to define his vision. He once said that he builds his plays of "an argument, a refutation, then a rebuttal of the refutation, then a counter-rebuttal, so that there is never any point in this intellectual leapfrog at which I feel *that* is the speech to stop it on, *that* is the last word."[1] This is a telling passage for several reasons. First of all, Stoppard describes his method in terms of a child's game, both for the sake of witty discrepancy as well as for accuracy since he plays with the blocks and slabs of Western civilization—to borrow a concept from *Dogg's Hamlet, Cahoot's Macbeth* that in turn was borrowed from Ludwig Wittgenstein. Exploiting every work of art and thought with which he is familiar for his games of intellectual leapfrog turns everything into a parody that combines a child-like exhilaration with despair at the loss of meaning. For it is significant that underlying these games is the desire for the last word: Childish, perhaps, but more importantly for Stoppard the farceur it signifies the ambition for the ultimate witty line; for the playwright it is the need for structure; and for the moralist it is the search for an absolute truth. If leapfrog repudiates the control of logic, causality, and form, it does so for the sake of truth; but this activity results in a substitution of non-sequiturs, "a compound of two opposite half-truths,"[2] creating an endless process that is beyond control. Thus, it leads to the paradox of fracturing meaning in the search for it, of becoming infinite in the process of trying to establish a beginning, middle, and end. Such a proliferation of perspectives is one of the main structural elements of Stoppard's plays. Not restricted to arguments, leapfrog generates constant shifts in levels of reality, styles, and roles, "every exit being an entrance somewhere else."[3] This shifting creates not only farcical slipperiness and incoherence but also menace, as is evident in the corpses that litter the stage, in the characters' farcical sufferings, and in their sudden reversals from victim to murderer—such as Guildenstern stabbing the Actor or George Moore shooting the rabbit and crushing the turtle. Stoppard therefore frequently parodies the detective story with its causal plot and clear beginning, middle, and end, making his plays circular and his characters detectives who in trying to hunt down the truth are hunted themselves.

Stoppard's characters are leapfroggers themselves, which is a sign of their child-like naiveté and vitality as well as of their desperate quest for the last word. As Moon explains in *Lord Malquist and Mr. Moon*: "[I am] leapfrogging myself along the great moral issues, refuting myself and rebutting the refutation towards a truth that must be a compound of two opposite half-truths. And you never reach it because there is always something more to say" (p. 53). But ultimately the characters enjoy not even this amount of control of their leapfrogging as they are swept along in the madly proliferating action unable to sift design from chance, order from "shambles." They are trapped and betrayed by this leapfrogging plot "without possibility of reprieve or hope of explanation" (*Rosencrantz and Guildenstern*, p. 121). Feeling thus "trapped in a complex of shifts . . . being edged towards panic," Moon experiences the proliferation of infinite leapfrog and its lack of control: "It's all multiplying madly" (*Malquist and Moon*, p. 51). The characters frantically substitute a series of jokes, puns, and half-truths for a vaguely glimpsed truth, in a process that, while not infinite, ends only with their deaths. When Moon for once feels near a moment of truth, an end to leapfrog, all that comes to him, typically, is a joke that he begins to tell but cannot finish until the end of the novel. It is a joke moreover that is also an ambush: A drunk actor takes a friend to see a play, saying, "Keep your eyes shkinned, hic, because I come on in a minute" (p. 175). This situation is a parody of Malquist's position of spectator as hero, the man who "withdraws with style from the chaos" (p. 21). The final irony in this sequence is Moon's death, when he "comes on" by being killed in mistake for Malquist.

Yet leapfrog creates an incoherence with a design of its own by which Stoppard can define his world. A farcical and ever-changing half-truth, it entails not only menace and disillusionment but also liberation and insight. Like Moon, who mistakes Malquist's words, Stoppard turns "cosmic accuracy" into "comic inaccuracy," "trusting the echoes in his skull to reproduce a meaning that had not touched him" (*Malquist and Moon*, p. 8). Comic inaccuracy is a parodic leapfrog substitution for cosmic accuracy. Although generated by accident and destructive of sense, it nevertheless creates a sense of its own. Cosmic accuracy is static and restrictive—it may even be meaningless—whereas comic inaccuracy is freewheeling and offers a way of capturing a reality "where all the absolutes discredit each other" (p. 52). It is the direction of a directionless world, necessarily deceptive and inconclusive: "Now you see me, now you don't" (*Ro-*

sencrantz and Guildenstern, p. 84). It is the correlative for a perception where "everything reaches me at slightly the wrong angle" *(Malquist and Moon, p. 54).* On the one hand, then, leapfrog fractures meaning, as with Tristran Tzara's cut-up Shakespeare sonnet; it shatters the coherence of reality, subjecting it to constant substitutions and changing perspectives; it produces a fantasy in which cosmic accuracy is fragmented into a mosaic of farcical incidences and coincidences. On the other hand, it keeps alive the possibility of meaning since it gains its parodic significance in the search for cosmic accuracy. And in the meantime it provides a way of dealing with life and art, thereby helping to express Stoppard's vision. Although Tzara's sonnet accidentally pieces together random blocks of Shakespeare, it also offers a new freedom, a new form and meaning. Thus, leapfrogging serves as a structure against chaos as well as an "ambush" of structure, so that everything paradoxically gains and loses meaning, infinitely teasing the audience.

Ambush, itself a leapfrog substitution from a different metaphorical sphere, is closely linked to leapfrog. It, too, is an expression of incoherence that leaves one out of control and of comic discrepancy that carries with it the hope of revelation. To see life in terms of leapfrog and ambush is to experience wondrous dislocations as well as disillusionments that lead to feeling "trapped and betrayed." Characters experience frequent ambushes just as Stoppard ambushes the audience and apparently feels ambushed himself. For his characters the ambush can break forth unexpectedly from the trivial, inspiring them to find meaning and value in the commonplace. In *Jumpers*, George, "ambushed by some quite trivial moment," sees that "life itself is the mundane figure which argues perfection at its limiting curve."[4] Such ambush is an epiphany as well as a half-truth substituting for cosmic accuracy. More often, ambush causes a less epiphanic dislocation of reality, as expressed by Guildenstern, who feels that living is like being "ambushed by a grotesque" (p. 39). This feeling corresponds to Moon's undergoing the most bizarre and the most commonplace experiences, feeling at the mercy equally of the ordinary that appears fantastic to him and the fantastic that seems ordinary. Looking at his wife's made-up face, he is puzzled and estranged by a vision of pink lips and green eyes. "Its familiarity ambushed him. . . . Once more the commonplace had duped him into seeing absurdity, just as absurdity kept tricking him into accepting it as commonplace" (p. 33). But this form of ambush still heightens one's world with wonder and excitement. This heightening effect is also true, at least in part, of Stoppard's desire to ambush the audience; like the painter, Martello, in *Artist Descending a Staircase*, he aims "to paint an utterly simple shape in order to ambush the mind with something quite unexpected about that shape by hanging it in a frame and forcing you to see it, as it were, for the first time."[5] So while ambushes generate incoherence, they also create meaning.

This, however, is not to forget the essential violence of an ambush. Stoppard's characters suffer above all violent ambushes that turn out to be fatal or farcical or both: blasted by a bomb, shot out of a human pyramid, abandoned on the moon, struck by lightning while wearing a Mickey Mouse gas mask, or, like Crouch, "knocked arse over tip by a naked lady" swinging from a chandelier (*Malquist and Moon*, p. 18). Likewise, Stoppard's ambushes for the audience imply violence as well as wit when, he cites as examples, an unexpected word appears in a sentence or a body falls out of a cupboard.[6] To experience life through ambushes injects the fantastic into the everyday and wrenches meaning from the commonplace, but it also traps one into an endless succession of half-truths and ends in violence. Moon's life exemplifies all these aspects. He is ambushed by his wife's make-up, a lilac-gloved Lord in a pink coach, a lion in Hyde Park, the Risen Christ on a donkey loaded with a carpet roll of bodies. He himself is planning an ambush with a bomb on a "huge, disproportionate" world (p. 12). But the bomb ambushes him, going off accidentally and blossoming into a balloon with an obscene message. At last Moon is also accidentally blown to bits by the bomb of an anarchist who mistakes him for Malquist.

Ambush works for Stoppard himself with similar ambivalence. Watching rehearsals of one of his plays, he is "ambushed by the wondrous feeling that it's my play."[7] He needs an ambush to find meaning and coherence in the disparate details that his infinitely leapfrogging mind presents to him. "I'd like to be struck by lightning, so to speak,"[8] he admits in an interview, in order to write a new play. Like the Player he might then extract a significance from melodrama "which it does not in fact contain" (*Rosencrantz and Guildenstern*, p. 83). But being subjected to ambushes also disrupts any order and upsets any assertion Stoppard might like to make, leaving him, instead of with the last word, with only "the courage of my lack of convictions."[9]

Stoppard's plays are caught up in a proliferation of parodic half-truths that cause a para-mystical affirmation and another dislocation that continues the leapfrogging. Stoppard shows this process chiefly in three interrelated areas—philosophy, politics, and art—and involves variations of three male characters: the average man, always central in his plays; the power figure; and the artist–stylist. The latter two manage to impose their own kind of order even if it is an act. Thus, the Player finds "a kind of integrity" (*Rosencrantz and Guildenstern*, p. 28) in seeinig life as performance. The performance gives a form, even if it is only an artificial and relative one, to inchoate life, while regarding action as a matter of acting makes it possible to act at all. Similarly, Archie creates his own self-serving fantasies with which he rules the Jumpers both physically and mentally; in his world physical examinations are indistinguishable from seductions or suicides from murders—as a murder victim is said to have shot himself inside a plastic bag.

Stoppard's main character, however, the average man, is condemned to fight a losing battle against the inconclusiveness of his world, which throws him into a state of permanent perplexity and leads to paralysis and martyrdom. Like Moon these characters are Boswellians, historians of life who try to pin down a pattern but meet only accidents, getting pinned themselves. Their urge to order and limit reality expresses itself in their search for a beginning, middle, and end. "Everything has to begin somewhere," asserts George when trying to prove the existence of God, yet he asks himself immediately, "except why does it?" (*Jumpers*, p. 29). Nevertheless he opens his lecture optimistically with, "To begin at the beginning" (p. 24). Similarly, Albert flees from the chaos of everyday life, "the enormity of that disorder," to take refuge atop a bridge that he plans to paint methodically for the rest of his life.[10] The bridge is "separate—complete—removed, defined by principles of engineering which makes it stop at a certain point, which compels a certain shape . . . the whole thing utterly fixed by the rules that make it stand up." Looking for the cause and effect, the characters are frustrated by an infinitely receding series in which straightening a tie leads back to the shift of glaciers, and, seeking consistency in words, they find that language "transfixes" nothing except, as in *Jumpers*, the hare. Dotty's cry of "Fire!" makes George inadvertently shoot off an arrow so that the only result of his search for a beginning, a First Cause, is the poignant end of that animal. Therefore, the characters are not only historians but also detectives who, while dedicated to solving mysteries, turn murderous themselves. But in either role they are forever out of their depths or in over their heads, left high and dry, at any rate out of control and abandoned to a madly multiplying world. It is they who fall victim to the farcical and often fatal accidents of life that overtake them in all aspects of their existence, philosophically, politically, and sexually.

Dogg's Hamlet, Cahoot's Macbeth again involves the paradoxes of leapfrog and ambush, but Stoppard deliberately seems to have reduced the scope of both, which leads to a reduction of his themes of philosophy, politics, and art to language games, freedom of expression, and slapstick. Moreover, the split into two plays increases the disorientation. In a sense, *Dogg's Hamlet, Cahoot's Macbeth* takes off from *Travesties* with its linguistic farcical first act followed by a switch to more serious political themes in the second; but this time Stoppard treats these subjects in two only loosely connected plays.

Dogg's Hamlet builds on examples from Wittgenstein's *Philosophical Investigations*, dramatizing and parodying Wittgenstein's language games with Block and Slab. The play is set on the speech day of a public school where a language known as Dogg is spoken, Dogg also being the name of its headmaster. Dogg consists of English words such as Block, Slab, and Cube with different meanings. Moreover, on this day the students are putting on a performance of *Hamlet* in English, a foreign language to them. Into this world stumbles Easy, the Moon figure of the play, speaking only English. Easy is delivering a load of lumber with which he is to help build a wall and rostrum serving as platform for the ceremony and as ramparts for *Hamlet*. Easy's ambush results in many slapstick misunderstandings, especially since English insults are Dogg politeness and vice versa; so "useless" means "good day" in Dogg and "squire," "bastard." A good part of the play is occupied in arranging and rearranging these blocks and slabs or just throwing them about on stage. It is a game one has to learn to play.

Altogether Dogg's world is one of play: language games, ball games, building games, acting in *Hamlet* and in the ceremony—it is all performance, and every exit is indeed an entrance somewhere else.

Dogg's Hamlet resumes the discussion of language so prominent in Stoppard's plays, particularly, of course, in *Jumpers, Travesties*, and *Professional Foul*. Dogg ambushes Easy and the audience at first with its nonsense—"pelican crash"—then with its sense as it becomes a parody not only of English but of our world, and then again ambushes with its ultimate inconclusiveness. Dogg mocks the pretensions of education and the hypocrisies of social intercourse. The students speak Shakespeare's lines as nonsense that, to them, they are, and they respectfully address their headmaster with "Cretinous, git?" which is Dogg for "What time is it, sir?"[11] Dogg shows a pervasive dirt and dung imagery that is climaxed in the Lady's speech, the highlight of the speech day ceremony. Speaking "nicely" she begins, "Scabs, slobs, yobs, yids, spicks, wobs" and then outlines a dirt and dung vision of man's progress: "Sad fact, brats pule puke cap-pot stink, spit; grow up dunces, crooks; rank socks dank snotrags, conkers, ticks..." ending with "nick swag, swig coke, bank kickbacks;... frankly can't stand kids. Mens sana in corpore sano" (p. 28).

The farcical rendition of *Hamlet*, introduced by an overture of famous lines from the play and concluded by a ninety-second "encore" of the entire plot, makes no more sense than Dogg. It underscores the separation of language and meaning and the substitution of playing and acting. The boy who won every one of the speech day awards plays Hamlet, thus leaving one farcical performance to enter another and suffering a double collapse. Like Dogg the seemingly random Shakespearean slabs create multiple perspectives, each with a fragmentary design of its own. As a reprieve from Dogg, the prologue suitably begins, "For this relief, much thanks." One of Stoppard's favorite puzzles about chance and design is suggested by the juxtaposition of "a divinty that shapes our ends" with "though this be madness, yet there is method in it." The prologue ends with "Cat will mew, and Dogg will have his day!" (pp. 31–32). Dogg, of course, does have its day; using *Hamlet* for its celebration annihilates Shakespeare and substitutes its own fragmented and parodic world, while in *Cahoot's Macbeth* the subversion of Dogg has its day as an affirmation of freedom in repressive Czechoslovakia. Dogg, moreover, is a leapfrog reversal of God: The blocks that are meant to announce "Dogg's Hamlet" instead spell "God Slag Them"; and in *Cahoot's Macbeth* Easy exclaims, "So help me Dogg" (p. 79). Dogg appears as another instance of comic inaccuracy replacing cosmic accuracy. It also shows the dissociation of language and meaning that plays havoc with one's urge for understanding as well as for ultimate values, engendering at best a half-truth of its own. One such instance is the momentary leap of faith that shows, as is said in *Professonal Foul*, the power of "the contextual force" so that "the essentials of a given situation speak for themselves."[12] Thus, Easy and the boys work together harmoniously without or despite language. Like every other order, however, it is a half-truth, and the building blocks with which they are attempting to do something constructive end up ambushing them with nonsense of a violent sort: "Meg Shot Glad" and "God Slag Them." Dogg, seeing these messages, again and again knocks Easy through the wall, which disintegrates and has to be rebuilt; while Easy, in his turn feeling insulted by Dogg-speaking Abel, cuffs the boy repeatedly. This action is the most overt use of slapstick in Stoppard so far.

Like the metaphor of the wall itself, language and communication are both limiting and liberating, a barrier in both senses. The building blocks are destructive as often as constructive; they wall all of us in and get us hurt, but then again they also link us momentarily in a "human chain," as happens particularly in *Cahoot's Macbeth*.

Moreover, language can ambush Stoppard into a fantastic logic of its own that helps to determine, or sometimes even to inspire, the changing directions of his leapfrogging plot. Stoppard told an interviewer that *Jumpers* started with an exchange from *Rosencrantz and Guildenstern Are Dead* that provided him with the image of acrobatics and mental acrobatics:

Rosencrantz: Shouldn't we be doing something constructive?

Guildenstern: What did you have in mind? A short, blunt human pyramid?[13]

Used in connection with Wittgenstein's blocks, doing something constructive may have played its part also in *Dogg's Hamlet, Cahoot's Macbeth*.

The jump to *Cahoot's Macbeth* is one of the logic of leapfrog and ambush. Instead of Dogg's public school, Stoppard switches to a private living room in Czechoslovakia. Easy, speaking English in Dogg's world, returns having learned Dogg, only to find everyone speaking English. The farce of *Hamlet* becomes the serious performance of *Macbeth* put on by a group of artists in "normalized" Czechoslovakia, who, forbidden to pursue their careers, stage plays in the living rooms of friends. Otherwise they have been forced into deadly and dead-end labor, such as being nightwatchmen, trolley porters at a mortuary, and newspaper sellers at a tram terminus.

The party is interrupted by the Inspector who, entering in the place of the drunken porter from *Macbeth*, threatens the actors, the hostess, and the audience; there is, after all, only one party, as he reminds us. Once again, Stoppard mixes levels of performance. In *Dogg's Hamlet* we saw adult actors playing schoolboys playing Hamlet parodically; now it is actors seriously acting *Macbeth* and "acting out of hostility to the state" (p. 61). They act differently when among themselves; in the Inspector's presence they speak their lines without meaning so that on one level they are just words—like Dogg—yet on another take on subversive connotations. Context determines meaning, and *Macbeth* gains a new topicality in this setting: "Bleed, bleed, poor country."

The Inspector is a master at linguistic ambiguity. Like Archie he twists language in the service of politics: "Words can be your friend or your enemy depending on who is throwing the book" (p. 59). His mistreatment of language implies a disregard for values and the dignity of the individual: "the public, or, as we call it in the force, the filth" (p. 60). His language recalls Dogg, now intended as an act of deliberate degradation. Dogg also appears metaphorically in what seems another instance of the logic of leapfrog, when the Inspector says to the actors, "And now you're in the doghouse," at which point Banquo, alias Cahoot, "howls like a dog, barks, falls silent on his hands and knees." Continuing the linguistic associations, the Inspector asks in bewilderment, "Foul . . . fair . . . which is which? That's two witches" (p. 62). The Inspector, representing a real regime, is a more crudely menacing power figure than Archie, but he is also shown his comeuppance, unlike Archie. His professed bewilderment, which is an act, becomes his apparent surety, which is a cover-up for his real bewilderment, as he finds himself increasingly out of control.

Easy, returning at the end of the play, unwittingly doubles as Banquo's ghost, his appearances noted by Macbeth only. He now speaks Dogg and is once again out of his depth. But recognizing Cahoot he can communicate in Dogg, and the two start building. Dogg takes on conspirational inflections that leave the Inspector "high and dry"; his last speech, delivered from the completed platform, sounds like the Lady's address in the first part. It may express his madness and frustration, or it may even signify the victory of "the infection of an uncontrolled idea" (p. 62), for one does not learn Dogg, one "catches" it, as indeed does the hostess. Although Easy built this platform, the final wall is erected by the Inspector's minions, Boris and Maurice, and it walls in the actors, who finish *Macbeth* in Dogg while being gradually immured behind it. Presumably, this act proves their inalienable freedom even in the most threatening of situations, but it could also mean their defeat in captivity.

Several indications suggest that conditions in Stoppard's world have tightened, restricting the freewheeling aspects of leapfrog and ambush as well as of the quest for the last word, and making reality grimmer while increasing the incoherence. In *Cahoot's Macbeth* freedom of expression and repression are set against each other in a narrowing of both the political and the artistic themes; art becomes, as Stoppard now says he believes, "the moral matrix from which we draw our values";[14] yet this assertion is mocked in the Dogg-speaking school with its travesty of *Hamlet*. In *Dogg's Hamlet* acting substitutes for meaning, while in *Cahoot's Macbeth* it provides meaning. *Dogg's Hamlet, Cahoot's Macbeth* combines a darkened world view with a happy ending. The dirt and dung imagery is at once more powerful and less significant, being distanced by Dogg. The theatricality is stronger than ever, yet it is intentionally impoverished and reduced to slapstick: Acting takes place in a foreign language and without an audience. The futility of building and breaking walls becomes both visually and theatrically deadening and finally hides the play from view. While other possibilities of slipping into different roles are still there, such as the Inspector's unwittingly taking the place of the porter in *Macbeth*, they play a less meaningful role in the thematic structure of the work. The stylish Malquist character has disappeared, and the power figures have become cruder and less effective; schoolmaster Dogg and the party functionary lack the mastery and sophistication of Archie. Finally, Easy, the last of the Moon figures, is an altogether more ordinary common man. He has lost much of the capacity for amazement and bewilderment; he is less articulate, vital, and eccentric; he is spared the moral dilemmas that unsettled all Stoppard's characters up to and including Anderson, who is the first of these men, however, to find an answer to them and act on it. Yet Easy gets through the world unscathed. As his name implies, life does not pain him; he adapts. In an ambush characteristic of Stoppard's world, Easy escapes the fatal blow that overtakes his mate. But while this bolt from the blue is typical in its mixture of absurdity and commonplace and the farcical fate it brings to its victim, it is treated as only a peripheral joke. The mate "got struck down in a thunderstorm on the A412 near Rickmansworth—a bizarre accident . . . a bolt from the blue, zigzagged right on to the perforated snout of his Mickey Mouse gas mask. He was delivering five of them at the bacteriological research children's party—entering into the spirit of it—when, shazam!—it was an electrifying moment, left his nose looking more like Donald Duck and his ears like they popped out of a toaster" (*Cahoot's Macbeth*, p. 20).

There is, however, no Shazam for Easy or for the actors, which makes for a happy ending of sorts: no corpses this time. Like his counterparts, Easy has the last word in both plays. In *Dogg's Hamlet* where he speaks English, he ends in Dogg, and in *Cahoot's Macbeth* speaking Dogg, he closes in English: "Well, it's been a funny sort of week. But I should be back by Tuesday" (p. 79). If not fatally ambushed, Easy has not been ambushed by insight either, and his banal inconclusive "last word" is itself a parody of what went before. Perhaps together with Dogg, the end is intended to return us to the beginning, to create a circular structure, if not a beginning, middle, and end.

As before, Stoppard, Moon-like, has set off a farcical bomb to ambush us into "a moment of recognition" (*Malquist and Moon*, p. 108), and like Malquist has carried it out in style. Yet his leapfrog and ambush, on the one hand, increase the incoherence, while his political concerns combined with a gloomier world view have, on the other, hampered the jumping. Perhaps Stoppard is working toward a compromise between leapfrog and a leap of faith, tired of the fact that, in Moon's words, "my emotional bias towards the reactionary and my intellectual bias towards the radical do not survive each other" (p. 80); or, in Carr's terms, he is trying to give up Switzerland during a world war and yet survive.

NOTES

1. Tom Stoppard, "Ambushes for the Audience: Towards a High Comedy of Ideas," *Theatre Quarterly* 4 (May-July 1974): 6–7.

2. Tom Stoppard, *Lord Malquist and Mr. Moon* (London: Faber and Faber, 1966), 53. Further references appear in the text.

3. Tom Stoppard, *Rosencrantz and Guildenstern Are Dead* (New York: Grove Press, 1967), 28. Further references appear in the text.

4. Tom Stoppard, *Jumpers* (London: Faber and Faber, 1972), 71. Further references appear in the text.

5. Tom Stoppard, *Artist Descending a Staircase* (London: Faber and Faber, 1973), 39.

6. Stoppard, "Ambushes for the Audience," 6.

7. Barry Norman, "Tom Stoppard and the Contentment of Insecurity," *London Times* (11 November 1972): 11.

8. Tom Stoppard, Interview, *New York Times* (25 November 1979): 5.

9. Tom Stoppard, interview with Ronald Hayman, 12 June 1974, in Ronald Hayman, *Tom Stoppard* (London: Heinemann, 1979), 2.

10. Tom Stoppard, *Albert's Bridge* (London: Faber and Faber, 1969), 16.

11. Tom Stoppard, *Dogg's Hamlet, Cahoot's Macbeth* (London: Faber and Faber, 1980), 28. Further references appear in the text.

12. Tom Stoppard, *Professional Foul* (London: Faber and Faber, 1977), 62–63.

13. Kenneth Tynan, "Profiles," *New Yorker* 53 (19 December 1977): 82.

14. Mel Gussow, "*Jumpers* Author Is Verbal Gymnast," *New York Times* (23 April 1974): 36.

Bibliography

The books here listed include major studies of fantasy, both fantasy literature in general and theory of fantasy.

Attebury, Brian. *The Fantasy Tradition in American Literature from Irving to Le Guin*. Bloomington: Indiana University Press, 1980.

Barnes, Myra. *Linguistics and Languages in Science Fiction/Fantasy*. New York: Arno Press, 1975.

Bessière, Irène. *Le Récit fantastique, la poétique de l'incertain*. Paris: Larousse, 1973.

Bradley, Ian. *William Morris and His World*. New York: Scribner's, 1978.

Carter, Lin. *Imaginary Worlds: The Art of Fantasy*. New York: Ballantine, 1973.

De Bolt, Joe, ed. *Ursula Le Guin: Voyager to Inner Lands and to Outer Space*. Port Washington, NY: Kennikat, 1979.

Hassler, Donald M. *Patterns of the Fantastic*. Mercer Island, WA: Starmont House, 1983.

Hillegas, Mark R., ed. *Shadows of Imagination: The Fantasies of C. S. Lewis, J. R. R. Tolkien, and Charles Williams*. Carbondale: Southern Illinois University Press, 1969.

Irwin, W. R. *The Game of the Impossible: A Rhetoric of Fantasy*. Urbana: University of Illinois Press, 1976.

Jackson, Rosemary. *Fantasy: The Literature of Subversion*. London: Methuen, 1964.

Kennard, Jean E. *Number and Nightmare: Forms of Fantasy in Contemporary Fiction*. Hamden, CT: Shoe String Press, 1975.

Manlove, Colin N. *The Impulse of Fantasy Literature*. Kent, OH: Kent State University Press, 1983.

————. *Modern Fantasy: Five Studies*. Cambridge: Cambridge University Press, 1975.

Prickett, Stephen. *Victorian Fantasy*. Hassocks, Sussex: Harvester Press, 1979.

Rabkin, Eric S. *The Fantastic in Literature*. Princeton: Princeton University Press, 1976.

Schakel, Peter J., ed. *The Longing for a Form: Essays on the Fiction of C. S. Lewis*. Kent, OH: Kent State University Press, 1977.

Schlobin, Roger C. *The Literature of Fantasy: A Comprehensive Annotated Bibliography of Modern Fantasy Fiction*. New York: Garland, 1979.

Schneider, Marcel. *La Littérature fantastique en France*. Paris: Fayard, 1964.

Slusser, George E., Eric S. Rabkin, and Robert E. Scholes, eds. *Bridges to Fantasy*. Carbondale: Southern Illinois University Press, 1982.

Swinfen, Ann. *In Defense of Fantasy: A Study of the Genre in English and American Literature Since 1945*. Bowling Green, OH: Bowling Green University Popular Press, 1983.

Todorov, Tzvetan. *The Fantastic: A Structural Approach to a Literary Genre*. Cleveland: Case Western Reserve University Press, 1973; Ithaca: Cornell University Press, 1975.

Vax, Louis. *L'Art et la littérature fantastique*. Paris: Presses Universitaires de France, 1960.

Index

About the Editors and Contributors

D. L. Ashliman has studied at Gottingen University, the school that ingloriously dismissed Jacob and Wilhelm Grimm from their academic positions in 1837. He is currently Associate Professor and Chairman of the Department of German at the University of Pittsburgh.

David J. Bond is Professor of French and Head of the Department of French and Spanish at the University of Saskatchewan. His interests in contemporary French and French–Canadian literature have produced books about Quebec novelist André Langevin and André Pieyre de Mandiargues as well as a substantial number of articles.

Mike Budd is Chairman of the Department of Communication at Florida Atlantic University. His major publications include articles on film theory and television criticism.

Michael R. Collings teaches English, including courses in science fiction, at Pepperdine University. He has written about fantasy and science fiction, has published his own poetry and science fiction stories, and has a book in press on Brian Aldiss.

Robert A. Collins, Associate Professor of English at Florida Atlantic University, has published essays on fantasy and science fiction writers and a critical biography of Thomas Burnett Swann. He founded the International Conference on the Fantastic in the Arts and edits *The Fantasy Review*.

Donald H. Crosby, Professor of German literature at the University of Connecticut, has extended his interests to the study of piano, music theory, and the history of music. In addition to his many publications in the area of German literature, he has composed a verse translation of Wagner's *Flying Dutchman*, which has been widely performed in this country.

Margaret M. Dunn has taught literature and composition courses at Stetson University and at the University of Central Florida. She is presently completing her doctorate at Indiana University, specializing in twentieth-century literature and composition, and she has articles forthcoming on Faulkner and H. D.

Joseph J. Feeney, S. J., is Professor of English at Saint Joseph's University, Philadelphia. In addition to scholarly articles in major periodicals, his work includes popular essays and book reviews. In 1983 he was a winner of the international James Joyce Literary Award, given to commemorate the novelist's centenary.

Kurt J. Fickert, Professor of German at Wittenberg University, Springfield, Ohio, is the author of books on Friedrich Dürrenmatt, Hermann Hesse, and Franz Kafka and the forthcoming *Franz Kafka: Life, Works, and Criticism*. He has published extensively about these and other writers in scholarly journals of contemporary German literature.

Paul L. Gaston teaches English at Southern Illinois University at Edwardsville.

Francis Gillen is Professor of English and Director of the Honors Program at the University of Tampa. His essays on drama and the novel have appeared in major periodicals, and in 1982 he won the University's Louise Loy Hunter Award as its outstanding teacher. He is currently working on books about the literature of the aging and about Harold Pinter.

Richard E. Hersh, currently employed by IBM as a technical writer, is completing his dissertation at the University of Florida and has published an essay on T. E. Lawrence.

Jan Hokenson is Associate Professor of French at Florida Atlantic University and Director of the Program in Comparative Literature. Although she has published essays about British and American literature, her major interests and publications are in modern European fiction. She is completing a book on the Fool Figure in modern European fiction.

Frederick Kirchhoff is Associate Professor of English at Indiana University/Purdue University at Fort Wayne. He has published articles on various aspects of Romantic and Victorian literature and is the author of monographs on William Morris and John Ruskin.

Raymond G. LePage is Associate Professor of French at George Mason University. His areas of specialization are seventeenth-century French literature and French–Canadian studies. In addition to articles and reviews appearing in numerous publications, he has contributed several articles to Frank McGill's *Masterpieces in Literature* series and is presently writing a book on the major illustrators of the French fabulist writer Jean de La Fontaine.

Jeannette Hume Lutton has been coordinator of an interdisciplinary program in the humanities that served Morehouse, Clark, and Morris Brown Colleges, and she is presently Professor of English at Morehouse College. An active participant in the Conference on the Fantastic, she has had three of her papers accepted for publication, and she is working on a book-length study of Chaucer.

Peter Malekin is currently a Senior Lecturer at the University of Durham, England. He has taught in Germany, Iraq, and Sweden. His interests include philosophy and the arts, Eastern and Western, as well as science fiction and the fantastic. His publications encompass these topics and others, including Shakespeare, Wordsworth, myth and art, and Modernist ideas, and his current projects range in addition to a translation of Jacob Böhme.

Nancy Caplan Mellerski is Assistant Professor of French at Dickinson College in Carlisle, Pennsylvania. Her research interests other than the fantastic include the contemporary French novel, theories of prose, nineteenth-century fiction and poetry, and detective fiction. She has published French language textbooks and is currently working on a book about the fiction of the *nouveau romancier* Claude Ollier.

Ann R. Morris is Professor of English at Stetson University, where she teaches nineteenth- and twentieth-century American literature. She frequently offers a course on the death experience as portrayed in literature, and it was this course out of which grew her essay on the interweaving of sex and death in Robert Coover's books. She is the author of two books and a frequent participant at conventions throughout the Southeast.

Howard Pearce, Chairman of the English Department at Florida Atlantic University, has published articles about British and American writers as well as comparative and theoretical essays developed from phenomenological insights.

Gabrielle Robinson is Associate Professor of English at Indiana University, South Bend, and specializes in modern drama. She has published essays on George Bernard Shaw, John Whiting, Tom Stoppard, Friedrich Dürrenmatt, James Joyce, and Flannery O'Connor and is presently finishing a book on Whiting.

Stephen J. Robitaille teaches English at the University of Florida.

William Schuyler is Professor of Philosophy at the University of Louisville and has published papers on problems with identity and on ethics in contexts not limited to merely human concerns. However, his published work covers a much broader range, including philosophy of language and philosophy of history.

J. P. Telotte is Assistant Professor of English at the Georgia Institute of Technology, where he teaches courses in film and drama. A member of the editorial boards of *Literature/Film Quarterly* and *Film Criticism*, he has published a variety of articles on film and literature and is the author of a forthcoming study of film fantasy.

Jean Tobin teaches courses in writing and literature at the University of Wisconsin Center at Sheboygan and has studied at Edinburgh University and the Université de Paris.

Robert Wolf is Associate Professor of Philosophy at Southern Illinois University at Edwardsville and is Assistant Editor of *Philosopher's Index*. His recent publications include articles in *Philosophia, Review of Metaphysics*, and *Proceedings of the Illinois Medieval Association*.

Chester Wolford is Associate Professor of English at Pennsylvania State University.

Jules Zanger is Professor of English at Southern Illinois University, has published articles about American writers, and has been a regular participant at the Conference on the Fantastic.